HISTORY OF
WHITE OAK SPRINGS
BAPTIST CHURCH
OF PAULDING COUNTY
GEORGIA: 1856-2018

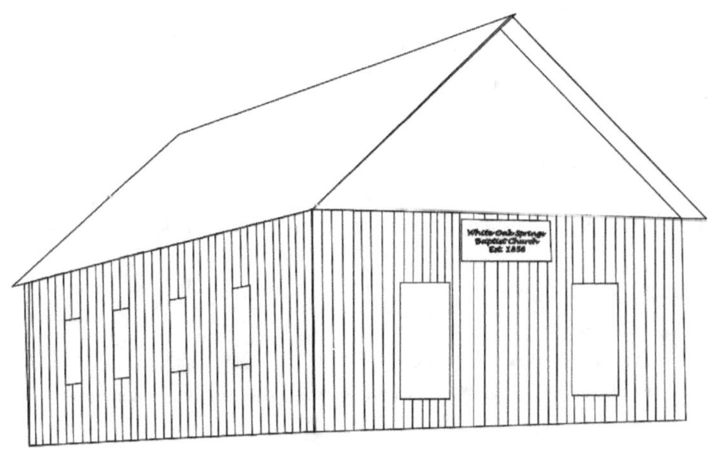

S. DAVID SMITH

History of White Oak Springs Baptist Church of Paulding County, Georgia: 1856- 2018

All Scripture quotations are from the King James Version (KJV).

Smith, Samuel David

    History of White Oak Springs Baptist Church of Paulding County, Georgia: 1856 – 2018.

Edited by: Nancy Freund

Front and back cover design: Rebecacover/Fiverr.com - *#FO8FDB54D363*

Photo credits:

    Church photo: McKenzie Lee

    Open Bible: kevron2002/depositphotos.com. Image number: 30832405

    Covered wagon: goodynewshoes/depositphotos.com. Image number: 9076101

Printed by: CreateSpace.com

CreateSpace, Charlestown, S.C.

ISBN-13: 978-1984121462
ISBN-10: 1984121464

This book is dedicated to

Clara Mae Baggett

She loves the Lord and loves this church.

Presentation

This is an honored opportunity for me to express my thanks and appreciation for the time and effort put forth in preparing this history of White Oak Springs Baptist Church. This record will, for all time, afford a glimpse into the early days, as well as the present time, of the God-given lessons and examples of those who have provided the leadership to make this His blessed house of worship. Throughout the ages, White Oak Springs Baptist Church has been the center of daily spiritual strength and a source of peace and comfort for generations of my own family and for the countless souls of this rugged Appalachian foothill area of southwestern Paulding County.

As we look back, we can see how the hand of God has directed the work of White Oak Springs Baptist Church, and as we look forward we are assured that He will lead White Oak Springs Baptist Church to even greater things in the years ahead. "Praise God from Whom all blessings flow."

Honorable Don Edwin Wix
Georgia House of Representatives, 1998–2010

Photo of the 1889 Sanctuary
This photo was taken in October 1918
Photo used with permission granted by Rev. Jeff Byrd

Preface

"Render therefore to all their dues: tribute to whom tribute is due; custom to whom custom; fear to whom fear; honour to whom honour." – Romans 13:7

In July 1933, Lucien E. Roberts published the book *A History of Paulding County*. It was a history of Paulding County, Georgia, and it included information on White Oak Springs Baptist Church and its cemetery. The church clerk, George W. Cole, gave information to the person writing the book. That book lists Jasper Smith as the founding pastor and lists Jesse Hitchcock as being a former pastor of the church. The historical information that White Oak Springs had in its files in October 2016 quotes that 1933 book.

The following is the historical information that the church had in its file in October 2016:

1.   In 1966, when the new church sanctuary was being dedicated, the November 1966 edition of the Challenger, published by the Concord-Tallapoosa Baptist Association, included a four-paragraph article on the new church building, along with a photo of White Oak Springs' new sanctuary. The first paragraph gave a brief history of the church and described the construction of the new building. The second paragraph was verbatim of the 1933 information about the church's pastors with the additional mention of the last few pastors. The third paragraph gave the names of current leaders and builders who were responsible for the new sanctuary. The last paragraph gave thanks to the Lord, to the church, and to its then-current pastor (This article is included as Appendix One).

2.   In April 1977, an updated Paulding County cemetery list was published. There were separate entries: one for the Old White Oak Missionary Baptist Church Cemetery and a second for the New White Oak Springs Missionary Baptist Church Cemetery. A historical description was presented for each cemetery and the church that met at each of the two properties. These two descriptions were given by George Ernest Gober. He cited the 1933 information and added some new facts about both properties.

3.   February 2, 1975, "Youth Sanctuary Dedication." This information lists the same pastors as the 1966 *Challenger* article, with the addition of the name of Charles Williams. (The article is included as Appendix Four).

4.   In 1987, Jeff Byrd (now Pastor Jeff Byrd) wrote a one-page history of the church. This brief history had new information about the church's ministry during the 1970s. It told of the 1985 fire that destroyed the fellowship hall. (This information is included as Appendix Two).

5.   A copy of the two-page *History of White Oak Springs Missionary Baptist Church* cites the 1987 brief history, with an additional sentence about the February 16, 2000, purchase of land and about the March 13, 2003, purchase of an additional 3.3 acres. (This document is included as Appendix Three).

6.   A copy of the three-page *History of White Oak Springs Pastors as Remembered by Gloria Caldwell Byrd—with current additional comments from her daughter Jo Ann Allen, last updated about 2010.* This information is included in the main text of this

book. She wrote that information over 20 to 30 years ago, and her daughter updated it in 2010.

7.   A two-page list of deacons ordained at White Oak Springs Baptist Church from 1908 to 1974 was taken from the church minutes on hand at the time. (This information is included as Appendix Seven).

8.   The early records of the church were lost in a fire when the church clerk's home burned down. The more recent records and church minutes were lost when an elderly church clerk moved from his home to temporary housing with limited space. His belongings were placed in storage at different places. In the shuffle, the box with the church minutes was lost.

9.   In January 2017, Clara Mae Baggett shared a little booklet that was written in 1978 when Larry G. Davis was pastor. This little booklet gives a short biography on the 12 men that were serving as deacons in 1977.   It also lists some very brief information on some of the other men that had served as deacons from 1908 forward. This booklet provided much firsthand information about their salvation and ministry. No author was listed. This untitled booklet will be called *The Deacons of White Oak Springs* when it is referenced in this text.

10.   White Oak Springs Baptist Church produced photo church directories in 1971, 1977, 1987, 1993, and 1998. These directories were used as membership lists for this book. The 1977 directory had two paragraphs that contained some new information that was used in this book.

11.   Jeff Byrd found some old church minutes that he transcribed and typed when he was working on the history of the church about 30 years ago. He typed up the monthly church business meeting minutes from the original minutes from the April 25, 1908, to April 22, 1911, meetings.

12.   Don Wix (former member of the Georgia General Assembly for the 33rd district from 1997 to 2010) shared some information that his father, Rev. J. Edwin Wix, had shared with him. Don Wix provided definitive information on where the first church building had been located. He learned that information from his father.

Research

To gain more historical information about the church, I made three trips to Macon, Georgia, to the Mercer University Baptist Historical Archives to copy the yearly "Tallapoosa (GA) Baptist Association" minutes from 1855 to 1982. These minutes later were transcribed, noting the pertinent information about White Oak Springs Baptist Church. The third trip was to follow up on information about Rev. J. A. Smith and Rev. Jasper Smith.

Then I began the research work to identify the first and last names of pastors and members mentioned in the Tallapoosa Baptist Association minutes. The Tallapoosa Baptist Association minutes are the primary sources for names of members and pastors of White Oak Springs Baptist Church from 1856 to 1985. In March 2017, most of the missing Tallapoosa Baptist Association records (1863, 1882, 1884-89) were secured from the Baptist Archives at the Southern Baptist Convention in Nashville, Tennessee.

Then U.S. census information was consulted. The 1850, 1860, 1870, 1880, 1900, 1910, and 1920 Paulding County, Georgia, Censuses were consulted. The internet was used, and many genealogical resources were consulted to find something about former members so that this book will be of use to others doing genealogical research on their families. One site that was very helpful was www.findagrave.com. That website on occasions had obituaries of past members. Ancestry.com was also consulted for some census information.

Pastor Keith Lee was very helpful to this author. He shared the information the church had on hand, and he arranged interviews with Clara Mae Baggett, Gloria Caldwell Byrd, Jeff Byrd, Ernest Gober, and Kenneth Cohran. He set aside a few days out of his busy schedule to accompany this author to visit these people. Brother Keith also rounded up the old photos included in this book. The Jeff Byrd family (Harris family) had a photo taken in 1918 of the church building and a 1929 photo of Bennett Bullock's baptismal pool.

Contents

Preface

I. Section One: Our Start   **01**

1. Why White Oak Springs Was Started   03

2. When White Oak Springs Was Started   05

3. Names of White Oak Springs Baptist Church   07

4. Two Locations of White Oak Springs Church   11

5. Our Three Houses of Worship   17

6. Baptismal Holes of White Oak Springs   27

II. Section Two: Our History   **29**

7. Pastors of White Oak Springs   31

8. Chairmen of the Deacons   33

9. Founding Members and Families: 1856–1858   35

10. The Early Years: 1859–1869   57

11. A Little Church in the Woods: 1870–1888   73

12. New Property, Sanctuary, & Cemetery: 1889–46   93

13. New Way of Doing Church: 1947–1963   131

14. A New Sanctuary Is Built: 1964–1966   243

15. Our Most Recent Pastors: 1967–2018   251

16. Looking Forward   242

III. Section Three: Our Appendixes   **243**

Appendix One: Article from Association Newsletter   245

Appendix Two: History of White Oak Springs – 1978   247

Appendix Three: History of White Oak Springs – 2000   249

Appendix Four: Youth Sanctuary Dedication   251

Appendix Five: Old White Oak Springs Cemetery   253

Appendix Six: First Families Buried in Church Cemetery   259

Appendix Seven: Deacons Ordained by Church   267

Appendix Eight: Sunday School Superintendents 270

Appendix Nine: Men Ordained at White Oak Springs 272

Appendix Ten: Rev. Jasper Smith 273

Appendix Eleven: Rev. J. A Smith (born 1806) 277

Appendix Twelve: Intriguing Mystery Membership List 279

Appendix Thirteen: 1970s Singing Trio of Church 283

Appendix Fourteen: Primitive Baptist Controversy 285

Bibliography **287**

Indexes **289**

Index of Pastors 289

Index of Churches 231

Index of Newspapers 293

Index of People 295

Section One

Our Start

Why Was White Oak Springs Baptist Church Started?
"And they continued steadfastly in the apostles' doctrine and fellowship, and in breaking of bread, and in prayers." —Acts 2:42

White Oak Springs Baptist Church was started because some of the members of Pumpkinvine Baptist Church were living west of that church in what today is called the White Oak Springs community, and others were living even farther west on the Haralson-Paulding County line.

Starting a new church in that area at that time (1856) made sense for the following reasons:

1. Pumpkinvine Baptist Church had dedicated members who lived in that area who were willing to form the core group of the new church.

2. Most of the core group were related to each other either by blood or by marriage.

3. The core group was large for that time period. It numbered 31 members a few months after the church started.

4. This group had a pastor who was willing to help them get started: Rev. James I. Harris. Pastor Harris was related to Craven Harris and his kinfolk.

5. A very experienced retired pastor (Rev. James Roberts) was part of the core group, and J. I. Harris was one of his preacher boys. It could be that Rev. James Roberts was the main person behind starting the new church and he put James I. Harris as its

new pastor since Pastor James Roberts' health was declining. Rev. James Roberts could possibly be named as the founder of White Oak Springs Baptist Church.

6. Paulding County was growing, and starting a new missionary Baptist church in that area would be a strategic move.

7. It was part of God's plan to establish a Christian witness in this part of Paulding County.

When Was White Oak Springs Baptist Church Founded?

"To everything there is a season, and a time to every purpose under the heaven."
—*Ecclesiastes 3:1*

"Known unto God are all his works from the beginning of the world."
—*Acts 15:18*

The April 19, 1856, church minutes for Pumpkinvine Baptist Church has the following entry:

> April 19, 1856 – The church met in conference. Invited visiting brethren to seat with us. 2nd opened the doors of the church. 3rd read the minutes of the last conference. 4th called over the items of business. Granted letters of demission to brethren Craven Harris, and sister Amy Harris, Celia Harris, Penelope Harris, Sarah Harris, Elizabeth Harris and Frances Burns in order for them to help constitute another church.

Another source of useful information is the September 13, 1856, minutes of the Tallapoosa Baptist Association. Their third order of business for that year reads: "Gave an invitation to churches desiring to become members of this body. White Oak Springs applied and after reading their faith received all their delegates named enrolled."

These two sources do not give the exact date the church was founded, but they give some very good hints. Pumpkinvine Baptist Church met in conference once a month in 1856. In April 1856, the church granted letters of demission to seven of its members to help constitute a new Baptist church. In April 1856, plans had already been made, or were in the process of being made, to start the new church. In 1856 White Oak Springs Baptist Church was holding its once-a-month church meeting on the fourth Sunday. The church preferred meeting on the fourth Sunday of each month throughout its history.

From the Pumpkinvine Baptist Church and Tallapoosa Baptist Association minutes, it is possible to say with certainty that the church was started in the spring of 1856. From here it gets "iffy." Pumpkinvine issued letters of dismissal on April 19, 1856, to seven of its members to form White Oak Springs Baptist Church. Therefore, White Oak Springs Baptist Church was started around or after that time.

Gloria Byrd shared that White Oak Springs Baptist Church has always commemorated the fourth Sunday of May for their church anniversary "for as long as I can remember." The fourth Sunday in May in 1856 was May 25. So May 25, 1856, was probably the day they held their first services at the new church.

Names of White Oak Springs Baptist Church

"A good name is rather to be chosen than great riches, and loving favour rather than silver and gold." ——*Proverbs 22:1*

Some of the information White Oak Springs Baptist Church has about its history was given by someone who was 80 years removed from its founding. In some of the information the church has, it states that the name "Springs" was added to the White Oak Baptist Church name in 1889 when they moved from their old location to the current property. It is great to have information of that type. It serves as a good road map for historians to use. However, that information, in this case, was not as correct as they originally thought.

Since this church was part of the Tallapoosa Baptist Association, their written yearly minutes dating back to 1856 were decisive in helping the church know its original name.

White Oak Springs Baptist Church

In September 1856, when the church was accepted into the Tallapoosa association, it used the name "White Oak Springs Baptist Church." In all the yearly minutes of that association, from 1856 to 1982, this church was referred to as "White Oak Springs Baptist Church." The word "Springs" has always been included in its name since the church was founded in 1856.

New White Oak Springs Baptist Church

The Paulding New Era newspaper called the church the "New White Oak Springs Baptist Church" in an 1892 obituary notice.

They used the word "new" to distinguish the new cemetery from old one.

The Baptist Church of Christ at White Oak Springs

The church business meeting minutes from April 25, 1908, to April 22, 1911, list the church name as "the Baptist Church of Christ at White Oak Springs." This form of the church name was very common for many Baptist churches started in the mid-1800s.

White Oak Springs Missionary Baptist Church

The church has been called "White Oak Springs Missionary Baptist Church" for many years. The church has always been a missionary Baptist church rather than a primitive Baptist church; therefore, the name "Missionary" was used to distinguish it from the primitive Baptists. The church was part of the Tallapoosa Baptist Association, which was a missionary Baptist group. The church sign out on Buchanan Highway uses the name "White Oak Springs Missionary Baptist Church." The church buses had the name "Missionary" painted on the sides of the buses as well. That is a name the church has used in a nonofficial way for at least 100 years. As signs were repainted and replaced over the years, the name "Missionary" was retained in the name and, hence, it is still on the sign today.

White Oak Springs Baptist Church, Inc.

The internet site www.ishcc.org gave the following information about the church:

"On May 16, 1966, White Oak Springs Baptist Church, Inc. located at 139 White Oak Church Road, in Dallas, Georgia 30157-

3236, was incorporated as a non-profit corporation."[1] Even though the church was organized in 1889 when they moved from their old location to the present one, evidently they were not incorporated until May 1966 when they were building the new church facilities. The name they incorporated as was "White Oak Springs Baptist Church, Inc." which is the official name of the church today.

---

[1] http://www.ishcc.org/GA/Dallas/white-oak-springs-baptist-church-inc.

Two Locations

"Moreover thou shalt make the tabernacle with ten curtains of fine twined linen, and blue, and purple, and scarlet: with cherubims of cunning work shalt thou make them." — Exodus 26:1

White Oak Springs Baptist Church has used two properties throughout its history. Part of their first property or meeting place is now called the Old White Oak Springs Missionary Baptist Church Cemetery.

There are over 100 graves at the old cemetery property. Kenneth Cohran said that when graves were dug at the old cemetery property, they would fill up with water. For some reason, some of the tombstones from the old cemetery were moved to the new cemetery. Many of the first families of Paulding County are buried in that cemetery, but only four have tombstones. The four people with tombstones at the old cemetery in 1977 were: Hamon Roberts (1799-1882); Nancy Roberts (1826–1900); Mary J. Hitchcock (1845–1892); and Cumi Hitchcock (1869–1883). Sixty years later, someone placed a tombstone for Jesse Leatherwood (1947). In the 1980s or 1990s, someone placed a tombstone for Bill Postell.

The thirty years following the Civil War were hard times in this part of Paulding County. Family members knew where their relatives were buried, and they probably kept up their graves. Most families did not have extra money available to purchase tombstones. An occasional simple bouquet of wildflowers and a lot of love would have to suffice. Unfortunately, as time has passed, those who knew who was buried there have passed on to their eternal reward, and now there is no record of those that are buried there. Those people with no tombstones to mark their final resting place are our spiritual forerunners that had the vision to start White Oak Springs Baptist Church and that ministered spiritually to this community. They are the ones who left the church the spiritual heritage it has today.

Location of Original Church Building

The original church building at the old property was located on the west side of Old White Oak Cemetery Road. This location is across the road from where the old cemetery is located.

1. Don Wix said that his father, Rev. J. Edwin Wix, mentioned that the original church building was believed to be located across the road from the cemetery.

2. There is an old 1896 map of Paulding County, Georgia, that shows the land lot numbers and roads where family homesteads, schools, and churches were located. There is a black dot where the old cemetery is on that 1896 map. On the other side of the road, there is another dot that has "White Oak Springs" listed by it. The original church building was located on the west side of the road across the street from the old cemetery.

When the church met at its first property, its membership remained fairly small. It started with 31 members. Shortly after the Civil War, its membership jumped to 88 members in 1866. However, within two years its membership was back down to the upper 30s and the low 40s. Many families were still moving west as the frontier expanded.

The New Location at the Second Property: 1889

In August of 1889, White Oak Springs moved from its original property located at what is now the Old White Oak Springs Cemetery to its current location. The street address of this new property today is 139 White Oak Springs Church Road.

The old location was marshy and was not very good for burials since the water table was only a few feet below the ground. On damp days, church members had to walk in the mud. Someone said that the church moved from the old location to the new location because a new road was cut and the old location was no longer on the main road from Dallas to Draketown. That may be correct or it may not be. The move was a good one because they moved from an inferior property (marshy) to a location on higher ground.

According to the descendants of Jacob and Betsy Cole, Jacob Cole donated the property where the cemetery is located today for the purpose of establishing a new cemetery beside the church at its new location. The first interment at the new cemetery was Elizabeth "Betsy" Cole, wife of Jacob Cole. She died on June 24, 1891. Therefore, the cemetery property was donated to the church about that time. Her husband, Jacob Cole, died about a year later, on July 23, 1892, and is buried beside his wife in the New White Oak Springs Cemetery.

There must have been a good bit of enthusiasm in the church shortly after the move to the new location: They had a new church property, a new larger sanctuary, and a new cemetery.

The Purchase of Additional Properties

In the last 30 years, small tracts of land have been acquired that have given the church more property.

The current parsonage was built in the early 1960s. Gloria Byrd thinks that Rev. Charles Williams was the first pastor to use it.

In the February 16, 2000, minutes, item 9.2 lists the following: "Church voted to buy land to trade with the city of Atlanta for land near the new parsonage. Price of land *[is]* $27,000.00." There is a hand-written notation beside that entry that says "barn and house."

On Thursday September 26, 2002, *The Dallas New Era* carried the following article: "Senator Nathan Dean Honored by White Oak Springs Baptist."

> White Oak Springs Missionary Baptist Church honored Senator Nathan Dean and Mrs. Dean on Sunday, August 18, 2002, with a banquet after the evening services for his assistance in helping them secure property adjoining the church from the city of Atlanta. Senator Dean worked extensively many months to help White Oak secure this property. His tireless efforts are greatly appreciated by the pastor and the members of White Oak. Of special interest was the parable about a mule told by Senator Dean regarding how much easier it is to accomplish a mission when people work together. White Oak Church is located at 139 White Oak Church Road off Highway 120 west in Dallas. The pastor is Johnny Simpson. Again, White Oak deeply appreciates everything Senator Dean did to help them secure this property.

Acquiring the additional property was a very good decision. It gave the church the area between their property and Buchanan Highway. It guarantees that the church will not be blocked off by new development between the sanctuary and the highway. The additional property will be a great place for additional buildings when they are needed.

- - - -

This article goes with photo on next page

Published in the Dallas New Era c1966

"White Oak School Class, 1903; Professor J. H. Lester, Superintendent."

Pictured, left to right, first row, are: Oscar Wilson, a Head child, a Wilson child, John Thompson, Jessie Neal, unknown, Lassy Neal, Jeneva Neal, Rosy Thompson, Ana Cole, unknown, Maudie Cole, Belle Haney, a Carter child, Annie Wix.

Second row: Issac Wix, Paul Head, Layfett Cole, Press Osborne, Dan Head, Zannie Wix, James Carter, John Osborne, Charlie Thompson, Quiller Cole, Jessie Harris.

Third row: Tempy Raney, Lily Wilson, Jane Cole, Venie Carter, Odesa Raney, Delia Carter, Mellie Wilson, Georgie Wix, Lizzy Thompson. The two attractive ladies on the end are Pearl Wix and Daily Cole, visitors.

Fourth row: C. O. Head, Rade Cole, Ramy Cole, Tim Cole, Bob Wilson, Cary Hitchcock, and Professor Lester.

Photo of 1856 Building

This is the only photo we have of the 1856 White Oak Springs Church Building. It had two doors on the end of the building that served as its entrances. The names of the children are on page 15. (Photo used with permission from Rev. Jeff Byrd)

Three Sanctuaries of White Oak Springs Baptist Church

*"Then a cloud covered the tent of the congregation,
and the glory of the LORD filled the tabernacle." —*   *Exodus 40:34*

First Sanctuary of White Oak Springs
Built 1856

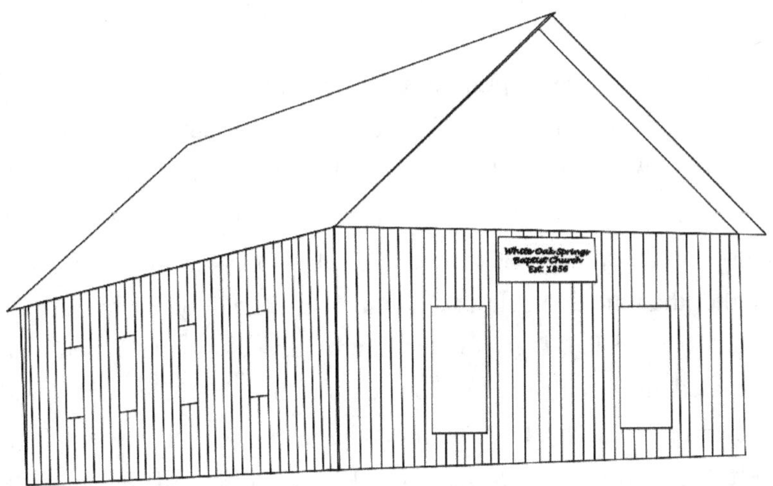

This wooden church building was located across the street from the old cemetery

The church erected a small wooden building and met at that location from the spring of 1856 until the fall of 1889. The size of that building is not known. The 1987 one-page history of White Oak Springs Baptist Church states that a "small building was built and a new church was born." The first sanctuary of the church, being small, probably held only 50 to 100 people.

The Dallas New Era newspaper published a photo taken in 1903 of the students that were meeting in the old sanctuary building. The White Oak Springs School was meeting in the old White Oak Springs Church building. That photo was taken outside of the building and has the school children standing in front of the building. Very little of the building can be seen; however, what can be seen does show that the building had a high roof and ceiling. The photo shows that the building was not made like a log cabin, but rather more like a warehouse. The building had long 1" x 10" planks nailed vertically to the outside of the building. This is similar to the way the 1889 building was built.

Description of the 1856 Sanctuary

From the photo taken in 1903 of the White Oak School (meeting in the old White Oak Baptist Church sanctuary building), the following information can be shared: (1) the 1856 church had two doors on the front of the church; (2) both of these doors were much higher than the doors now used in homes. The doors were close to eight or nine feet high; (3) the church also had a flat porch that spanned the width of the front of the building. This porch, or platform, came out from the building about five or six feet. The left corner of this porch was about 18 to 24 inches off the ground; (4) centrally located on the platform were stairs that might have been five to eight feet wide; (5) from the ground step (a piece of wood on the ground level) to the top of the platform, there were only two steps. The drawing of the 1856 building was based on this information and from other buildings built about that time in the same area.

Still Standing in 1909

The January 23, 1909, church business meeting minutes has one paragraph that mentions the White Oak Springs School and the old church building. In December 1908, the school gave the church some money for use of the old church building. The church decided to not accept the money from the White Oak School and recommended the school use that money to build a new school building.

From those minutes it can be deduced that: (1) the original church building was still standing in January 1910; (2) the old church building was being used as a schoolhouse called "White Oak School"; (3) the original church building was getting old and was in need of repair; and (4) members of White Oak Springs Baptist Church felt it would be better for the school to build a new building rather than repair the old building. No records have been found about the White Oak School or if a new building was built in 1910 or for how much longer the original 1856 building remained erect on the old property.

The 1926 minutes of the Tallapoosa Baptist Association stated that White Oak Springs was constituted or chartered in 1889. That was the same year the church moved to its current location at 139 White Oak Springs Church Road.

The August 9, 1889, edition of the *Paulding New Era* newspaper had the following article about the new church building being built.

> White Oak Springs Church are *[sic]* building a new church house on Dallas-Draketown road near William Clark, where the general meeting of the 2nd district will convene this year commencing on Friday before the 4th Sunday in August.

The August 9, 1889, *Paulding New Era* said that the new White Oak Springs Baptist Church building was built by the house of William Clark on the Dallas-Draketown Road. A Civil War soldier named Samuel Clark (b. August 8, 1839 and died February 1, 1930) is buried in the New White Oak Springs Cemetery. His parents were William M. Clark and Lucy Leathers. William M. Clark's tombstone has the inscription "Asleep in Jesus," attesting to his faith in Jesus Christ as his Savior. Samuel Clark married Celicie Moody on December 15, 1867. Celicie was born in 1839 and died in 1928. (Source: *Confederate Veterans and Widows Pensions,* Paulding County, Georgia, p.10).

1889 Church Sanctuary[2]

Second Sanctuary of White Oak Springs

In August 1889, the church moved to its new property and started meeting in their new sanctuary. This was the church's second sanctuary.

The newly built sanctuary was ready to be used on August 25, 1889 (fourth Sunday of that month). The *Paulding New Era*

---

[2] Photo used with permission granted by Rev. Jeff Byrd.

newspaper mentioned the weekend festivities in its August 30, 1889 edition: "Services at White Oak Springs in the afternoon was rained out."

From this article, one may deduce that the Sunday services were held in the afternoon. Many churches held their one service a month at 2 pm on their Sunday. This still gave those who attended time to make their horse and buggy ride home before it got dark.

White Oak Springs Sanctuary – date uncertain – c1945 -50

The wood frame of the 1889 sanctuary was a "log frame" building. This building had two windows on the front and two main entrance doors on the side of the building facing the road (west side). Each side of the building had three large windows. The second church building had weathered boards on the side. They were unpainted wooden planks. These unpainted planks were 1" x 10" by 12' or 14' long. These boards were nailed to the framework of the building vertically. Where these boards met, there was a little crack or space between the planks. To cover that, long strips of wood two inches wide were nailed to cover the spacing between the boards and to better seal the outside of the building.

The third (1966) building was built alongside the 1889 building, which was then dismantled. The front doors of the 1889 building were on the same side (west side) of the building as the 1966 sanctuary. There were only five feet separating the two buildings.

The inside of the 1889 building was basic. It had wooden floors, wooden walls, and wooden trusses holding up the roof. The people entered the church from the road side of the building. There was no choir loft or raised platform for the pulpit area. It was all on the same level. Clara Mae Baggett said that in the 1950s, the old 1889 church had a piano in it, and the doors were always left unlocked so people could come and pray as they wanted. For heat, this building had a wood-burning stove placed in the building's center. On cold mornings, deacon Tom Fuller would come and start the fire most of the time. There was no electricity in the building until the mid- to late-1920s. There were no bathrooms installed. They had outhouses on the back of property on the cemetery side of the building.

Later on, date uncertain, the church covered the rustic planks on the outside of the building with some type of more weather-resistant coving that they painted white. This gave the very old building a more modern look for a time.

Water for the Thirsty

1. At the church's new location, there was no running water, so they brought water up from the creek on the church's west side.

2. In the 1950s or so, a well was being used that was located nearby. People would bring a bucket of water from the well to the church so that those attending would not have to walk as far to get water. People all drank from the same ladle.

3. In 1966 there was a well on the north side of the main sanctuary entrance about 10 to 15 feet from the stairs. This well house had a water spigot.

Let There Be Lights

Hurricane lamps (kerosene oil lamps) were used for night revival services when they were held once or twice a year. The church borrowed their hurricane lamps from Pumpkinvine Baptist Church whenever they held protracted services (revival meetings from two to four weeks in length, with both am and pm services).

One day, when J. Edwin Wix was young, he made the recommendation they buy lights and have them installed. This was when J. Edwin Wix was younger, in the late 1920s or early 1930s.

Third Sanctuary House

In 1963 it was decided to build a new church sanctuary. The basement was completed first, and three more years were needed to complete the sanctuary. On October 2, 1966, the new sanctuary was dedicated. Guy Gazaway was a deacon at church and was in charge of the building committee when the 1966 sanctuary was built.

Jeff Byrd said that when construction started on the new sanctuary, the basement of the sanctuary was built first and then they gave a pause for three years to raise the funds for the rest of the construction. When the basement was finished, they started using it for Sunday School classes. Jeff Byrd remembers how he would leave the old wooden sanctuary and walk behind the new building while it was being built. One day he went out the wooden building, and the church sanctuary was there. It was like the church sanctuary "popped up" all of the sudden. He said it seemed like the construction of the main part of the sanctuary went up very quickly, at least through the eyes of a five-year-old boy.

Third Sanctuary - Built in 1966

Photo used with permission from McKenzie Lee

The 1977 White Oak Springs Baptist Church photo book gives the following information on the other buildings that the church has built since 1966.

> White Oak Springs Baptist Church was constituted in 1856. In 1963, the basement of the present building was built to be used for Sunday School rooms. In 1966 the new sanctuary was built. After beginning a bus ministry in 1970, the church outgrew its space. The children then had Sunday School while the adults had their worship service. In 1974, a sanctuary for the children and 12 additional Sunday School rooms were started and [were] completed in 1975. In 1976, the children had outgrown their space and a second children's church was being renovated.

The 1889 wooden building was dismantled after the new and more modern church sanctuary was built in 1966. Kenneth Cohan shared that Raymond McClarity bought the old 1889 church building for lumber.

In 1974 and 1976, two more buildings were built to help with the children's ministry. In 1968, a wood-frame fellowship hall was built. Unfortunately, that building caught fire during a Sunday evening service on September 8, 1985, and burned to the ground. A larger fellowship hall was completed in 1987.

Two Baptisms at Bennett Bullock's Baptismal Pool
July 1929

Rev. Fred Wigley baptizing in Bennett Bullock's baptismal pool in July 1929

Another Baptism from the 1930s or 1940s

Baptismal Holes of White Oak Springs Baptist Church
"Then they that gladly received his word were baptized." —Acts 2:41a

When the 1856 building was built, it is very unlikely that it had a baptismal pool. Baptisms were held in nearby streams or borrowed ponds. The old mill at Manor's Mill on Manor's Mill Road had a nice area of water where people could swim and fish. People would arrive by foot, horse, or horse-drawn carriage at these baptisms.

When the church moved to its new location in 1889, it still did not have a baptismal pool in it. Creeks, streams, and ponds continued to be used as needed. None of the current members interviewed for this book could recall any stream or pond that was used for baptisms other than the Bennett Bullock's baptismal pool, with the exception of Lucious Baxter's Lake.

Bennett Bullock's Baptismal Pool

J. Bennett Bullock (b. August 16, 1887–d. July 6, 1980) married Willie Mae Mobley on April 23, 1909. Willie Mae Mobley Bullock was born in 1892 and passed away in 1972. They are both buried in the Smyrna Methodist Church Cemetery on Buchanan Highway a few miles west of the church. Some of Mrs. Bennett Bullock's relatives (the Mobleys) were founders of White Oak Springs Baptist Church. Bennett Bullock and Willie Mae Mobley Bullock are mentioned because they provided a baptismal pool that they allowed all churches in the area to use. This pool was located on the Bullocks' property.

The rectangular baptismal pool had steps that led down to the pool and formed an "L" shape to the pool. It was large enough to hold the person being baptized plus the pastor without any problem. The water could come up a little above waist high on the adults. There are pictures of people being baptized at this pool, which show 10 or 12 folks in the water awaiting their turn to be baptized. The church has a photo taken in 1929 of a baptism being held by White Oak Springs at the Bennett Bullock's baptismal pool.

People interviewed for this book said "all the churches in the area" used that location for their baptisms. The Baptist churches in Paulding are grateful for the Bullocks' generosity and willingness to provide a place where baptisms could be held on their property.

Lucious Baxter's Lake

When Vernon Cole decided to get baptized, it was a Sunday morning in February during a prolonged arctic cold snap. They had to break the ice in order to baptize him in the lake after church that morning. He was baptized at Baxter Lake on Buchanan Highway. That was not the only baptism that is known to have been held there. Other baptisms were held at that lake, but they were held in more hospitable weather conditions.

The church used Bennett Bullock's baptismal pool until the 1966 sanctuary was built. It had its own baptismal pool built inside the building.

Modern Baptismal Pool Installed in 1966 Sanctuary

Since the dedication of the new church sanctuary in 1966, the church has used its own baptismal pool located in the main sanctuary behind the choir loft.

Section Two

Our History

Pastors of White Oak Springs Baptist Church
Dallas, Paulding County, Georgia

"Obey them that have the rule over you, and submit yourselves: for they watch for your souls, as they that must give account, that they may do it with joy, and not with grief: for that is unprofitable for you." —Hebrews 13:17

Please note: The dates given in this list of pastors who served at White Oak Springs Baptist from 1856 to 1963 were taken from the Tallapoosa Baptist Association minutes. That association held their annual conference in the fall of the year. The original White Oak Springs Church minutes were lost in a fire about 90 years ago (about 1930).

1. James I. Harris   1856-58
2. Charles Cheek   1859
3. No pastor listed   1860
4. No pastor listed   1861
5. Charles Cheek   1862
6. No pastor listed   1863

No report from Tallapoosa Association for 1864 (Civil War)

7. F. M. Smith   1865
8. N. W. Eubanks   1866-68

No report from Tallapoosa Association for 1869

9. William Coalson   1870
10. W. B. Smith   1871-72
11. J. M. Key   1873-74
12. W. B. Smith   1875
13. J. S. Reynolds   1876-77
14. J. H. Ogle   1878-81
15. D. Wortham   1882-83
16. M. F. Waddell   1884-85
17. D. Wortham   1886
18. J. H. Ogle   1887-91
19. M. F. Waddell   1892-93

20.	G. B. Jenkins	1894
21.	S. T. Gilland	1895
22.	T. B. McClung	1896-98
23.	J. H. Ogle	1899-1905
24.	H. T. R. Marks	1906-07
25.	J. H. Davis	1908-17
26.	J. W. Womack	1918-25
27.	G. Fred Wigley	1926-31
28.	Marion B. Moon	1932-38
29.	James A. Crabb	1939-41
30.	E. J. Cain	1942-46
31.	Herman H. Long	1947-56
32.	Roy Goodson	1957-59
33.	Paul E. Carter	1960-61
34.	Charles E. Williams	1962-63
35.	George Barnett	Sept. 1964- Feb. 18, 1967
	Grover Cook	3/18/1967 – 8/20/1967 - interim
36.	Charles Williams	8/20/1967 – February 6, 1977
	Roy Stanford	5/18/77 – 6/26/1977 - interim
37.	Larry G. Davis	6/26/1977 -3/14/1979
	Clarence Harris	3/14/79 – 9/12/1979 - interim
38.	Druey Tierce	9/12/1979 – 6/2/1981
	Fred Watts	9/15/82 -11/6/1983 - interim
39.	John Robinson	11/6/1983 – 2/17/1985
40.	Ken Martin	5/19/1985 – 12/14/1985
41.	Earl Partain	2/19/1986 – 11/16/1994
42.	Willard Toney	11/30/1994 – 6/14/1995
43.	Johnny Simpson	9/13/1995 – October 2007
44.	Chris Simpson	3/9/2008 – 2013
45.	Keith Lee	2013 to date

Chairmen of the Deacons
White Oak Springs Baptist Church
Dallas, Paulding County, Georgia

"Likewise must the deacons be grave, not double-tongued, not given to much wine, not greedy of filthy lucre; Holding the mystery of the faith in a pure conscience. [10] And let these also first be proved; then let them use the office of a deacon, being found blameless." —1 Timothy 3:8-10

1.	1856 -1888	Unknown
2.	1888-1908	G. W. Cole.
3.	1908 -1943	Moses Barto Roberts
4.	1943-1963	J. N. Wix
5.	1963-1973	Ben Carter
6.	1973-2004	Kenneth Cohran
7.	2004 to date	David McKenzy

Founding Members and Families of White Oak Springs Baptist Church: 1856–1858

"For who hath despised the day of small things? for they shall rejoice. . ."
Zechariah 4:10a

The Tallapoosa Baptist Association held its annual meeting in 1856 at the Springville Baptist Church in Cobb County. The Tallapoosa Baptist Association was one of the first Baptist associations in the western part of the state. At that time, it encompassed Baptist churches from Paulding, Cobb, Haralson, Carrol, Polk, Douglas, Campbell (now Fulton), Cass (now Bartow), Fayette, and even one church that joined in 1835 that was located in Alabama (Arbacoochee).

The third item of business treated at that associational meeting was to receive new churches into its fellowship. That year they received only one new church. The minutes from September 13, 1856, of the Tallapoosa Baptist Association read: "Gave an invitation to churches desiring to become member of this body. White Oak Springs applied and after reading their faith received all their delegates named enrolled."

The report from White Oak Springs Baptist Church listed in the 1856 Tallapoosa Baptist Association records show that the newly formed White Oak Springs Baptist Church had, during the past year, baptized five, received eleven by letter, and had a total membership of thirty-one. This means the church had an original core group of 15 that started the church. This yearly report also lists J. I. Harris as its pastor and lists two delegates who were sent to represent the church. They were J. H. Edwards and J. Roberts.

Rev. James I. Harris
First Pastor of White Oak Springs Baptist Church

Rev. J. I. Harris pastored White Oak Springs Baptist Church from 1856 to 1858. James I. Harris is sometimes listed as J. J. Harris in items that have been transcribed by others from the original documents. This is due to the difficulty that modern readers have while transcribing old-style cursive writing and is also due to the closeness of the capital "J" with the old capital cursive "I." When someone over 100 years later transcribed the handwritten minutes of the Tallapoosa Baptist Association to a typed form, that person listed James I. Harris as "J. J. Harris" rather than "J. I. Harris." The 1868 Tallapoosa Baptist Association minutes does list James I. Harris as a pastor of one of the churches. In the 1850 Census for Paulding County, Georgia, his name is listed as James I. Harris.

Rev. John H. Ogle's obituary states that he was baptized by Rev. James I. Harris. Rev. J. I. Harris died between September 1870 and September 1871. The first pastor of White Oak Springs Baptist Church in 1856 was Rev. James I. Harris.

Pastor Harris was born in South Carolina in about 1812. He was married to Mary Amy Miller Hollis, who was born in about 1810. In the 1850 Census, James and Mary had two children, who were James J. Harris (age 3) and Thomas J. Harris who was less than a year old. Mary was a widower when she married James, and in 1850 she was listed as having six children of her own whose last names were Hollis from her first marriage. The names of her children living in the home were Mahala Hollis (age 22), Jane Hollis (age 20), Sarah Hollis (age 18), Mary Hollis (age 16), Amy

Hollis (age 12), and Evaline Hollis (age 10). All the Hollis children were born in South Carolina. The two Harris children were born in Georgia.

James Harris is listed in the Pumpkinvine Baptist Church records as a deacon of that that church when Rev. James Roberts was the pastor. James Harris' name is also mentioned in connection with selling or donating land to Pumpkinvine Baptist Church during the church's early years[3].

A Quarter (1/4) Church

White Oak Springs Baptist Church was a quarter-church until 1951. This means that the church held one preaching service each month. For most of its history White Oak Springs Baptist Church held its one service a month on the fourth Sunday or weekend. From 1952 to 1956 the church was a "half church," which means it met two weekends a month. They met on the first and third Sundays from 1952 to 1956. In 1957, White Oak Springs Baptist Church started holding services each weekend of the month.

Baptist pastors back in the 1800s would be the pastor or preacher of anywhere from one to six churches at the same time. They could preach at the same church on a specific weekend each month. Sometimes at new churches they could hold the once-a-month services on a Saturday. On rare occasions, a pastor could preach at two churches on the same day, if the churches were not too far apart. Sometimes churches would hold their once-a-month service on a Saturday or even a Friday.

---

[3] htttp://freepages.genealogy.rootsweb.ancestry.com/~freehouse/New%20Adair%20Web%2 0Site/County%20Records/Paulding%20County,%20GA/Church%20Records/Pumpkinvine %20Church%20Front%20Page.htm

In the late 1770s and early 1800s, the Methodists had circuit-riding preachers who traveled far and wide in their travels. The height of the circuit-riding preacher movement in the United States was about 1810. Some Methodist preachers had 600-mile circuits at that time. Most circuit riders had four- to eight-week circuits. They would visit the same circuit (or route) and preach at the same places every four, six, or eight weeks. These circuits would require that these preachers be absent from their families for many weeks at a time and then they would see their wife and kids only a day or two before heading off again.

By the time White Oak Springs was founded in 1856, many Baptist pastors lived at their homes with their families during the week and just traveled to a different church each weekend. On many occasions, the Baptist pastor could get up early Sunday morning and ride by horse or surrey to the church, fulfill his preaching and pastoral duties, and then be back at home before dark. If the church was farther away, the preacher could go to the church on Saturday and stay with a family that had an extra room or cabin for his use.

Pastor James I. Harris preached at White Oak Springs once every month on the fourth Sunday. During 1856, he also was the once-a-month preacher at Pleasant Planes Baptist Church in Carroll County, Georgia. In 1857, Pastor Harris preached at Pleasant Plains Baptist Church in Carroll County, Georgia, on the second Sunday; at Double Springs Baptist Church in Paulding County on the third Sunday; and at White Oak Springs on the fourth Sunday.

The pastors who ministered at White Oak Springs Baptist Church from 1856 to 1957 were never full-time pastors working only at White Oak Springs Church. They were more like circuit-riding preachers who had a home in the four-county area and made trips each weekend to preach at their churches. Their churches paid them a salary, which was more like an offering. The churches usually elected their pastors to a one-year term, and many would call a different pastor each year. Most of the early pastors of White Oak Springs Baptist Church were farmers during the week, and they traveled to their churches on the weekends.

When White Oak Springs Baptist Church started in 1856, they were already calling themselves the White Oak Springs Baptist Church. When the church joined the Tallapoosa Baptist Association a few months after it started in 1856, they were already calling themselves "White Oak Springs Baptist Church."

In the early 1900s, there was a school in the area that was named White Oak School. The school met in the old White Oak Springs Baptist Church building at the 1856 property. If the school using the old church property called itself "White Oak School," and the church at the new property was using the name "White Oak Springs Baptist Church," then members could have surmised the name "Springs" was added to the church name when the move was made in 1889 from the original property to the new property.

This church was officially accepted into the Tallapoosa Baptist Association on September 13, 1856. It had 31 members and a pastor. However, they started meeting sometime before that September 1856 date. The church lost its original records in a fire over 90 to 100 years ago, so a complete list of the founding members does not exist.

In 2016, the church knew that it was started with some members from, or with the help of, Pumpkinvine Baptist Church. The church minutes of Pumpkinvine Baptist Church are transcribed in the book *First One Hundred and Fifty Years of Pumpkinvine Baptist Church.* Their minutes from April 19, 1856, read as follows:

> April 19, 1856—The church met in conference. Invited visiting brethren to seat with us. 2nd opened the doors of the church. 3rd read the minutes of the last conference. 4th called over the items of business. Granted letters of demission to brethren Craven Harris, and sister Amy Harris, Celia Harris, Penelope Harris, Sarah Harris, Elizabeth Harris and Frances Burns in order for them to help constitute another church.[4]

These seven names are part of the core group that helped start White Oak Springs Baptist Church at the old cemetery property. In 1856 J. H. Edwards and J. Roberts were the delegates of White Oak Springs to the annual Tallapoosa Baptist Association meetings. In 1857, John H. Eubanks was the church's lone delegate to the associational meetings. In 1858, Moses Cooper and Craven Harris were the representatives. In 1859, H. Eubanks and N. Cooper were the appointed representatives to the annual conference. In 1860, Mr. M. Mobley was the church's representative.

---

[4]*First One Hundred and Fifty Years of Pumpkinvine Baptist Church.*

If we use the seven names from Pumpkinvine Baptist Church plus the two delegates that were the official representatives from White Oak Springs Baptist Church to the Tallapoosa Baptist Association meeting in September 1856, these names compose nine of the 31 charter members of the church. If we use the names of the five other messengers to the conference from 1857-60, along with their wives and older children, this author believes that those names will represent most, if not almost all, of the founding members of the church.

In 1857 two people joined the church (one by baptism and one by transfer of church letter). Two members died that year, leaving the church with 29 members. In 1858 one member died and no one else joined. Total membership in 1858 was 28. In 1859 four people joined (one by baptism and three by letter), three were dismissed by letter to join another church, and one person was expelled. That left a total membership of 28 for 1859. In 1860, there were no additions or dismissals. The membership remained the same at 28. From 1857 to 1860, the church received a total of six new members. There was not significant change in the membership list from 1856 to 1860.

Craven Harris and His Extended Family

Caren Harris and James I. Harris were brothers. In the 1860 Census of Paulding County, p. 211, District 1083, Family number 749, gives the following information: Craven Harris, age 33, born in SC (born about 1833). His wife is Elizabeth Harris, age 33, was born in SC. They had one daughter named Nancy that was two years old, born in 1858 in Georgia.

In 1847, the family of Samuel and Amy Harris moved from Union County, South Carolina (near Spartanburg) to Paulding County, Georgia. They had the following children: Elijah Harris (born about 1800), Celia Harris (born about 1804), Penelope Harris (born about 1806), Daniel Harris (born about 1810), James I. Harris (born about 1812), Hannah Harris (born about 1813), Pleasant Harris (born about 1824), Sarah Harris (born about 1826), Thomas A. Harris (born about 1828), and Craven Harris (born about 1833). Samuel's first son, Elijah, had a daughter named Frances Elizabeth Penelope Harris (born about 1838) who married Henry Hayes Burns. Elijah Harris migrated to Arkansas with the Burns family after the Civil war.[5]

In the 1860 Paulding County Georgia Census, Pumpkinvine District, p. 819, Elijah Harris (born about 1800) lived beside Daniel T. Harris (born about 1810) and his family. Elijah Harris is the eldest son of Samuel and Amy Harris and is the brother of Celia, Penelope, Daniel, Hannah, Pleasant, Sarah, Thomas A., and Craven Harris. In the Elijah Harris household, the following people are listed: Elizabeth C. Harris (born about 1816); Cilia C. Harris (born about 1843); William J. Harris (born about 1848 in South Carolina); and Celia Ann L. Harris (born about 1854). William J. Harris later married Mary Ann, and they had two children named William Alonzo Harris (born about 1868) and David Harris (born about 1870). William Alonzo Harris later became a deacon and served for many years at White Oak Springs Baptist Church.

---

[5]http://www.reocities.com/Heartland/Pines/5077/harris.htm

The seven people who transferred their membership from Pumpkinvine Baptist Church in April 1856 were "Brethren Craven Harris, and sister Amy Harris, Celia Harris, Penelope Harris, Sarah Harris, Elizabeth Harris, and Frances Burns." Craven Harris was the only male mentioned. Amy Harris was Craven's mother. Amy was born between 1780 to 1790. Her daughters that were members of Pumpkinvine were Celia Harris, Penelope Harris, and Sarah Harris. The Elizabeth Harris mentioned was either Craven's wife (Elizabeth Harris) or Elijah Harris's wife (Elizabeth Harris). Frances Burns was Frances Elizabeth Penelope Harris who had married Henry Burns.

J. H. Edwards

The other two delegates from 1856 were J. H. Edwards and J. Roberts. Unfortunately, no information could be found on J. H. Edwards. In the *New Era* newspaper published in Dallas, Georgia, February 1, 1883, edition, there is the following advertisement: "If anyone wants their sewing machine repaired, call on me at Dallas, where I will sojourn for only a few days. I am a machinist of 16 years experience and guarantee all of my work. J. H. Edwards." That is the only reference that could be found of a J. H. Edwards. There is a possibility, that "J. H. Edwards" could be "J. H. Eubanks" if the photocopy of the original was not of good quality, or if there was a blemish on the page or photo, which made transcription of that name difficult.

J. Roberts is James Roberts, whose wife was Martha. His name will be addressed after the others have been presented.

John and Hosea Eubanks

The lone White Oak Springs delegate for 1857 was John H. Eubanks. In the 1860 Paulding County, Georgia, Census, a John Eubanks (age 60) and his wife Sarah (age 61) are listed along with their daughter Lenaan (Leann) Eubanks (female, age 30—born about 1830) and son Newton Eubanks (age 14, born about 1846). This John Eubanks had a son named Hosea Eubanks in the same 1860 Census, and he was living nearby. Hosea was 20, his wife, Angeline, was 22. He is listed as Hared in one of the censuses. His tombstone reads Hosea, so that name will be used. They had a daughter named Sarah who was two years old and a son, James, who was less than a year old. Hosea was born in South Carolina. His wife, Angeline, and children were all Georgia-born.

Hosea Marion Eubanks married Angeline McBrayer, the daughter of John H. McBrayer (1812–1900) and Susana B. Leathers McBrayer (1816–1900). John H. McBrayer (Angeline's father) and H.M. Eubanks (Angeline's husband) were the delegates to the Baptist associational meeting from White Oak Springs in 1867. Hosea M. Eubanks served in the Confederate Army CSA 40th Georgia Regiment Infantry Company A. He served in the same company and regiment as N. W. Eubanks.

Angeline Eubanks (born March 5, 1838–died July 3, 1928) and her husband Rev. H. M. Eubanks (born Oct 28, 1839–died 1923) are buried in Mount Olive Church Cemetery (Methodist) in Cherokee County, Alabama.

Moses Cooper and N. Cooper

In 1858, Moses Cooper and Craven Harris were the church's representatives. In 1859, H. Eubanks and N. Cooper were the appointed representatives to the annual Baptist conference. Moses Cooper appears in the 1860 Paulding County Census. Moses Cooper was 54 (born about 1806). His wife was Jane (age 52—born about 1808). Their children were James Cooper (age 21), John Cooper (age 18), Mary Cooper (age 13), Sarah Cooper (age 12). Another son, Nathan Cooper (age 19), was living beside Moses and Jane Cooper in the next household.

The following information was posted online by a descendent of Moses Cooper. This was written by Robert Croft:

> Moses Cooper was born in 1806. He joined the Confederate Army on May 31, 1861, in Atlanta, Ga. with two of his sons and one nephew. They were all assigned to the GA 7th Infantry Regiment—Company C—Paulding County Ga. ("Paulding Volunteers") He was 55 years old when he enlisted as a private, which was unusually old at that time…

> Moses fought in the first Battle of Manassas, Virginia. (Also called: The Battle of Bull Run). He was wounded during that battle and died in the hospital on August 31, 1861. He is buried in the Confederate Cemetery in Warrenton, Va. He was in the service exactly 3 months.[6]

---

[6] https://sites.google.com/site/cooperandcroftcivilwar/150-years-ago.

Moses Cooper's two sons that joined the CSA army with him were James Neighbors Cooper and John F. Cooper. James N. Cooper (born in SC in 1838–died March 13, 1901, in Caddo, OK) married Lucy Hitchcock (born 1846 in Paulding County, Georgia–died 1917 in Caddo, OK). Lucy Hitchcock was the daughter of John Hitchcock (b. 1805) and Mary Hitchcock (b. 1817). Mary Hitchcock was Rev. James (b. 1791) and Martha (b. 1798) Robert's daughter, two of the foundering members of White Oak Springs Baptist Church. John Hitchcock and Mary Hitchcock were living beside John and Sarah Eubanks another founding family of the church.

James N. Cooper and his wife, Lucy Hitchcock Cooper, moved to Caddo, Oklahoma, about 1892[7]. Sherry Cooper Sanders is a descendant of the Moses Cooper and in the epilogue of her book *My Brother ... My Son,* states that "James became a schoolteacher, preacher in the Church of Christ faith, and a farmer. He died on March 12, 1901, in Bryan County, Oklahoma near Caddo, (then known as Indian Territory)." Both James N. Cooper's and Lucy Hitchcock's parents were founding members of White Oak Springs Baptist Church.

Moses Cooper's wife was Jane Neighbors Mann Cooper. She was born on September 19, 1807, in Ireland and died on December 7, 1884. Chapter one of *My Brother ... My Son* states that Jane Neighbors migrated from Belfast, Ireland, in 1819 when she was 12 years old. She and many of her children are buried in the New Georgia Baptist Church Cemetery. Her parents, Thomas and Mary

---

[7] http://mem55.typepad.com/caddo_my_home_town/2007/03/ (on Nov. 23, 2016).

Ann Nash Neighbors, are also buried in that cemetery. Another of Moses and Jane's daughters was Sarah Cooper (1848–1932) who married W. B. Cole. They both are buried at New Georgia Baptist Church cemetery in Villa Rica, Georgia.

The book *My Brother ... My Son* by Sherry Cooper Sanders shows what life was like in the Pumpkinvine District of Paulding County, Georgia, during the Civil War years. This book revolves around Jane Cooper and shows her point of view of what life may have been like in the area during that time. This book also gives information on Moses Cooper and two of his sons as they served in the Confederate Army during the Civil War. Moses and Jane Cooper, along with Nathan Cooper, were members at White Oak Springs Baptist Church during this time period

Nathan Cooper

Nathan Cooper was born in 1840. He was about two years younger than his brother James and about two years older than his brother John. He was first cousin to Uncle Bud.

Nathan did not join when his father and two brothers did. His wife, Martha, was expecting their first child, so he stayed home to be with her and to take care of his mother, the farm, and the rest of folks at home. This was the best decision he could have made, but it didn't last long.

The South needed every man available. He was "drafted" 11 months after his daddy and two brothers went in. He was assigned to the GA 56th Infantry Regiment Company E–May 1st 1862. He was captured at Baker's Creek, Miss. May 16th 1863 and released June 15th 1864.

Nathan became a wealthy landowner and politician in Paulding County after the war. He died June 24th, 1898.[8]

N. Cooper first appears as a delegate of White Oak Springs Baptist Church to the Tallapoosa Baptist Associational meeting in 1859 when the church was three years old. He also served as a delegate of White Oak Springs to the association in 1866, 1870, 1871, 1872, 1875, and 1877. The last year that his name appears in the White Oak Springs records was 1877.

Thomas and Retincy Moody

Information from *Georgia Frontier*, Vol 3, p. 282

Thomas Moody was born on October 26, 1811, and died in Paulding County, Georgia, October 29, 1864. He married Retincy Hill Champman in 1835. The 1850 and 1860 Paulding County Censuses list the following children living with them: Sarah (b. 1837), Mary (b. 1838), William T. (b. 1840), Calista (b. 1841), Leander (b. 1842), Elizabeth (b. 1843), Greenberry (b. 1845), Ezekiel (b. 1846), Martha Jane (b. 1849), Samuel (b. 1851), John (b. 1852), Retincy (b. 1853), Sophronia (b. 1857), and Eller (b. 1859).

Thomas Moody and his wife, Retincy, were living beside Rev. James Roberts and his wife and in very close proximity to many of the founding members of this church. Some of their children

---

[8] https://sites.google.com/site/cooperandcroftcivilwar/150-years-ago

married members of the church. Thomas and Retincy are both buried in the Old White Oak Springs cemetery, and their tombstones were moved to the new cemetery. Over 100 years later, they still had descendants in this church that were regular attenders.

There are no written records that Thomas Moody and his family were members of White Oak Springs, but the church has no records from that time period. It is very possible that Thomas and Retincy Moody were indeed founding members of White Oak Springs Baptist Church.

Meridy & Rebecca Mobley

The next name of the founding or charter members of White Oak Springs is Meridy Mobley (according to his tombstone). His family is listed in the 1860 Paulding County Georgia, Census: Meridy Mobley (age 48—born about 1812 in South Carolina), wife Rebecca Mobley (age 37), and children Susan Mobley (age 19), Jesse M. Mobley (age 17), Matthew J. Mobley (age 14), Newton B. Mobley (age 13), Merida Mobley (age 3), and Allen Mobley (age 2). Meridy Mobley's tombstone inscription states he was born on November 9, 1812, and died December 20, 1870. His wife, Rebecca, was born March 27, 1822, and she died on October 18, 1866. Both Meridy and Rebecca Mobley as well as many of their children and grandchildren are buried at Mt. Zion Baptist Church Cemetery (#1) in Paulding County, Georgia.

Pastor James and Martha Roberts

The last of the founding members' names are James Roberts and his wife Martha. James Roberts was born in 1791 in North

Carolina and died in October 1860 in Paulding County, Georgia. He is listed as "J. Roberts" in the information about White Oak Springs Baptist Church. He represented the church as its delegate in its first year of existence at the Baptist association in 1856.

"J. Roberts" could be just about anyone. When doing the research for this book, this author figured that J. Roberts would just be one of those nice guys whose identity would never definitely be known. However, that was not the case. When researching Hamon Roberts, who is buried in the Old White Oak Springs cemetery, this author noticed that he was born in North Carolina in 1799. There were only three families with the last name of Roberts listed in the 1860 Paulding County, Georgia Census that had been born in North Carolina.

In the 1860 Paulding County, Georgia, Census, there was a person listed as "A. Roberts," age 43, born in North Carolina; Hamon Roberts, age 60; and a James Roberts, age 69. Both Hamon and James Roberts were born in North Carolina. Hamon Roberts and James Roberts are brothers, and their father was Ryland Roberts (born about 1760–65 in Randolph County, North Carolina, and died in 1834 in Newberry, South Carolina). (*Georgia Frontier—* Vol 3, Jeannette Holland Austin, p. 305-06).

James Roberts is listed in the 1860 Census of Paulding County, Georgia, along with his wife, Martha, and two children named W. E. Baxter and E. E. Baxter. W. E. Baxter married L. J. Tucker in 1867. E. E. Baxter could probably be Emily E. Baxter who married Mr. C. Brown in 1867. Emily's mother was Muscoga Catherine Roberts. Muscoga died in 1854 in Paulding County, Georgia.

Research revealed that James Roberts was born in 1791 in North Carolina and died in Paulding County, Georgia, in October 1860. His wife, Martha, was born in South Carolina in 1798. His last will and testament names their five children: Polly Roberts Hitchcock w/o (wife of) John Hitchcock; Fanny Roberts Cogburn w/o Zachariah Cogburn; Susanne Roberts Starnes w/o Thomas Starnes; Wesley Hogan Roberts, and Sarah Roberts Boone w/o Matthew Boone. (*Georgia Frontier*—Vol 3, Jeannette Holland Austin, p. 305-06).

Mary "Polly" Roberts married John Hitchcock on September 4, 1845, in Paulding County, Georgia. Polly is a nickname for Mary. John and Mary Hitchcock were living beside John and Sarah Eubanks in the 1860 Paulding Census. Living 10 households away were James and Mary Roberts. Living five households away in the other direction was Hosea (Hared) Eubanks, John's son. Living beside Hared Eubanks is the Elijah Harris family and the Craven Harris family who were from Pumpkinvine Baptist Church. Frances Burns was also living a house or two away.

Another of James Roberts' daughters (Susannah Roberts) married Thomas Stearns[9], who was the great-great grandson of Shubal Stearns, the founder of the now-famous Sandy Creek Baptist Church in Randolph, North Carolina. That church was a very missionary-minded church, and its members became the founders of hundreds of missionary Baptist churches in the South in the early 1800s.

---

[9] https://trenttibbitts.com/tag/paulding-county/

In 1850, James I. Harris was living beside James Roberts and his wife, Martha. Both James I. Harris and James Roberts are listed as "Missionary Baptist Pastors" in the 1850 Paulding County, Georgia, Census. James I. Harris was the first pastor of White Oak Springs Baptist Church when it was started in 1856. James Roberts was the first pastor of Pumpkinvine Baptist Church from 1845–1848. James I. (J) Harris was ordained as deacon in 1849 (from the History Book of Pumpkinvine Baptist Church).

The former pastor of Pumpkinvine Baptist Church, James Roberts, was serving as a mentor and helping the new church get started since he lived near the church. Craven Harris, along with six other people, had been members of Pumpkinvine Baptist Church when they received a transfer of letter to help start a new church. Rev. James Roberts, husband of Martha, had many ties to the new White Oak Springs Baptist Church. James' brother Hamon is also buried in the Old White Oak Springs Cemetery.

Further research needs to be done to see if the Rev. James Roberts' grave can be found. He could be buried anywhere, including his own homestead. However, it is very possible that he could have been buried in the graveyard at the Old White Oak Springs Cemetery.

Brother Elder James Roberts
Committee on Deceased Ministers
(1860 Tallapoosa Baptist Association minutes)

Your committee beg leave to report that we feel renewed obligation to thank God for his great mercy and love in sparing the lives of so many of the ministers of His Word during the past year.

But while we return to Him thanks for His infinite mercy and goodness in the preservation of the lives of so many of his ministers, we are made to bow low in humble submission in the loss of one of the Watchmen of Zion, our aged Brother Elder James Roberts, who departed this life after a short time since, having been in a very low state of health for several years and unable to preach for some years before his death. We learn that he died strong in a triumphant hope of a blessed immortality beyond the grave.

Dear Brethren, let us pray our heavenly Father to spare the lives of his ministers for the years to come; and that He would send more laborers into His vineyard and for which we would recommend that a few minutes be spent in prayer. All of which is respectfully submitted. Rev. W. New—Chairman.[10]

Rev. James Robert's brother, Hamon Roberts (born 1799–died 1882), is buried in the Old White Oak Springs Cemetery along with his wife, Nancy Roberts (1826–1900). Hamon and Nancy Roberts had the following children listed in the 1860 Paulding County, Georgia, Census: Susan (born 1846), Franky [aka "Frances"] (fem.—born 1852), Delilia (born 1855), June (born 1858), Moses Barto Roberts (born 1862–died 1943) and Zellie Roberts (born 1851–died 1941). Moses married Sarah "Sallie"

---

[10] 1860 Tallapoosa Baptist Association minutes

Cole on September 23, 1883, and they were active members in White Oak Springs Baptist Church, especially in their later years. Zellie Roberts married Jacob Sinyard.

Founding members of White Oak Springs Baptist Church in Paulding County, Georgia

These members transferred from Pumpkinvine Baptist Church on April 19, 1856.

1. Craven Harris

2. Amy Harris

3. Celia Harris

4. Penelope Harris

5. Sarah Harris

6. Elizabeth Harris (w/o Craven or Elijah Harris). Both their wives were named Elizabeth Harris.

7. Frances Burns (w/o Henry Burns and daughter of Amy Harris).

8. Rev. James Roberts

9. Martha Roberts (Mrs. James Roberts)

10. J. H. Edwards

11. Mrs. J. H. Edwards

12. John (H.) Eubanks

13. Sarah Eubanks (Mrs. John. Eubanks)

14. Lenaan Eubanks

15. Hosea Eubanks (also listed as Hared Eubanks)

16. Angeline Eubanks (Mrs. Hosea Eubanks)

17. Moses Cooper

18. Jane Cooper (Mrs. Moses Cooper)

19. Nathan Cooper

20. Martha Cooper (Mrs. Nathan Cooper)

21. Meridy Mobley

22. Rebecca Mobley (Mrs. Meridy Mobley)

Children of founding members that are also very probably founding members of the church.

Rev. James Roberts' relatives or wards

23. E. E. Baxter

24. W. H. Baxter

Marity and Rebecca Mobley's children

25. Susan Mobley

26. Jesse M. Mobley

27. Matthew J. Mobley

28. Newton B. Mobley

29. Merida Mobley

30. Allen Mobley

Moses and Jane Cooper's children

31. James Cooper and wife Lucy Hitchcock Cooper

32. John Cooper (married Mary Catherine Wheat on April 1, 1866)

33. Mary Cooper (married N. T. Bullock on December 27, 1865)

34. Sarah Cooper

Due to the close connection of Hamon and Nancy Roberts to James Roberts and many of the founding members of White Oak Springs, this author is adding their names to the list of probable founding members of the church.

35. Hamon Roberts (h/o Nancy Roberts)

36. Nancy Roberts (w/o Hamon Roberts)

Due to the connection of Thomas and Retincy Moody to James Roberts and many of the founding members of White Oak Springs, this author is adding their names to the list of probable founding members of the church.

37. Thomas Moody

38. Retincy Moody

The Early Years: 1859–1869

"In the beginning God ..." —*Genesis 1:1*

Rev. Charles Cheek

Rev. Charles Cheek was the second pastor of White Oak Springs. He is listed as pastor of White Oak Springs only in 1859 and 1862. During 1859, he preached not only at White Oak Springs on the fourth Sunday of each month, he also was pastoring Mt. Olivet Baptist Church in Paulding County, where he preached on the second Sunday of each month. He also pastored a third church at the same time and preached at Floyd Creek Baptist Church in Polk County, Georgia, on the third Sunday of each month. He also pastored Friendship Baptist Church in Paulding in 1879.

Rev. Charles Cheek is listed as living in Van Wert, Georgia, in Paulding County (now Polk County) Georgia, in the 1860 Census. Van Wert had been the county seat of Paulding until 1851, when it was moved to Dallas. In 1851, Polk County was formed from part of Paulding County.

The Committee of Deceased Ministers at the meeting of the 1881 Tallapoosa Baptist Association presented the following obituary for Rev. Charles Cheek on September 12, 1881.

Brother Charles Cheek was born on March 17, 1817, in Cabarrus County, N.C., joined the Baptist Church at Shiloh, Fayetteville, GA in 1840. He was licensed to preach at Mt. Moriah Church, in Paulding County, GA., July 22d, 1854, and was ordained to the gospel ministry at Mt. Moriah Church on the Friday before the third Sabbath in July 1858. Died January 22d, 1881, at 66 years, 10 months, and 18 days. We tender to the bereaved family our sympathies and prayers. Let us be grateful to Almighty God that he has so graciously spared the lives of our ministering brethren and spend a few minutes in humble, grateful prayer in behalf of those still on the watchman's tower. Respectively submitted, J. S. Reynolds. On the adoption of the above report, the association spent a few minutes in humble prayer, led by Elder J. S. Reynolds.[11]

White Oak Springs Baptist Church members from 1859 to 1862 when Charles Cheek was pastor: H. Eubanks, N. Cooper, and M. Mobley (1860 and 1862).

Paulding County, Georgia, during the Civil War Days

In December 1863, the Union armies arrived in north Georgia and wintered there. Beginning in April 1864, the war began again in northwest Georgia and started winding its way southward. When the northern war machine moved into Paulding County, its residents were not exempt from hardships. On May 25, 1864, the Battle of New Hope Church occurred. Two days later the Battle of Pickett's Mill was fought. These two battles were victories for the Confederates, but they were just the prelude for the battle of Atlanta. Union troops were in the area until after the battle of Kennesaw Mountain, which ended on July 2, 1864. After that date, the War and the Union Army went further south, heading to Atlanta and then to Savannah, Georgia. After the dangers of having a Civil War battle in one's front yard had passed, there still were other dangers, like the occupying troops or even worse, dealing with army deserters.

---

[11] Minutes of the 1881 Tallapoosa Baptist Association

Paulding County historian Lucien E. Roberts gives the following account in his book *History of Paulding County* (page 48):

> The wounds inflicted by the Federals on the Civilian population were far deeper than the military accounts indicate. The Federal Army foraged more than usual in this county (Paulding), located twenty or twenty-five miles from the railway base. The invasion occurred at a season where the wheat was ready to harvest, the corn was beginning to grow, and at such a time that at least twelve months would be required to get another harvest. Hogs, cows, horses, poultry, bees—neither beast nor insect was spared. Numerous stories are told of Federal troops taking the last chicken or hog from an already destitute family. This meant that shortly women and children would be seen plodding their way to Cartersville to secure a few pecks of meal with which to keep body and soul together.[12]

The same author goes on to say that "by the end of the year (1864), two thousand Paulding County citizens alone lacked bread for a Christmas dinner."[13] The Civil War brought hard times to Paulding County and to the members of White Oak Springs Baptist Church. Things got worse when the carpetbaggers came after the civil war was over. The White Oak Springs folks fought through these difficulties, and served the Lord at their church.

---

[12]*History of Paulding County*, by Lucien E. Roberts, July 1933, p. 48.

[13] Ibid, p. 47.

Rev. F. M. Smith

The first pastor of White Oak Springs Baptist listed after the Civil War was F. M. Smith. There are two F. M. Smiths listed in the 1860 and 1870/1880 Censuses of Paulding. There was also a third F. M. Smith (Francis Monroe Smith) listed in the Bartow County Georgia Census. In some genealogy sites, people have difficulty distinguishing these three families. Since F. M. Smith was a pastor of several Baptist churches in the area, a more complete history is being presented for him.

There is an F. M. Smith (Francis Monroe Smith) listed in Bartow County Georgia, in 1840 and 1850 that moved to St. Clair County, Alabama, by 1860. He is listed there in the St. Clair County, Alabama, 1860, 1870, and 1880 Censuses. He married Martha Ann Miller in Cass County, Georgia, on November 3, 1854. He was born in 1824 in South Carolina and died in 1882 in St. Clair County, Alabama. That Rev. Francis Monroe Smith was a Baptist minister. This Rev. F. M. Smith was not the Baptist minister who pastored White Oak Springs Baptist Church in 1865.

The second F. M. Smith is Fielding M. Smith and his wife Susan. This F. M. Smith had seven children listed in the 1860 Census. His professions are listed as carpenter, master carpenter (1860), and blacksmith (1870) in the censuses. This Fielding M. Smith (whose wife was Susan) is not a candidate either.

Rev. F. M. Smith and wife, Virginia Shelton Smith

The F. M. Smith believed to be the Baptist minister of White Oak Springs is listed in the 1860 Paulding County, Georgia, Census. He was born about 1830 in South Carolina. He is listed with his wife,

Jane (Virginia/Jenny/Jane) and son Eligah (Elijah) Smith. Jane was born about 1834 in South Carolina. Their son, Elijah, was born about 1858 in Georgia. F. M. Smith's occupation listed in the 1860 Census is M.G.B. That stands for "Minister of the Gospel—Baptist."

This F. M. Smith is identified as Francis M. Smith by Smith family researchers. He was born on February 5, 1829, and died in Augusta, Georgia, on June 13, 1890, while he was traveling. He was married to Virginia Caroline (Jenny) Shelton. She was born on September 10, 1835, and died in Paulding County, Georgia, on November 17, 1910. She is buried in the Holly Springs Baptist Church Cemetery in Paulding County, Georgia. They had nine children. In 1870, F. M. and Virginia Smith were living beside Martin Shelton, who was Virginia's father.

Some Smith researchers identify this F. M. Smith as the one listed in the 1850 Anderson County, South Carolina, Census with his parents Wyatt and Hannah Guyton Smith. That F. M. Smith is listed as Francis Smith (age 24). This Francis M. Smith is not the one who pastored White Oak Springs Baptist Church.

Pr. F. M. Smith

In the 1860 Paulding County, Georgia Census Pastor Smith is listed as F. M. Smith (born in South Carolina—age 30) with his wife, Jane C. Smith (born in South Carolina—age 26), along with their one child, Elijah Smith (born in Georgia—age 2). F. M. Smith is listed as a Baptist minister (M.G.B.).

The 1870 Paulding County, Georgia Census lists Francis N. (or M.) Smith (age 38), wife Virginia (age 35), son Elijah (age 11), Henry (age 9), Jerry (age 7), Jasper C. (age 4). A Catherine Smith, age 62, was also living in the same household. In that census, she is identified as Frances Smith's mother.

In the 1850 Cobb County, Georgia Census (Baits Community), Francis Smith is listed along with his mother, Catherine. Family number 1199 lists his family: James Smith (b. 1788), Catherine Smith (b. 1801), Charles (b. about 1827), Francis (b. about 1829), Nicy (b. 1832), Jane (b. about 1835), Thomas (b. about 1838), Simpson (b. about 1840), and Mancel (b. about 1844). All of these family members were born in South Carolina.

F. M. and Virginia's child Jasper was born in 1866. He later became the Rev. Jasper C. Smith who pastored Baptist churches in Paulding county and surrounding areas in the 1910s, 1920s, and 1930s. He passed away in 1941. Jasper C. Smith and his wife are buried at the New Georgia Baptist Cemetery in Paulding County, Georgia. Some of White Oak Springs Baptist Church members in the 1970s thought this Jasper C. Smith was the Jasper Smith was the founder of White Oak Springs Baptist Church mentioned in the 1933 *History of Paulding County*. However, the dates do not match up. This Jasper C. Smith was born while his father, F. M. Smith, was pastoring this church in 1866.

F. M. Smith is listed in the 1880 Polk County, Georgia Census (Cedartown). F. M. Smith was 50 years old and was listed as a lawyer. His wife was Virginia (age 48). Their children were Elijah (age 22), Henry E. (age 19), Jerry F. (age 16), Jasper C. (age 14), Wyatt (age 7), and Tom L. (age 5).

The following is an advertisement placed by Rev. F. M. Smith in the March 9, 1888, Carroll Free Press (placed 23 years after he pastored White Oak Springs Baptist Church). It is assumed this F. M. Smith is the same one that pastored at White Oak Springs; however, it may be a different person. Today, White Oak Springs Baptist Church would respond negatively to such an advertisement.

I Cure Cancer

With a vegetable preparation (no drugs or poisons in it). I give no pain nor unpleasant feeling. My specific is a balm to the sufferer. It counteracts the disease, is certain relief to the afflicted, and cures the patient of cancer, which has so long stood in defiance of wisdom and skill of the medical fraternity. Address, enclosing a 2 cent stamp for answer, or apply to: Rev. F. M. Smith, Temple, Carroll Co. GA."[14]

This author believes that there was some kinship (or at least friendship) between F. M. Smith and W. B. Smith (b. February 18, 1810–died in Douglas County, Georgia on February 26, 1880), but more research needs to be done to prove that. That W. B. Smith was nicknamed "Doc." People came to him from far and wide to be treated by him with secret medicines he had learned from the Indians.[15]

---

[14] https://www.newspapers.com/clip/461545/smith_rev_fm_cure_cancer/ (Nov. 12, 2016).

[15] https://www.findagrave.com/cgi-bin/fg.cgi?page=gr&GRid=69971742.

William Wilder Wells

W. W. Wells is listed as a member who represented White Oak Springs at the Tallapoosa Association meeting in 1865. W. W. Wells' name is William Wilder Wells. He was born in 1822 and died in 1889. W. W. Wells' wife was Mary A. Wells, and she is buried alongside her husband at the Mount Beulah Cemetery in Cobb County, Georgia. In 1868, W.W. was a member at Mt Zion Baptist Church in Cobb County, Georgia. His brother was James Henry Wells (J. H. Wells) and he also was a member of the church in the 1880s. Mr. W. W. Wells was musically inclined and helped with the church choir and music (according to the 1880s newspaper articles).

Rev. Newton W. Eubanks

Rev. Newton W. Eubanks pastored White Oak Springs Baptist Church from 1866 until 1868. Newton W. Eubanks was the son of John and Sarah Eubanks. In most references he is named N. W. Eubanks. In the 1860 Census of Paulding County, Georgia, Newton is listed with his father, John Eubanks (age 60), and mother, Sarah (age 61). His sister Lenaan is also listed, and she was 30 years old. The John Eubanks family was also living beside the John and Mary Hitchcock family.

The November 23, 1867, minutes of the "Baptist Church in Van Wert", Paulding County, Georgia, notes that the church called Newton Eubanks to be their pastor.

> At Van Wert, met in conference. John R. Heaton, Moderator Pro Temp. 1st, went into choice of a preacher for the ensuing year and chose Reverend Newton Eubanks, unanimously. 2nd, appointed Brethren Moses McCarley and Jesse Hitchcock as a

committee to see Brother Eubanks and notify him of the selection the Church has made.

Newton's father, John H. Eubanks, was a founding member of White Oak Springs Baptist Church and served as one of its delegates from the church to the local Baptist associational meetings in 1857, in 1867, and probably some years in between since some of those minutes are incomplete.

After the civil war, N. W. Eubanks was listed a licensed preacher living in Dallas, Georgia, in the associational minutes, but not as a representative of White Oak Springs. In 1867 and 1868, N. W. Eubanks is listed as the pastor of White Oak Springs Baptist Church. Newton was also the pastor of Pumpkinvine Baptist Church in 1867.

Jesse Hitchcock moved his membership from the Van Wert Baptist Church on February 22, 1868. This information is from the minutes of the Baptist Church in Van Wert, Paulding County, Georgia, February 22, 1868. There were two Jesse Hitchcocks residing in Paulding County and nearby cities in the 1860-70s.

February 22, 1868. The Baptist Church at Van Wert. Brother Heaton, Moderator. 1st, opened the door of the Church for the reception of members, and Sister Mary Jane Hunt presented a Letter of Dismission from the First Baptist Church at Atlanta, and was received. 2nd, taken up the reference in regard to a colored sister Perlina, case. The committee's report was heard and said committee dismissed, and the Church excommunicated her from their fellowship. **4th, granted Sister Harriet Rogers and Brother Jesse Hitchcock Letters of Dismission.** 5th, the committee appointed to notify Brother Camp and Eubanks of the calls of the Church had made are hereby dismissed. Jesse Hitchcock, Church Clerk.[16]

The representatives of White Oak Springs Baptist Church to the Tallapoosa Baptist Association from 1866-68: J. Carter, N. Cooper, H. M. Eubanks, N. W. Eubanks, and J. L. McBrayer.

It is uncertain who "J. Carter" could be. There are three Carters listed in the 1860 Paulding County Census that have a first name that starts with the letter "J" and that are over 20 years of age: There is a "J. Carter," age 35, listed on page 863. There is a James Carter, age 45, born in South Carolina, and a Joseph Carter, age 25, who was born in Georgia. James and Joseph Carter are listed side by side on page 801 of the census and may be related.

Richard J. and Judy Carter

Richard J. Carter would probably be related to the "J. Carter" of White Oak Springs Baptist Church. In 1895, a Joseph Carter was a messenger from White Oak Springs Baptist Church to the association meeting.

Judith "Judy" Adair Carter Bullock Hitchcock

The following information was gleaned from the book: *Georgia Frontier,* Volume 3, by Jeanette Holland Austin (pages 8–9 and pages 50–51).

Judith "Judy" Adair is the daughter of James Lee Adair (b. 1805–d. 1864) and Caroline Evans. James Lee Adair was the first postmaster of Villa Rica, Georgia. James Lee Adair was also the

---

[16]http://www.usgennet.org/usa/ga/county/paulding1/church/VanWert.05.html

son of Bozeman Adair, who was a member of Pumpkinvine Baptist Church. Judith Adair outlived three husbands. She married (1) Richard J. Carter on January 8, 1858. He died during the Civil War. They had three children: James Rufus Carter (b. 1858), Josephine Carter (b. 1860), and Thomas B. Carter (b. 1862). Their daughter Josephine Carter married (1) Zachariah Wix (b. 1855–d. 1892) and then (2nd) John Mathew Hitchcock (1847–1923).

Judith "Judy" Adair Carter married (2) Nickalus Hawkin Bullock in 1866. Nickalus was born in 1825. Judith had two children with Nickalus: William Bullock (b. 1862) and John Pickney Bullock (b. 1871). In the 1860 Paulding County Census, they were living in very close proximity to many of the founders of White Oak Springs Baptist Church: the Mobleys, the James N. Coopers, and others.

Judith "Judy" Adair Carter Bullock married (3) Jesse Hitchcock on October 13, 1892. Together they had no children.

Judith Adair had five children during her lifetime. Many of her children, grandchildren, great-grandchildren, and other descendants have attended White Oak Springs Baptist Church since its inception. Judith "Judy" Adair Carter Bullock Hitchcock was born July 1, 1838, and she died June 22, 1919. She is buried in the White Oak Springs Cemetery. Judith had a very close connection with White Oak Springs Baptist Church since before the Civil War when she married Richard J. Carter. It is possible that she might have been a member of White Oak Springs all her life.

Rev. N. W. Eubanks (Newton) is listed as serving as the second pastor of the Union Primitive Baptist Church in Paulding County, Georgia. That church started on September 4, 1868. The Baggett family history website gives the following information:

> Ordained Ministers and Deacons of the New Hope (Primitive) Baptist Association assisted in the constitution of the Church. Elder Burrell Camp was elected Pastor, and Zebulon Little was elected Clerk for the coming year. The Church remained in the New Hope Baptist Association for several years. It is now a member of the Euharlee Primitive Baptist Association.[17]

J. L. McBrayer is James L. McBrayer. His tombstone inscription indicates he was born on March 31, 1840, and died on January 20, 1919. His wife was Mary C. Moody (born July 18, 1842–died January 13, 1932). Mary's tombstone reads: "Gone, but not forgotten." James and Mary McBrayer are both buried at Friendship Primitive Baptist Church Cemetery in Paulding County, Georgia. James L. McBrayer's sister, Angeline McBrayer, married Hosea Marion Eubanks (H. M. Eubanks).

Missionary Baptists and Primitive Baptists

White Oak Springs Baptist Church was in the Tallapoosa Baptist Association, which was a Missionary Baptist association. White Oak Springs also maintained fellowship with other Missionary Baptist churches.

From 1813 to 1830, Rev. Luther Rice worked to establish the Triennial Baptist Convention. He was able to unify the Baptist

---

[17] http://baggetthistory.com/union.html

churches in the United States to work together to support Baptist missionaries on the foreign fields, and he started Bible colleges to train pastors. Missionary Baptist churches, as they were called, also donated funds to help publish Sunday School quarterlies, tracts, and Bibles.

In the 1830s there was a strong backlash against this missionary or cooperative spirit in sending funds from the local church to support these various parachurch organizations. In 1832, the Primitive Baptists, as they called themselves, organized into a national fellowship of churches. Most of these churches were in the Deep South, where most Baptist churches were located at the time. The use of the word "primitive" in their name means "original" Baptists as opposed to those that were in favor of supporting missions, Bible colleges, Sunday School societies, etc. in the 1830s.

These Primitive Baptists were also called hard-shell Baptists and "old-school Baptists." Old school Baptists described them well in the 1830s because they did not adhere to the new idea of working together to help promote the cause of Christ's church here on earth. They were also called anti-missional or anti-missionary Baptists.

The Primitive Baptists did not support the idea of sending money from their local church to anything outside their local church. Primitive Baptists were Calvinistic in doctrine and did not promote the use of musical instruments in their churches. Being strongly Calvinistic in doctrine, they were usually opposed to evangelistic meetings called protracted meetings. Primitive Baptists also held that foot washing was one of the three ordinances of the church. They sang *a cappella* in all of their services. These Primitive Baptists did not support Bible colleges, so their ministers were not formally trained in a theological setting.

The "Primitive Baptist—Missionary Baptist" controversy came to a head in the 1830s and 1840s when the Primitive Baptists began to form their local, state, and national associations. During this time, one-third or more of the Baptists in the Deep South became Primitive Baptists. During that time, the United States was expanding its territory farther westward toward Texas, and thousands of new Baptist churches were being started as Baptist families moved to new areas and then started Baptist churches. The churches that were lost to the Primitive Baptists were soon replaced with many new churches being started all over the Deep South that were Missionary Baptists.

Newton Eubanks, his brother Hosea "Hared" Eubanks, his father John Eubanks, and James L. McBrayer do not appear in the White Oak Springs Baptist Church minutes after 1868. Newton Eubanks (N. W. Eubanks) is listed as serving as the second pastor of the Union Primitive Baptist Church in Paulding County, Georgia. That church started on September 4, 1868. James L. McBrayer and many of his descendants are buried in the Friendship Primitive Baptist Church Cemetery in Paulding County, Georgia.

Difficult Times

In 1867, White Oak Springs Baptist Church had 88 members. Pumpkinvine Baptist Church had 79 members. Pastor Newton Eubanks was pastoring both of those churches. There are no records for 1869. However in 1870, White Oak Springs Baptist had 34 members. During that year, they dismissed four members by letter and expelled 13 members. In 1869, White Oak Springs Baptist Church had 52 members (including the members excluded during 1870). From 1867 to 1868, White Oak Springs Baptist Church lost an additional 36 members for some reason. All total, White Oak Springs Baptist Church lost a total of 54 of its members in less than three years. That is a loss of 61 percent of its membership for some reason or another. The 13 members that were expelled in 1870 could have been expelled for Primitive Baptist doctrines.

On November 23, 1867, the Baptist Church in Van Wert, Georgia, called Newton Eubanks to be their pastor for the coming year. Four months later, on February 22, 1868, the same church withdrew their call for him to be their pastor. The same church also withdrew their call to Pastor Burrell M. Camp at the same time. Motion five of the February 22, 1868, meeting of the Van Wert Baptist Church states:

> "5th, the committee appointed to notify Brother Camp and Eubanks of the calls of the Church had made are hereby dismissed."

Four months later, on September 4, 1868, Pastor Burrell M. Camp became the first pastor of the newly formed Union Primitive Baptist Church in Paulding, and N. W. Eubanks became its second pastor.[18]

---

[18] http://baggetthistory.com/union.html

Pastor N. W. Eubanks' name does not appear in the Tallapoosa Baptist Association minutes after 1868. For the descendants of Rev. Eubanks and Rev. Camp, no sin or wrongdoing was involved in taking away their calls. From the 1830s to the 1880s, Baptist churches all across the South were defining their position on what the mission of the church is and what a local church's participation should be in helping further the cause of Christ at home and abroad. In 1867 and 1868, Baptist congregations in Paulding County, Georgia, including White Oak Springs Baptist Church and the Baptist Church in Van Wert, were defining their positions.[19]

White Oak Springs Baptist Church's membership went from 88 in late 1867 to only 34 in late 1870. That is a loss of 54 members in a short time. That is a loss of 61 percent of its membership. Other Missionary Baptist churches could have been started during that time, and many people moved out of the area after the Civil War. However, Pumpkinvine Baptist Church's membership numbers did not plummet during that time period. If Primitive Baptist doctrine was involved, then White Oak Springs Baptist Church made the hard decisions, bit the bullet, and came out a stronger Missionary Baptist church than it was before. In October 1870, a very strong Missionary Baptist pastor was pastoring White Oak Springs: Rev. William Coalson.

---

[19] For more information on why the Primitive Baptist Controversy occurred in Paulding County, Georgia in 1867 and 1868, see Appendix 14.

A Little Church in the Woods: 1870–1888

"He said, I am the voice of one crying in the wilderness,
Make straight the way of the Lord, as said the prophet Esaias." —John 1:23

Rev. William Coalson

Rev. William Coalson[20] pastored many churches in Paulding County, but he pastored only one year at White Oak Springs. That year was 1870. William Coalson was born on September 8, 1823, and he passed away on June 18, 1888, in Paulding County, Georgia. He married Harriet Eady in Wilkinson County, Georgia, on December 26, 1842. They are both buried in the Old Garner Cemetery in Haralson County, Georgia. "He lived in the northeast corner of Haralson County where Paulding and Polk Counties meet Haralson." That area later became known as "Coalson Corner." (*Paulding County History Book,* p. 147, 1999).

His obituary was published in the Christian Index on Thursday, July 5, 1888:

---

[20] The Mercer University Archives granted permission to use this photo.

COALSON – Elder Wm Coalson died on June 18, 1888. Many hearts were made sad by the death of this father in Israel. He had been afflicted with heart disease for several years. Like Moses of old, he died without one eye beholding his falling asleep, but God's. In the evening of the 18th of June, he walked across his farm into the woods beyond, and there as we believe, he fell asleep in Jesus. Night came on, and he did not return; a search was instituted, but not until midnight was his body found. While there was no earthly friend near in his last moments, that Friend that sticketh closer than a brother was with him, making the cold earth upon which he fell, "feel soft as downy pillows are."

Brother Coalson was born in Sumter County, GA, on September 8th, 1823. He married December 26, 1842, to Harriet Eady, who is left to mourn his loss. She has been a helpmate to him indeed, in his ministerial work. Fourteen children were born unto them, five of which have preceded their father to the better land. Our brother lived to see all of his children, except one, members of Baptist churches, and he was permitted, a few months ago, to assist in the ordination of one of his sons, Brother A. J. Coalson. The heart of the father rejoiced to know that his mantle had fallen upon his youngest son. May God make him as strong in the defense of the gospel as his father was.

Brother Coalson obtained a hope in Christ and joined Corinth Baptist Church, Sumter County, GA in 1843. He soon was ordained as a deacon, served in the capacity for several years. He then exercised his gifts under a license for some time. In the meantime, he removed himself to Carroll County, GA, where he was ordained for the gospel ministry April 7th, 1860, Elders Burke, Shoss [?] and Harris presbytery. He rendered pastoral services to churches in Carroll, Paulding, Polk, and Haralson Counties. He was instrumental in constituting many of the churches in these counties. Holly Springs church in Paulding County, which numbers over two hundred at present, was constituted in his house some twenty years ago. His remains rest near this spot.

He served as moderator of the Tallapoosa Association 12 years in secession. Five years ago he was appointed by the state board to travel as a missionary in the bounds of the Tallapoosa Association, which work he was engaged in at the time of his death. Let us bow in submission to God's will; our loss is Brother Coalson's eternal gain. A. J. Morgan"

White Oak Springs Baptist Church members in 1870 when William Coalson was pastor: J. Carter, and N. Cooper.

Rev. W. B. Smith

Rev. W. B. Smith pastored White Oak Springs Baptist Church in 1871 and 1872. He pastored here again in 1875. In 1878, Rev. W. B. Smith was living near the Brownsville community in what today is Douglas County, Georgia. In 1879, he was pastoring the Sweetwater Baptist Church and was living near Chapel Hill.

The Carroll Free Press from Carrollton, Georgia, June 18, 1886, page 3.

Rev. W. B. Smith was in town last Wednesday evening on the hunt for his mule which had been stolen from his premises near Mr. McWhorter in Douglas County. The thief tried to sell the mule to Mr. Rooks, four miles west of town at the same evening Mr. Smith was here and no doubt tried to sell it to others, [???] where he succeeded in swapping the mule to Mr. Pearce for a horse. The mule was turned in the lot and when the thief rode off on the horse the mule jumped out of the lot and ran off after the horse and thief. Mr. Pearce started in pursuit hollering to the thief to stop, and he becoming frightened, jumped from the horse and took to the woods and on arriving there look chagrined. Of his mule … ??????. Pearce kept his horse. But the thief at last accounts had not been captured.

The Carroll Free Press from Carrollton, Georgia, October 29, 1886, p 3: "Rev. W. B. Smith, a missionary in the Carrollton association, who was taken sick at the poor farm, this county, is still very sick at his home at McWhorter."

Rev. W. B. Smith was born Feb. 9, 1828, and he passed away on April 18, 1887. He is buried in Prays Mill Baptist Church Cemetery in Douglas County, Georgia. His tombstone states that he was ordained for the ministry in October 1869. In the same cemetery is another W. B. Smith [aka "Doc Smith"]. That W. B. Smith was born Feb. 18, 1810, and died in Douglas County on Feb. 26, 1880. This person could be his father; however, some researchers believe they may be unrelated.

Rev. W. B. Smith was probably the Rev. Walter B. Smith who pastored Pumpkinvine Baptist Church in 1871 and 1872.

In the 1880 Carroll County, Georgia, District 642 Census, there was a William B. Smith listed as being 52 years old (born about 1828). His wife was Sarah Smith (born about 1829), and their children were listed as Columbus Smith (born about 1858), Harry Smith (born about 1861), Susan Smith (born about 1864), Mary Smith (about 1867), and John T. Smith.

White Oak Springs Baptist Church members in 1871-72 when W. B. Smith was pastor: J. Carter, N. Cooper, and Elizabeth Ann Cole.

Elizabeth Ann Cole was a member of White Oak Springs Baptist Church from at least about 1870 until her death in 1891.

Elizabeth Ann Cole's obituary published in the *Paulding New Era* on July 3, 1891, states that she had been a member of White Oak Springs Baptist Church for "over 20 years." Elizabeth was born in 1807 and died on June 24, 1891. She and her husband, Jacob Cole (b. 1809–d. 1892), are buried in the church cemetery. Elizabeth's tombstone states that she was the first person to be buried in the New White Oak Springs Baptist Church cemetery. Since she is a known member of the church from at least 1870 until her death, her name will be added to the list of members of the church along with those who represented the church at the associational meetings.

Rev. J. M. Key

Rev. J. M. Key pastored White Oak Springs Baptist Church from 1873 until 1875.

White Oak Springs Baptist Church members from 1873–75 when J. M. Key was pastor: N. Cooper, J. S. Garner, S. L. Garner, C. Harris, John Hitchcock, J. N. Smith, and Elizabeth Ann Cole.

John Hitchcock's name first shows up as a messenger of White Oak Springs Baptist Church to the Tallapoosa association in 1873. This John Hitchcock is not the John Matthew Hitchcock born in 1805, because he died in 1870. However the John Hitchcock listed in the 1873 Tallapoosa association minutes is probably John Matthew Hitchcock who was born in 1847. These two John Matthew Hitchcocks were father and son.

Rev. J. S. Reynolds

Rev. J. S. Reynolds pastored White Oak Springs Baptist Church in 1876 and 1877.

White Oak Springs Baptist Church members from 1876–77 when J. S. Reynolds was pastor: C. Harris, J. S. Smith, J. Hitchcock, N. Cooper, and Elizabeth Ann Cole.

J. Hitchcock could be one of any five J. Hitchcocks. The good news is that they are all related, and most attended this church.

John Matthew Hitchcock (b. 1805–d. 1870) married Tabitha Herrin (b. 1814). They had two children: Louise Hitchcock (b. 1834) and Jesse William Hitchcock (b. 1836). Jesse was the Rev. Jesse Hitchcock. When Tabitha Herrin passed away, John Matthew Hitchcock married Mary "Polly" Roberts, the daughter of Rev. James and Martha Roberts. John Matthew and Mary Roberts Hitchcock had four more children: Lucy Ann Hitchcock (b. 1846), John Matthew Hitchcock (b. 1847), Overton Alberton Hitchcock (b. 1849), and John H. Hitchcock (b. 1854 or 1857).

In the 1860 Paulding County Georgia, Census, Joseph Hitchcock (b. 1853) is listed as John and Mary Hitchcock's son, along with his older siblings except for Jesse and Louise, who were much older. Joseph Hitchcock is listed in the Paulding County, Georgia Census along with his wife, Martha (age 26), daughter Bell (age 3), son A. Jack (age 2), and daughter "Merucey" (age 1).

Jesse Hitchcock (b. 1836) married Mary Jane Toler. They had 11 children. Many attended White Oak Springs, and many are buried in the church cemetery. Their children were: William Oscar Hitchcock (b. 1862), John Oliver Hitchcock (b.1866), Leona Madora Hitchcock (b. 1867), Talithia Cumi Hitchcock (b. 1869), Estella Louisa Hitchcock (b. 1871), Jesse D. Glen Hitchcock (b. 1874), Henry Grisson Hitchcock (b. 1878), Charles Toler Hitchcock (b. 1881), Lucy Elizabeth Hitchcock (b. 1883), and Jebez Caswell Hitchcock (b. 1885). Jesse married (1st) Mary Jane Toler on May 21, 1861. Then he married (2nd) Judith (Judy) Bullock on October 13, 1892, in Paulding County, Georgia.

Jesse and Mary's first child, Overton Hitchcock (b. 1849), was listed in the 1860 Census along with his wife, F. E. (age 23), son A. J. (age 3), and daughter M. S. (age 2).

Jesse Hitchcock and his wives Mary Jane Toler Hitchcock and Judith Adair Bullock Hitchcock are all buried in the new White Oak Springs church cemetery.

John Matthew Hitchcock (b. 1847) and his wife, Mary A. Hitchcock, are buried in the new White Oak Springs church cemetery.

Overton Hitchcock and wife, Frances Pace Hitchcock, are buried in the new White Oak Springs church cemetery.

As church clerk in the Van Wert Baptist Church, Jesse Hitchcock always signed his name as Jesse Hitchcock in the church minutes each month. Jesse Hitchcock was also the church clerk for Mount Olivet Baptist Church in Paulding County until 1871, and he signed his name in their records as Jesse Hitchcock. When he became the church clerk for White Oak Springs Baptist Church, he signed his name as Jesse Hitchcock. Although the J. Hitchcock listed in the 1876 Tallapoosa Baptist Association minutes could be Jesse Hitchcock, it could also be John Matthew Hitchcock (b. 1847) or another unknown Hitchcock whose name started with "J."

Lucien Emerson Roberts in his 1933 book *A History of Paulding County*, page 141, wrote that Jesse Hitchcock was the church clerk for Mount Olivet Baptist Church in Paulding County from 1866 to 1871. A Jesse Hitchcock transferred his membership out of the Baptist Church in Van Wert in February of 1868. Jesse Hitchcock's name first appears in the White Oak Springs Baptist church records in 1891. Jesse Hitchcock seems to have been very active in the leadership of every church he attended. However, it is possible that Jesse Hitchcock, his wife, Mary Jane Toler Hitchcock, and all their 10 children could have started attending White Oak Springs Baptist Church much earlier if they started attending there when they moved their membership from Mount Olivet Baptist Church in 1871.

N. Cooper is listed as a messenger of White Oak Springs Baptist Church several times in the 1870s. The last time he is listed is in

1877. This N. Cooper is believed to be Nathan Cooper, son of Moses and Jane Cooper. Moses Cooper died at the beginning of the Civil War. It is possible that the Cooper families were all members of White Oak Springs Baptist from 1856 until the late 1870s. New Georgia Baptist Church was started (according to their website ngbc.org) on July 18, 1873. It could be that one of the Cooper families started attending the New Georgia Baptist Church shortly after it opened, and Nathan Cooper moved his membership to that church after 1877. Jane Cooper died on December 7, 1884, and was buried in their church cemetery. Nathan Cooper died on June 24, 1898. He also is buried in the New Georgia Baptist Church Cemetery.

Rev. John. H. Ogle

Pastor John Harrison Ogle[21] pastored at White Oak Springs on three occasions. His first term of service was 1878 through 1881; his second was 1887 through 1891; his third time was 1899 through 1905. Pastor John Ogle's name is usually recorded as "J. H. Ogle" in the Tallapoosa Baptist minutes. Pastor Ogle was born on July 28, 1843, in Newton County, Georgia, and he passed away on December 19, 1910, in Paulding County, Georgia. He is buried at Holly Springs Baptist Church Cemetery. Pastor Ogle was married first to Nancy Caroline Haley on December 19, 1867. Then, after his first wife's death, he married Sarah Jane Sander on

---

[21] Photo used with permission from Margie Campbell Adair.

October 16, 1884. All total he had 14 children. He was baptized by Elder James I. Harris, the founder of White Oak Springs Baptist Church.

During the Civil War, Rev. John H. Ogle served in CSA GA 40th Infantry Regiment, Company F. Serving in the same regiment was his father, William Ogle, and a Jasper S. Smith.

Pastor John H. Ogle must have been a man of vision and action. He was the pastor of White Oak Springs Baptist Church when the decision was made to move from the old property to the new one and build the new church sanctuary.

In Memoriam
Elder John H. Ogle

Elder John H. Ogle was born July 28, 1843 in Newton County, GA. And departed this life December 19, 1910. He was born a poor boy [*and had*] limited [*access to*] education, was a good and obedient son to his parents. He entered the war in 1862. He joined the missionary Baptist Church in Paulding County and was baptized by Elder James I. Harris. He married first in Newton County to Miss. Caroline Haley. She was a good Christian woman and to them were born five children. She died, and he married Miss. Sarah J. Sanders, of Haralson County and nine children were born to them, being the father of 14 children all living to mourn his death except two. He was an affectionate husband and kind father in his family.

He pastored a number of churches: New Georgia; Mt. Zion Paulding; Popular Springs; Mt. Olivet; Draketown; Mt Zion; Bethlehem of Haralson county; Pleasant Hill of Polk county;

Pleasant Grove of Carroll county; Holly Springs; *and* White Oak. He was moderator of the Tallapoosa association in the year of 1900. He was very watchful all the time, following the footsteps of the lowly Galilean, always contending for the faith once delivered to the saints.

A collection of his dying thoughts as we gather them from the life he lived and the death he died: His last words were, "I am just as happy as I can be."

As attending on the death of the righteous who die in the Lord, nothing can give a more correct view of his own account of the life he lived.

The day drew on that he must be gone for the whole of his sickness was from Thursday till Monday: "I see myself now at the end of my journey; my toilsome days are ended. I am going to see that head that was crowned with thorns; that face that was spat upon for me. I have formerly lived by faith and hope, but now I go where I shall see by sight and shall be with him in whose company I shall delight and see him as he is and be satisfied with his likeness." Now, while he was thus in diresome, his countenance changed as his mortality gave way, immortality taking its place.

We as a church mourn his loss. But while it is our great loss, we feel that it is Heaven's great gain.

Written by orders of the Baptist Church of Christ at Fairmont (First Baptist Church, Fairmount, Georgia) in conference, this Dec. 31, 1910.

Elder J. H. Davis, Moderator.
J. A. Holcombe, Church Clerk.

W. C. Mosley, Jesse Hitchcock, W. A. Pool, committee.

White Oak Springs Baptist Church members from 1878–81 when John H. Ogle was pastor: J. Hitchcock, W. P. Whitlow, J. Singleton, W. P. Turner, and Elizabeth Ann Cole.

Mr. James Singleton (b. about 1813) and his wife, Elizabeth (b. about 1832), and their daughter, S. L. Singleton (b. about 1866) are listed in the 1880 Paulding County Census (Pumpkinvine District—1087). They are living beside Retincy Moody (b. about 1810) and many other of the first members of White Oak Springs Baptist Church. Retincy Moody was the widow of Thomas Moody.

The April 10, 1884, *Paulding New Era* published the following: "Retinsa Moody, an aged widow lady living in the upper part of the county, died last Monday."

Thomas Moody (b. 1811–d. 1864) and Retincy Hill Moody (b. 1820–d. 1884) are both buried in the Old White Oak Springs Baptist Church Cemetery. After the church moved to its new location in 1889, their tombstones were moved to the new cemetery, possibly by their daughter Sophronia Moody Wilson. It is said that the Moody tombstone was stolen from the old cemetery by vandals, found later, and then placed in the new cemetery for better protection.

The first interment at the new cemetery was Elizabeth "Betsy" Cole, wife of Jacob Cole. Her tombstone states she was born in

1807 and died on June 24, 1891. Her tombstone also states that she was the first person to be buried at the new cemetery.

Rev. Duncan T. Wortham

Rev. D. Wortham[22] pastored White Oak Springs Baptist Church in 1882–83. Duncan Wortham is buried in the Bethany Christian Church Cemetery in Paulding County, Georgia. His wife is buried there also. Pastor Wortham usually is listed as D. Wortham in the Tallapoosa Baptist minutes.

Pastor Duncan's tombstone states that he was born January 30, 1823. He was married on October 7, 1841. He joined the M. B. Church (Missionary Baptist Church) in 1845. He was ordained for the ministry in 1862. He died on August 12, 1907.

The May 1, 1884, edition of *Paulding New Era* newspaper published the death notice of his son John Wortham. In that article, it states that the son of Rev. Duncan Wortham passed away. A week later on May 8, 1884, the *Paulding New Era* gives more information about John Wortham's death and lists Pastor D. Wortham's wife's name as Malinda. Malinda's tombstone states she was born in 1823 and died in 1907. It also states she joined the

---

[22] Public domain photo of Duncan T. Wortham. He died in 1907.

M. B. Church in 1845. Their descendants state that they had eight children.

White Oak Springs Baptist Church members in 1882–1833 when D. Wortham was pastor: C. Harris, J. Hitchcock, Erastus Wells, Addie Wells (née Carter), and Elizabeth Ann Cole. It is uncertain when Mary Jane Toler Hitchcock became a member of White Oak Springs: however, she was a member at the time of her death in June 1892. G. W. Cole became a member of White Oak Springs Baptist Church on August 6, 1883. His wife was Louisa Sinyard Cole. The Sinyard family is related to the Rev. James Roberts family, which is one of the founding members of White Oak Springs Baptist Church. It is not known exactly when Louisa Sinyard Cole became a member of this church, but it is possible that this is the only church she where she was a member or attended.

The *Paulding County New Era* newspaper reported in the April 12, 1883, edition that "Brother Wortham preached at White Oak Springs Sunday to an attentive crowd."

Report from the Committee on Deceased Members of the Tallapoosa Baptist Association
Paulding County, Georgia, 1907

Your committee on deceased members beg leave to make the following report: Our association has lost one of its members during this year, our beloved Brother Elder D. Wortham passed away, he has served his day and fallen asleep. He lived to over 80 years of age, he was beloved of all who knew him, he was a good soldier of Jesus Christ, He lived a godly life, and died as he had lived in the full triumph of the faith of the son of God. We tender our hearty sympathies to his bereaved family and pray that they may follow his examples and their lives may be like his.

The obituary of Mr. L. E. Wells (Erastus Wells) appeared in the *Cullman* (Alabama) *Tribune-Gazette and Tribune* on February 21, 1908:

Mr. L. E. Wells (Erastus Wells) was a native of Georgia. He was born on March 13, 1861, and passed away February 5, 1908. He joined the Missionary Baptist Church at White Oak Springs, Paulding, Georgia, in 1883 and remained a devoted Christian, parent, and neighbor until his death. He was a member of the Center Grove Church when he died, having joined in 1906. He was ordained a deacon of the same church in 1907. His wife, Miss Addie Carter formerly, whom he married in 1885 still survives him. He was the father of seven boys and two girls who survive him. He is buried in the Center Grove Baptist Church Cemetery.

Rev. M. F. Waddell

Rev. M. F. Waddell pastored White Oak Springs Baptist Church in 1883–85 and then a second time in from 1892 -93.

White Oak Springs Baptist Church members in 1883–1885 when M. F. Waddell was pastor: J. R. Cole, C. Harris, J. Hitchcock, J. H. Wells were messengers to the Baptist Association during these years. G. W. Cole, Louisa Sinyard Cole, Erastus Wells, Addie Wells (née Carter), Elizabeth Ann Cole, and Mary Jane Toler Hitchcock were also members.

Rev. D. Wortham

Rev. Duncan Wortham pastored White Oak Springs Baptist Church for a second time in 1886.

White Oak Springs Baptist Church members in 1886 when D. Wortham was pastor: W. Chambliss, and C. Harris were representatives of the church to the local association. G. W. Cole, Louisa Sinyard Cole, Erastus Wells, Addie Wells (née Carter), Elizabeth Ann Cole, and Mary Jane Toler Hitchcock were also members.

Rev. John H. Ogle

Rev. John H. Ogle pastored White Oak Springs Baptist Church for a second time from 1887 until 1891. This pastorate became one of the most important ones in the history of the church since it was under his leadership that the church decided to move and build a new church meeting house.

White Oak Springs Baptist Church members in 1887–91 when John H. Ogle was pastor: G. W. Cole, G. Garner, Jesse Hitchcock, and F. J. (I.) Smith. Elizabeth Ann Cole was also a member during these years. L. E. Wells (Erastus Wells) was a member from 1882 until about 1905. Addie Carter Wells was a member from at least 1885 until about 1905. Louisa Sinyard Cole, and Mary Jane Toler Hitchcock were also members.

The Paulding New Era published the following on Friday, July 3, 1891.

Aunt Betsy Cole

"Old aunt Betsy Cole age 84 years, the wife of uncle Jacob Cole, age 82, who has been confined to her bed for some time, departed this life on last Wednesday night a week ago and was enterred [sic] at New White Oak Springs church where she chose to be buried, she joined the church at Old White Oak Springs over 20 years ago but for some cause was never baptized, but in her last hours was ready and willing to die, and chose to be buried at New White Oak, these two old people lived alone together after their children all left them 15 years and appeared to have great love for each other, she leaves a number of friends besides 3 sons and 4 daughters, and an old bereaved *(husband)* tottering and trembling over the dead body of his once near and dear friend for the last time in this life and said, 'farewell, farewell, to the last friend I have, no doubt but what the old gray headed tottering father felt that he was left without a friend, yet has a friend far superior to a companion who is able to land him safely over the cold icy stream of death into a land of peace where we should all strive and fight to win.'"

Jacob and Elizabeth Cole had many children that were active members of White Oak Springs Baptist Church. Many of their descendants attended this church for over a century and may still be attending today. Here is a list of their children: **William Cole**, married Dicy *(Dicey)* Sinyard; **Susanah Cole**, married John Sinyard; James M. Cole, married (1) Sarah M. Waites and (2) Mary Fuller; **John R. Cole**, married Elizabeth Neal; **Elizabeth Cole**, married Robert M. Treglown; **Sabra Cole**, married Henry H. Smith; **Mahala Cole**, married Macajah M. Ford.[23]

---

[23] www.genealogy.com/ftm/d/e/d/Diane-S-Dedmon/GENE5-0001.html - (Nov 3, 2016)

William and Dicy Sinyard Cole, John and Susanah Sinyard Cole, and John R. and Elizabeth Cole all have descendants that were active members and leaders of White Oak Springs Baptist Church.

The *Paulding New Era,* August 16, 1889, gives the following obituary: "Died. Old Uncle Elicia Harris, departed this life on the 16th inst. His remains were interred at the White Oak Springs Cemetery."

George W. Cole

G. W. Cole was George W. Cole, Sr. He was first listed as representative of White Oak Springs in 1891. His nickname was Brother Doc or Brother Dock. The nickname Doc does not have to mean he was a real doctor. The original meaning in Latin is *doctus* which means having been taught or that one is a learned person[24]. Brother Doc Cole became the secretary of every Baptist church he attended and even of the Tallapoosa Baptist Association shortly after he joined. He could read and write well. He at least had a superior education as a child and may have even studied in college. An educated man like Brother G. W. Cole would stand out in a frontier community where most people could not even read or write. Brother Doc was also the long-time postmaster for the community of Bud, which is the community where the old church was located two miles away.

Brother Cole is buried in the new church cemetery and his tombstone reads: "Remember youth while passing by, as you are now so once was I, as I am now so shall you be, prepare for death and follow me." George W. Cole, Sr. was born in 1849 and died in

---

[24] http://bestnicknametees.com/nicknames/doc/ on Nov 25, 2017.

1908. He married Mary Louisa Sinyard. She was born in 1853 and died in 1922. His son was also named G. W. Cole, and he served as a representative of the church after G. W. Cole's death in 1908.

Obituary of G. W. Cole

(from the *New Era* newspaper, May 21, 1908, p. 5)

Death comes equally to all and makes us all equal when it comes. On the night of March 26th, 1908, death visited the home of Louisa Cole and removed from this world of sorry and affliction her husband G. W. Cole. All that loving hands of his dear wife, children, relatives, friends could do to relieve him, death came. They did not expect but a few hours before it came, though Brother Dock was badly afflicted.

Brother Dock bore his afflictions with all the fortitude of a Christian. He never murmured or complained of his sufferings. He was ready and willing to go. He joined the missionary Baptist Church at White Oak Springs August 6th, 1883. He was elected clerk of the same church October 27th, 1883. Brother Dock was ordained a deacon at the same church June 23rd, 1888, and was elected clerk of the general meeting of the second district of the Tallapoosa Baptist Association July 27th, 1891. He was elected clerk of the Tallapoosa Association September 11, 1891, and treasurer of the same Association September 12, 1891.

Brother Cole was born in Harris County, Georgia, June 18, 1849; moved to Paulding County in 1858, where he spent the remainder of his life. He was married to Miss. Louisa Sinyard in the year 1870, November 6th.

Brother Cole leaves his wife and several children to mourn his loss. He was buried at White Oak Springs Church March 27th,

1908. The funeral services were conducted by Brother J. H. Ogle and Brother J. H. Davis.

Brother Cole lived a pious life and [was] a devoted Christian from the time he joined the church. The church has lost one of its best members, the county one of its best citizens, the community one of its best neighbors. He was always ready to defend the cause of Christ at any time he was called on to do so.

He was a good husband, a kind and loving father, a good neighbor and friend to all. He will be missed in the church, and in the community in which he lived, and those who will miss him the most are the heart-broken wife, children and grand-children.

He leaves a host of relatives and friend to mourn his loss. Those who knew him best loved him most. May the God of all the earth bless the family of the loved one that's gone before. May we all be prepared to meet our loved ones where the good are all at rest.

J. Robt. Cole

M. R. Adair

Jesse Hitchcock

New Property, New Church Sanctuary, New Cemetery:

August 1889–1946

"Behold, I make all things new." —Revelation 21:5

Rev. John H. Ogle, who pastored White Oak Springs Baptist Church on several occasions, was the pastor of the church when the church decided to move from its old location. He led the church during the construction, and he became its first pastor at the new location. White Oak Springs Baptist Church thanks the Lord for the vision of this pastor and for his leadership to make the move.

In August 1889, White Oak Springs was building their new church building so they could start using it the fourth Sunday of the month.

The move to the new church location was made during the fourth weekend in August 1889. The church held a special event on Friday, August 22, in which they received sister Baptist churches, and then they held services in the new church on Sunday, August 24, 1889.

Rev. M. F. Waddell

Rev. M. F. Waddell pastored White Oak Springs Baptist Church in 1892 and 1893.

White Oak Springs Baptist Church members from 1892–93 when M. F. Waddell was pastor: G. W. Cole, Jesse Hitchcock (a licensed preacher), L. E. Wells (Erastus Wells), Addie Carter Wells, and Mary J. T. Hitchcock.

Rev. G. B. Jenkins

Rev. G. B. Jenkins pastored White Oak Springs Baptist Church in 1894.

The tombstone of Elder G. B. Jenkins states that he was born on May 19, 1846, and that he died on December 14, 1895. The tombstone states he was 50 years, 6 months, and 25 days old. The title Elder means pastor or Reverend. It is a term that was commonly used in the mid- to late-1880s. Elder G. B. Jenkins is buried in the Pleasant Hill Baptist Church Cemetery in Villa Rica, Georgia. In the 1896 Tallapoosa Baptist minutes, G. B. Jenkins is named as the one pastor of the association that had died during the past year. Rev. Jesse Hitchcock led in a time of thanking God for G. B. Jenkins' years of ministry.

White Oak Springs Baptist Church members in 1894 when G. B. Jenkins was pastor: M. R. Adair, G. W. Cole, Jesse Hitchcock, L. E. Wells (Erastus Wells), Addie Carter Wells.

M. R. Adair is Milton R. Adair. According to his tombstone, Milton R. Adair was born February 4, 1857, and he died on January 22, 1936. He married Amanda S. Sinyard. She was born on May 13, 1859, and died May 28, 1931. They are both buried in the Gann Cemetery in Paulding County, Georgia. His parents were William Levi Adair (b. 1829) and Adaline Gann (b. 1835). William Levi Adair (b. 1829) was the brother of Judith "Judy" Adair Carter Bullock Hitchcock (b. July 1, 1838).

M. R. (Milton R.) Adair's name appears in many Civil War pension affidavits for people connected with White Oak Springs Baptist Church or who lived in the area. Mr. M. R. Adair is also listed as chorister or song leader of the church in the church records.

Rev. Stephen T. Gilland (S. T. Gilland)

Rev. Stephen T. Gilland[25] pastored White Oak Springs Baptist Church in 1895.

Rev. Stephen T. Gilland, according to his tombstone, was born on April 1, 1870, and died on April 12, 1950. His wife, Sarah Ida Wyatt Gilland, was born on March 22, 1877, and she passed away on June 20, 1945. Both Stephen and Sarah are buried in the Douglasville City Cemetery in Douglasville, Georgia.

White Oak Springs Baptist Church members in 1895 when S. T. Gilland was pastor: Joseph Carter, G. W. Cole, Jesse Hitchcock (a licensed preacher), L. E. Wells (Erastus Wells), and Addie Carter Wells.

---

[25] Photo used with permission granted by Mary Waldrop.

Rev. Thomas Burton McClung (T. B. McClung)

Rev. Thomas B. McClung pastored White Oak Springs Baptist Church from 1896 until 1898.

Pastor T. B. McClung was licensed to preach in 1893. He was living in Temple, Georgia, at that time. T. B. McClung's name was Thomas Burton McClung (tombstone info). According to his death certificate, he was born in Campbell County, Georgia, on October 25, 1852, and died on January 8, 1920. He married Susan E. Whitehead (born March 20, 1855, and died August 9, 1920). Thomas Burton McClung's nickname may have been "Bert." His parents were Samuel McClung and Debra Brown McClung.

Thomas Burton McClung's paternal grandfather, Ruben McClung (born 1777 in Ireland and died 1860), is buried in Sweetwater Baptist Church Cemetery in Paulding County, Georgia. Ruben's tombstone states that he was the first generation of McClungs to come to America. He was a (if not the) founder of Sweetwater Baptist Church. He also donated the first property to the church, which was his homestead.

White Oak Springs Baptist Church members from 1896–98 when Thomas Burton McClung was pastor: M. R. Adair, G. W. Cole, Jesse Hitchcock, J. Carter. L. E. Wells (Erastus Wells) was a member from 1882 until about 1905. His wife Addie Carter Wells was member from about 1885 until about 1905.

Jesse Hitchcock was the Rev. Jesse William Hitchcock.

Jesse William Hitchcock was born 07 May 1836 in Walton Co., GA, and died 29 Jul 1912 in Rockmart, Polk Co., GA. He married (1) Mary Jane Toler[26] on 12 May 1861 in Paulding Co., GA, daughter of William Toler and Elizabeth Creel. She was born 17 Jan 1845 in Bibb Co., AL, and died 10 Jun 1892 in Paulding Co., GA. He married (2) Judah Bullock 13 Oct 1892 in Dallas, Paulding Co., GA.

Rev. Jesse Hitchcock

In 1931 or 1932, church clerk George W. Cole (Jr), told Lucien E. Roberts, who was writing the History of Paulding County (1933), that Rev. Jasper Smith and Rev. Jesse Hitchcock were former pastors of the church. Tallapoosa Baptist Association minutes show no listing that these men ever pastored at White Oak Springs.

Rev. Jesse Hitchcock is first listed as a licensed minister of White Oak Springs in 1892. In 1902, Jesse Hitchcock is listed as an ordained minister who had his membership at White Oak Springs Baptist Church. The minutes of the Tallapoosa Baptist Association state in its rules of decorum that the Lord's Supper and Baptism could be administered only by ordained ministers. Jesse Hitchcock was probably ordained as a minister, so he could administer the Lord's Supper at White Oak Springs and other area churches when those churches had no pastor. The Tallapoosa Baptist Association minutes (1856 to 1982) never list Jesse Hitchcock as a pastor of any of the churches in the association. Jesse Hitchcock was a very active member and leader in the church.

---

[26] http://www.genealogy.com/ftm/h/i/t/Glenn-L-Hitchcock-GA/GENE1-0001.html

Jesse Hitchcock was also the local judge for the community of Bud (the community where the church was located in 1856). He served in this capacity for many years. Brother Jesse Hitchcock also was called upon to help write many of the obituaries for the Tallapoosa Baptist Association for pastors who had died during the past year. He also wrote some obituaries for deacons of the churches where he was a member.

The following obituary is from *The Atlanta Constitution Newspaper,* Atlanta, Georgia, on August 1, 1912:

Dallas, Ga. - July 31. Jesse Hitchcock, one of the pioneer citizens of Paulding County, died at 11 o'clock last night after a short illness. "Uncle Jesse," as he is familiarly known, was the father of Dr. W. O. Hitchcock, of this place, and is survived by a large number of relatives in this county.

From the *Dallas New Era,* 17 July 1892:

Mary Jane Toler married Jesse William Hitchcock May 12, 1861, Fish Creek, Polk Co., GA. She became the mother of 6 sons and 5 daughters, 9 still survive. She joined the Yorkville Baptist Church in 1869. She then moved her membership to Old White Oak Springs Baptist Church in Paulding Co. where she remained until her death. She was a good wife, a loving mother, and a remarkable Christian woman. She was confined to her bed for more than 3 months with an abscess in her right side. She suffered much. The eyes of a fond mother that sparkled with the light of love are closed forever. Earth is lost, but heaven is gained. We tender our sympathy to the bereaved companion and children left to mourn her. She was buried at Old White Oak Springs on the 11th of June 1892 at 4 o'clock P.M.

Rev. John H. Ogle

Rev. John H. Ogle pastored White Oak Springs Baptist Church for a third time from 1899 until 1905.

White Oak Springs Baptist Church members in 1899 when John H. Ogle was pastor: G. W. Cole, Jesse Hitchcock, L. E. Wells (Erastus Wells), and Addie Carter Wells.

White Oak Springs Baptist Church members from 1901 to 1905 when John H. Ogle was pastor: M. R. Adair, G. W. Cole, J. Robert Cole, W. J. Harris, Jesse Hitchcock.

W. J. Harris is William Jackson Harris. He and his wife are buried in the church cemetery. According to his CSA pension papers, William was born on March 22, 1841, and died on March 11, 1909. His wife was Mary Ann Harris, who was born about 1838. They had two children listed in the 1880 Paulding County Census: William Harris was born about 1868 and David was born about 1870.

Rev. H. T. R. Marks

Rev. H. T. R. Marks[27] pastored at White Oak Springs Baptist Church in 1906. H. T. R. Marks was born on June 26, 1853, and he died on March 13, 1930. His full name was Henry Thomas Reed Marks. His wife was Mary Marks. She was born on December 28, 1855, and she died on December 13, 1926. They are buried in the Mountain View Baptist Church Cemetery. That church is only a

---

[27] Photo used with permission from Howard Garrett on Nov. 30, 2017.

few miles from White Oak Springs Baptist Church. Their tombstone states: "We will meet again."

White Oak Springs Baptist Church members in 1906 when H. T. R. Marks was pastor: M. R. Adair, B. C. Cole, G. W. Cole—clerk, Radar Cole, J. Robert Cole, Wofford Cole, Jesse Hitchcock—ordained minister, H. H. Kemp, M. B. Roberts. H. H. Kemp is H. Hendred Kemp.

Moses Barto Roberts

M. B. Roberts is Moses Barto Roberts. He is the son of Hamon Roberts, who was one of the probable founders of White Oak Springs Baptist Church. Moses B. Roberts was also the nephew of known founding member Rev. James Roberts. Moses married Sallie Cole on September 23, 1883. They had 14 children. Most of them are buried in the church cemetery. Their children's names were; George R. Roberts (b. 1887), Vinnie Roberts (b. 1889), Pearlie Roberts (b. 1889), Omie Roberts (b. 1892), Hamon Jessie Roberts (b. 1894), Nath. C. Roberts (b. 1896), Sim Roberts (b. 1898), Tyra Roberts (b. 1900), Ada Beth Roberts Hicks (b. 1901), Ruben Arnold Roberts (b. 1905), Elmer Roberts (b. 1906), Dewey [Dean] L. Roberts (b. 1910).

Two entries about the death of G. W. Cole from the 1908 Tallapoosa Baptist Associational Minutes

Report of Committee of Deceased Ministers

We, your committee, submit the following report: We find that one of our deacons has been called to his reward above. Brother G. W. Cole, who was a good deacon of

White Oak Springs Baptist Church. Brother Cole was also the efficient clerk for seventeen years of our body. We sorely feel his loss.

Resolution of the death of G. W. Cole

Whereas, God in His all-wise providence has seen fit to remove by death our beloved brother and deacon G. W. Cole. Whereas, for a number of years he served us faithfully as clerk of the general meeting of the Tallapoosa Association, and whereas this body feels deeply the loss of so valuable a servant, therefore be it resolved, that we extend to his family all heartfelt sympathy in their sorrow. Resolved that a copy of these resolutions be printed in the Christian Index and that a copy be sent to his family, and a page of our minute be devolved to his memory. A.J. Coalson and R. E. L. Whitworth—commission.

G. W. Cole is the first person that the church has record of that served as a deacon of this church. He was the chairman of the deacons at White Oak Springs Baptist Church for many years.

The tombstone inscription of G. W. Cole, Sr (died 1908), gives the following reminder to all who stroll through the graveyard: "Remember youth while passing by, as you are so once was I, as I am now so shall you be, prepare for death and follow me."

Rev. J. H. Davis

Rev. J. H. Davis pastored White Oak Springs Baptist Church for nine years: from 1908 until 1917.

On July 24, 1908, White Oak Springs Baptist Church ordained H. H. Kemp and Moses Barto Roberts (M. B. Roberts) as deacons. On June 26, 1915, White Oak Springs Baptist Church ordained W. A. Harris and Walter Cole as deacons.

Moses Barto Roberts and wife Sallie Cole Roberts
Photos used with permission from Matt Bandy

Deacon Moses Barto Roberts

Moses Barto Roberts was a deacon of White Oak Springs Baptist Church from July 24, 1908, until his death in 1943. The biography of deacon J. N. Wix states that Wix had been the chairman of the deacons at White Oak for 20 years when he died in 1963. So, J. N. Wix was the chairman of the deacons from 1943 until 1963. Deacon Moses B. Roberts was probably the chairman of the deacons at the time of his death in 1943. He may have served as chairman of the deacons from 1908 until 1943.

Moses Barto Roberts Family

Back row (left to right): Elmer, Beth, Fannie, Bart, Vinnie, Ruth, Nathan, George
Front row (left to right): Sim, Hammie, Dean, Arnold.
Photo used with permission from Matt Bandy

More Information on the Moses Barto Roberts Family

The Heritage of Paulding County, GA 1832-1999 book, published by the Paulding County Historical Society, has two articles on Moses Barto Roberts and his family. Here are five quotes that give a glimpse into this beloved family of our church. The first four quotes are from article 1030, and the last quote is from article 1031.

In 1881, Mary Frances (Roberts) married a widower, Jesse Cole. He was the son of two other Paulding County pioneers, John and Sarah Cole. Two years later, Bart married Jesse Cole's daughter, Sallie. (Moses Barto Robert)'s oldest sister was then also his mother-in-law.

In the early 1900's, there were so many Roberts and Cole relatives living within a two or three-mile radius, they had their own private telephone system.

Bart was born, lived, and died in the same homestead.

Grandfather Bart was the most gentle of men.

Bart had a logging/sawmill company on his farm where most of his children helped.

Isaac Wix

The Isaac Wix family has many descendants that were active members of White Oak Springs Baptist Church. Their children married many of the children of the founding members of this church. Isaac and Missouri Wix were the Wixes connected to this church. They are buried in the Old White Oak Springs Cemetery. Isaac Wix is listed in the 1860 Paulding County Georgia Census as being born in 1815. His wife, Missouri, was listed as being born about 1825. Their last name in the 1860 Paulding Census is spelled "Weeks." In the book *1864 Census for Re-Organizing the Georgia Militia,* (page 816), Isaac is listed as being 51 years old, and his last name is spelled "Wicks."

The 1860 Paulding County Georgia Census lists the following children for Isaac and Missouri E. Wix (Weeks): Benjamin Wix (born 1852), Joseph H. Wix (b. 1853), Isaac Wix (b. 1855), Julia Ann Wix (b. 1856), Zachariah Wix (b. 1856), Mary E. Wix (b. 1858), Marion Wix (b. 1859), Adarine Wix (b. 1861), William H. Wix (b. 1859). Other children in this Wix family, according to their descendants, were Newton Wix (b. 1863), Salley Jane Wix (b. 1865), Rebecca Larena Wix (b. 1870). Joseph Hiram Wix and Zachariah Wix were Isaac and Missouri's sons, and they and their descendants were active members at White Oak Springs Baptist Church.

J. H. Wix

Joseph Hiram Wix was born on April 20, 1852 (according to his tombstone). He died on November 15, 1923. He married Nancy Alice Trapp, who was born on February 19, 1853, and died on July 6, 1936. Both J. H. Wix and Nancy T. Wix are buried in the White Oak Springs Cemetery. The 1880 Paulding County Georgia (Pumpkinvine) Census lists the following children: S. C. (Sarah) born about 1873; William (born about 1874); J. M. (John Newton) born about 1878; Adaline (born about 1880). They had other children, according to the descendants. The other children were Oliver (born about 1881); Alma Annie (born about 1891); Charlie R. (born about 1895).

Deacon J. N. Wix

J. N. Wix (John Newton Wix) is listed in the church records as having been born September 4, 1877. He died on November 12, 1963. J. N. Wix married Georgia O. Clark. Georgia Clark was the daughter of Samuel Clark and Cecilia Moody Clark. John Newton Wix served as chairman of the deacons for 20 years, served as church clerk for 36 years, justice of the peace for 64 years, member of Marchmon Lodge 57 years, served as treasurer and clerk from 1953–56 (from *Deacons of White Oak Springs*).

John Newton Wix was the son of Joseph Hiram Wix and Nancy Trapp. They had the following children: Ruthie P. Wix (born about 1907), Herbert Loring Wix (born about 1911), John Edwin Wix (born about 1914), Oma Lois Wix (born about 1917), and Vera I. Wix (born about 1923). In the 1920 Paulding County, Georgia, (Pumpkinvine) census, John M. (N.) Wix (age 42), wife Georgia (age 36), and children Pauline (age 12), son Lorsing (age 8), John E. (age 8), Lois (age 2) are listed. The 1920 Census lists the names the children went by.

The Wix family was participating in the ministries of this church from the 1860s or 1870s. The first time the Wix surname appears in the Tallapoosa Baptist Association minutes is 1914 when J. N. Wix was one of the church's delegates to the Tallapoosa Baptist Association. There are Wix descendants that are members of this church still today.

Deacon William Alonzo Harris

W. A. Harris is William Alonzo Harris. He went by Lanzo. William Alonzo Harris was born in 1869 and died in 1958. Lanzo married Mary Louise Leatherwood. She was born in 1872 and died in 1946. Jeff Byrd said that William and Mary Louise Harris built their house on Buchanan Highway in 1905 with a $200.00 inheritance they received from Mary Louise's side of the family. Jeff Byrd and his wife live in that home today (2018).

Deacon Walter Cole

Walter Cole served as deacon at White Oak. He was ordained at the same time as W. A. Harris on June 26, 1915. Brother Walter Cole married Mollie Wilson.

First Mention of Sunday School

The 1916 minutes of the Tallapoosa Baptist Association records for the first time that White Oak Springs Baptist Church had a Sunday School. Mr. G. W. Cole was listed as the superintendent, and the church had a Sunday School enrollment of 58. There are reports through 1919 about the Sunday School, but there is no mention of the Sunday School again until the 1927 minutes.

Sunday Schools were usually held weekly, even though most churches had a preaching service only once a month. It is possible that White Oak Springs has held weekly Sunday School services since 1916. It is also possible they held Sunday School for a decade or so and then did not start holding them regularly until about 1953. We do know that in the 1950s, White Oak Springs was holding Sunday School each week. Regular members and attenders brought their children to church to be systematically taught the Bible. Current Pastor Keith Lee says that "a church is only as good as its members." Sunday School attendance remained at only about 30 until 1953 when many changes were made at church.

White Oak Springs Baptist Church members from 1908 through 1917 when J. H. Davis was pastor: M. R. Adair, C. B. Bradley, Elder J. Robert Cole—ordained minister, Walter Cole, Z. C. Cole, W. A. Harris—clerk, C.B. Hitchcock, Jesse Hitchcock—ordained minister, T. J. Fuller, Jas. Lenzy (James M. Lindsey), H. H. Kemp, Jasper Rainey, C. A. Roberts, M. B. Roberts, H. R. Wilson, and J. N. Wix.

Business Meeting Minutes of White Oak Springs
(April 25, 1908–April 22, 1911)

White Oak Springs Baptist Church has old church business minutes that Jeff Byrd transcribed. He had an extra copy of these transcribed minutes in his possession, so they were not lost when the rest of the minutes were lost around the year 2000.

The monthly minutes he transcribed followed the same basic outline: 1. Invited visiting members to attend. 2. Opened the doors of the church to receive new members. Read the minutes from the last meeting. 3. Old business. 4. New business. 5. Read and adopted the minutes of the day and then adjourned. Today, the church office has a copy of these minutes. Many of these business meeting minutes list the church name as "The Baptist Church of Christ at White Oak Springs."

Here are the names listed in the church business meetings:

April 22, 1908: Elder J. H. Davis (pastor), Homer Cole to arrange shingles of the roof. W. A. Harris elected church clerk. Appointed J. Robert Cole, W. A. Harris, H. R. Wilson to visit member Warner Osborn.

May 23, 1908: Elder J. H. Davis (pastor), Received H. H. Kemp and wife Nara Kemp as members. Elected Z. C. Cole, H. H. Kemp, and Homer Cole, as delegates to associational meeting. J. R. Cole and W. T. Hollis listed as alternates. Elder H. T. R. Marks (moderator pro tem).

June 24, 1908: Elder Robert J. Cole preached the message. Warren Osborn explained why he missed last month's conference. Voted to ordain H. H. Kemp and M. B. Roberts as deacons. Selected Elder J. H. Ogle, E. Dyre, W. A. Dodd, and J. A. Jordan to act as presbytery at this ordination.

June 24, 1908: Ordination of H. H. Kemp and M. B. Roberts to be deacons. 1. Ordination sermon by J. H. Davis. 2. Ordination committee (presbytery): J. H. Davis, W. A. Dodd, J. A Jordan, Jesse Hitchcock, M. R. Adair, Andrew Kemp, and J. Robert Cole. 3. Appointed Z. C. Cole and Homer Cole mouthpiece of church. 4. Church was examined by Elder Jesse Hitchcock. 5. Candidates examined on articles of faith by Elder J. H. Davis. 6. Consecrating prayer given by Brother W. A. Dodd and charge by Elder J. Robert Cole.

July 25, 1908: Elected H. H. Kemp and W. A. Harris as delegates to associational meeting and M. B. Roberts and Z. C. Cole as alternates.

July 31, 1908. Met in conference and elected Elder J. H. Davis as pastor for the coming year.

August 22, 1908: Received Cinda Bulter (Butler) as member by transfer of letter. J. Robert Cole elected to assist Brother Davis in his pastoral work. W. A. Harris, church clerk.

September 26, 1908; Elder J. H. Davis (pastor). Received S. O. Hicks as member. Sent $25.00 to the Draketown school. W. A. Harris, church clerk.

October 24, 1908: Elder J. H. Davis (pastor). Jesse Hitchcock preached the sermon. W. A. Harris, church clerk.

November 24, 1908: J. Robert Cole and A. J. Coalson preached. O. J. Henderson, M. R. Adair, Jesse Hitchcock, and M. B. Roberts mentioned. W. A. Harris, church clerk.

December 26, 1908: John Hitchcock gave a statement why he missed last business meeting. Clark Gazaway, O. J. Henderson, and M. R. Adair mentioned. Elder Jesse Hitchcock moderator pro tem and W. A. Harris, church clerk.

J. A. Wilson transferred his membership to White Oak Springs in 1911.

Other notes from the minutes:
The church received Carrie Fuller by experience (testimony) on August 23, 1916. She was baptized August 27, 1916.

The church received Katie Fuller by experience (testimony) on August 23, 1916. She was baptized August 27, 1916.

The church received Alma Fuller and Ella Henderson as members (no date).

The church received Elmer Cole by letter in July 1917.

The church received Ola Caldwell by experience (testimony) in August 1919.

The church received Vonnie Wilson by experience (testimony) in August 1919.

Rev. John William Womack

Rev. John William Womack[28] pastored White Oak Springs from 1917 until 1925. Pastor Womack was born on September 17, 1874, and he passed away on December 13, 1948. His wife was Georgia Morgan Womack. She was born on May 29, 1873, and she passed away on May 22, 1937. Her first name may have been Savannah, thus making her name Savannah Georgia Morgan Womack. The pastor and his wife, Georgia Morgan Womack, are buried at Mount Olivet Baptist Church Cemetery in Dallas, Georgia. Pastor Womack's tombstone inscription reads: "A Sinner Saved by Grace." His wife's tombstone inscription reads, "As a minister's wife, she did what she could."

On October 23, 1920, White Oak Springs Baptist Church ordained T. J. Fuller and J. M. Daniel as deacons.

Former deacon Kenneth Cohran said John Fuller started the Sunday School program.

Deacon J. M. Daniel

Mr. J. M. Daniel was ordained October 23, 1920. Little is known of his ministry. He married Ida Bradley. The church records (Deacons of White Oak Springs) state that he was born August 7, 1871, and died on December 12, 1957. In the 1920 Paulding

---

[28] Photo used by permission granted by Larry Butler, a descendent of Pr. Womack.

County Georgia Census of the Pumpkinvine community, his family is listed as follows: J. M. Daniel (age 41), Ida (age 30), son Sam (age 10), daughter Josie (age 9), daughter Oda (age 7), daughter Opal (age 3), and daughter Emma (age 1).

White Oak Springs Baptist Church members from 1917 through 1925 when J. W. Womack was pastor: H. R. Adair, Henry Brown, J. Robert Cole—ordained minister, G. W. Cole, Lafayette Cole, Walter Cole, J. M. Daniel, Katie Fuller, G. W. Fuller, T. J. Fuller, John Hitchcock, Nettie Gamel, W. A. Harris—clerk, J. N. Nix (J. N. Wix?), H. R. Wilson, J. R. Wilson, Mary Wilson, Oscar Wilson, R. H. Wilson, and *J. N. Wix.*

Jesse A. Harris

Quiller Cole wrote the *Dallas New Era* newspaper in 1918 (exact date unknown) upon the death of Jesse A. Harris. Jessie died October 26, 1917. He was only one of seven servicemen from Paulding County, Georgia, who died during the Great War (World War I). His name is engraved on the WWI memorial in Dallas, Georgia. He was twenty-three years, three months, and four days old at the time of his death. Jesse Harris was a member of White Oak Springs at the time of his death. Quiller Cole concluded his remarks about his friend by saying: "The church will miss a good Christian, the younger set as well, the choir will miss his voice in the singing class. His voice is stilled here, his seat is vacant, his presence with us will be no more here on earth. We will see and hear him just beyond the Pearly Gates."

The oldest photo that White Oak Springs Baptist Church has of its 1889 building is one that was taken shortly after Jesse's burial in the church cemetery. The picture is of Jesse Harris' grave with newly lain flowers on it. The church is in the background. If it were not for that photo of Jesse's grave, the church would have no photo of the old church from the 1910s.

A Rev. George A. Maner is buried in the church cemetery. He was born October 16, 1856, and he died on September 25, 1917. He was a pastor because the title "elder" was on his tombstone. His descendants state that he was born in Smyrna, Georgia, and he married his second cousin Clameria on March 7, 1876, in Cobb County, Georgia. They had 11 children. He married a second time to Sally Ida Cole in 1895, and they had seven children.

Rev. G. Fred Wigley

Rev. Fred Wigley, wife Lona e James Robert Wigley

Rev. G. Fred Wigley[29] pastored White Oak Springs Baptist Church from 1926 until 1931.

In 1927, T. J. Fuller is mentioned as the Sunday School Superintendent at church.

Obituary for George Fred Wigley. He went by Fred Wigley.

George Fred Wigley was the son of John Jefferson Wigley and Ruthie Ann Miller Wigley, Paulding County, Georgia.

George married Lona Morgan, November 29, 1903, in Paulding

---

[29] Photo used by permission granted by Amy C. Parker.

County, Georgia. They had several children: Clarence F. Wigley, Paul Albert Wigley, Jewell Atcheson, Vassie J. Womack, Rilla Mae Wigley, Sue Ragsdale, Fred Lee Wigley, Virginia Louise Sewell, and Gay Lewis "G. L." Wigley.

Rev. Wigley was pastor of several churches in the Paulding County area, and he was also a farmer and owned a small country store. He was widely known throughout the county, and his influence for good will live on in the lives he touched through his ministry.

In 1921, Wigley was elected pastor of New Hope Baptist Church, and he served until 1926. Other churches he served were: Beulahland, White Oak Springs, High Shoals, McPherson and Pumpkinvine in Paulding County. He served other churches in Cobb and Floyd Counties.

The Rev. Wigley had a photographic mind and could quote scripture eloquently. He loved gospel music and singing and taught a number of singing schools. Fred sang solos and he and his sisters, Maud and Vennie, who played the organ, sang as a trio in weddings and funerals.

The funeral was held Monday, September 15, 1969, at New Hope Baptist Church at 2 PM. The Rev. J. E. Wix, Rev. C. R. Campbell, Rev. George Barnett, and the Rev. Henry B. Moore officiated.

At the time of his death, Fred was survived by 5 daughters, two sons, 23 grandchildren, 25 great-grandchildren and one great-great grandchild.[30]

---

[30] http://www.findagrave.com/cgi-bin/fg.cgi?page=gr&GRid=51356511 on Dec. 29, 2016.

According to his tombstone, George Fred Wigley was born on March 20, 1884, and died on September 13, 1969. His wife, Lona, was born on November 26, 1885, and she passed away on May 3, 1970. They are both buried in the New Hope Cemetery.

On October 22, 1927, White Oak Springs Baptist Church ordained D. E. Harris, J. O. Wilson, C. Gordon Baxter, and J. N. Wix as deacons.

Deacon Daniel Erving Harris

The following obituary was written at the church's request by J. N. Wix, Miss. Bessie Roberts, and H. M. Brown

We the committee appointed by the church in conference to write an obituary for our beloved Brother Daniel Erwin Harris, wish to contribute this memorial as a last tribute of our deepest respect and love. Brother Harris was born December 26, 1879, in Paulding County. He married Miss Metie Lindsey (Meedie Lindsey) in February 1896. Two children were born to this union. One died in infancy, the other, Mrs. Floy T. Cole, survives him. His companion died in February 1922. Later he married Miss. Bell Raney August 1922. To this union two children were born, Ruby and Agnes who survive him.... Brother Harris united with Pumpkinvine Church in 1910. He later moved his membership to White Oak Springs and remained a faithful member until his death. He was ordained as Deacon (10/22/1927) and served well in this capacity. He was always ready and willing to do anything for the upbuilding of his community and God's kingdom. A demonstration of his Christian life was invariably found in his love and kindness to his fellow man and in his deliberations of his church work. ... Brother D. E. Harris departed this life December 21, 1946.

Funeral services were held at White Oak Church December 22 with the Rev. J. E. Wix, M. B. Moon, and E. J. Cain officiating. Burial was in the church yard. He is survived by his wife and three daughters. A great number of relatives and friends mourn his going.... We the undersigned committee resolve: First, the family has lost a true and devoted husband and father. Second, the church suffers the loss of a consecrated and loyal member and deacon. Third, that a copy of this be furnished to his family and sent to the New Era, another spread on the minutes of the church. Respectfully Submitted, J. N. Wix, Miss. Bessie Roberts, H. M. Brown.

Deacon John Oliver "Dutch" Wilson

The following information is gleaned from his obituary published in the Dallas New Era on April 29, 1948. It was written by J. N. Wix, H. M. Brown, and Effie Carter

Brother Wilson was born in Paulding County April 12, 1883, and spent his entire life in this county with the exception of some 12 years he lived in Iradell, Texas. He returned to Paulding County in 1918, and on May 19, 1918, he married Monnie Cole; in August 1919, he joined White Oak Baptist Church by letter, he had previously joined in Texas by experience; his wife joined White Oak at the same time. Brother Wilson was ordained as a Deacon of his church and he served in this capacity at White Oak until his death. ... Brother Wilson's philosophy of life was to deal fairly, honestly, and faithfully with his fellowman and his church, he was always ready and willing to do all that lay in his power for the upbuilding and betterment of his church and community. He possessed that noble spirit of being firm in his faith, firm in his convictions in all matters that confronted him in life, always standing for the right of his church and state, ready to compromise when convinced that he might be wrong, which is a Godly and noble spirit for any man to possess.... Be it resolved that his wife has lost a kind and devoted husband, the church one of its best members, the community a good neighbor, and the county a good citizen. Respectfully submitted *(by)* J.N. Wix, H. M. Brown, Effie Carter.

Deacon C. Gordon Baxter

The Obituary for C. Gordon Baxter (Charles Gordon Baxter) states he was born in 1876 and died in 1955. He had been a member of White Oak Springs Baptist Church for about 50 years and a deacon for 28 years. His obituary listed two sons named D. P. Baxter and W. S. Baxter and five daughters named Mrs. Annie Mae Gurley, Mrs. Josie Cole, Mrs. Guy Gazaway, and Mrs. Henry Cochran.

White Oak Springs Baptist Church members from 1926 through 1931 when G. Fred Wigley was pastor: Glen Baggett, Buddie Baxter, C. G. Baxter, O. G. Baxter, Henry Brown, H. M. Brown, Mrs. Henry Brown, Mrs. Clara Clark, C. A. Cole, John Cole, T. J. Fuller, D. E. Harris, J. D. Harris, John D. Harris, G. L. Rakestraw, J. O Wilson, R. H. Wilson, H. R. Wilson, J. N. Wix, and Loring Wix.

White Oak Springs Baptist Church member H. R. Wilson died in 1930. H. R. Wilson was Harvey Rose Wilson (b. 1875–d. 1929). Harvey Wilson's wife was Martha Dora Harper Wilson. He was the son of George W. Wilson (b. 1850–d. 1896) and Saphronia Moody Wilson (1857–1893). Saphronia Moody was the daughter of Thomas Moody and Retincy Hill Chapman Moody.

Rev. Marion B. Moon

Rev. Marion B. Moon pastored White Oak Springs Baptist Church from 1932 until 1938.

Rev. Marion B. Moon was born on July 14, 1892, and he passed away on July 3, 1957. His wife was Nettie B. Moon, who was born on January 1, 1884, and died on October 12, 1983. They are both buried in the Yorkville Baptist Cemetery. Nettie B. Moon's parents were Thomas J. and Amanda Partain Brown (from her obituary published in *The Rockmart Journal,* on October 17, 1983).

Gloria Byrd remembers Pastor Marion Moon. She remembered that he would show her attention when she was small; so, she really liked him. She said she could not remember much about his wife. The reason, she wrote, was possibly because his wife did not show her as much attention as Pastor Moon did. The Moons had a daughter named Rosie Fae Moon.

Deacon Henry M. Brown

On October 22, 1936, White Oak Springs Baptist Church ordained H. M. Brown as a deacon. H. M. Brown is Henry M. Brown (b. 1892–d. 1953). He married Bessie Taylor. His name first shows up as a messenger of the church in 1923. He was ordained a deacon of the church in 1936. He remained active in the church throughout his life and even was active in the church at the time of his death. Clara Mae Baggett says that when she was a child, Henry and Bessie Brown would drop by on the way to church, pick her up, and take her to church. Bessie Taylor Brown was born in 1892 and passed away in 1978. She is buried in the church cemetery. She was the daughter of L. T. Taylor and Sally Field Taylor.

The booklet "Deacons of White Oak Springs" states that Brother Brown was the church clerk, and that he served his church well. He also served as chorister from 1947 to 1953.

Kenneth Cohran recalls that when Henry Brown was music leader, Brother Brown would come out the front door of the old wooden church as people were gathered before the service, take out his pocket knife and tap it a few times on the old wooden planks on the side of the church and say: "It's time to get started."

White Oak Springs Baptist Church members from 1932 through 1938 when Marion B. Moon was pastor: Ambrey Baggett, Lowell Baggett, Mrs. Grace Brown, Mr. & Mrs. H. M. Brown, Ola Caldwell, Herman Cole, W. T. Cole, Mrs. J. D. Daniel, Irwin Harris, Mrs. Lon Harris, Ralph Harris, W. A. Harris, T. J. Fuller, J. O. Wilson, Edwin Wix, Mrs. George Wix, J. N. Wix, Loring Wix, and Mrs. Virgie Wix.

Deacon William Timothy Cole

The following obituary was found in some loose papers in the back of one of the file cabinets at church.[31]

> W. T. Cole was William Timothy Cole. He went by Tim Cole. He is first mentioned in the Tallapoosa Baptist minutes in 1923, and he was an active representative of the church most of his life. His wife was Alma Cole. Tim and Alma were married February 21, 1911. The Heritage of

---

[31] Clara Mae Baggett deserves praise for going the extra mile to help find historical information in the file cabinets of the church office.

Paulding County, Georgia: 1832 – 1999 book, entry 471, states that Tim and Alma were life-long members of White Oak Springs Baptist Church. Tim was born in 1887 and died in 1966. His favorite verse, according to the Heritage of Paulding book, was Proverbs 22:1 (KJV): "A good name is rather to be chosen than great riches, and loving favor rather than silver and gold."

Ralph Harris served as Sunday School Superintendent from 1933 through 1937. He served again one more time in 1941. T. J. Fuller served as the superintendent in 1938, 1939, 1940, and 1947. Sunday School averaged about 30 during the 1930s and early 1940s.

Deacon Ralph Harris

The booklet "Deacons of White Oak Springs" gives the following on Brother Harris:

Brother Ralph Harris was ordained October 19, 1940. Brother Ralph was born September 8, 1907. He married the former Ruby Moore on July 18, 1931. They have four children, nine grandchildren, and two great-grandchildren. He retired in 1973. Brother Harris was saved and joined this church in 1930.

Clara Mae Baggett said that Ola Caldwell was a spiritual encourager to her and others. Ola Caldwell was a Sunday School teacher and was the pianist at church from the 1950s through the 1970s. The members of White Oak Springs loved their music, and their congregational hymn book of choice was the Stamps-Baxter hymnal. (Amazing Grace was page number 57 and Victory in Jesus was song 120).

Pastor J. Edwin Wix

Edwin Wix is Rev. J. Edwin Wix. His full name was John Edwin Wix. Pastor Wix attended White Oak Springs Baptist Church when he was younger and was called to preach at this church. He never pastored White Oak Springs, even though he did pastor many other churches in the area. The following excerpts are from his obituary that was published in the *Atlanta Journal-Constitution* on July 25, 2003.

> John Edwin Wix was born in West Paulding County, GA on February 24, 1915, and died on July 22, 2003. "He was ordained into the ministry on July 28, 1940, and on Christmas Eve of that same year, was married to Trumie Paris, 1915-2000. ... His first funeral service was on November 14, 1939, and since that date, he has conducted 3040 funerals, an average of one per week for the past 63 years. He joined 795 couples in marriage and received thousands in the fellowship of the churches he served. As Governor Roy Barnes, a lifelong friend, said of Brother Wix, "he has either married, baptized or buried just about everybody in Mableton." Pastor Wix also has "served as Chaplain for the GA State Senate and House of Representatives."

J. Edwin Wix was a representative of White Oak Springs Baptist Church from 1934 until 1938. He first attended the Tallapoosa conference in 1934 when he was 19 years old. Pastor Jeff Byrd said that Edwin Wix grew up at White Oak Springs Baptist Church. Once when the church was preparing for two weeks of protracted revival services, the church was talking about borrowing hurricane lamps from Pumpkinvine Baptist Church. Edwin made the suggestion that they buy lights and have them installed instead of using the old hurricane lamps. The lights were installed and, as a result, more people attended the meetings. The exact year when the lights were installed is not known, but Edwin Wix was young at the time he made the recommendation. The lights were probably installed sometime in the 1930s.

Jeff Byrd remembers a word of advice that J. Edwin Wix gave him early in his ministry (speaking of church finances): "If you buy a roll of toilet paper, make a record of it." Pastor Wix was emphasizing the importance of keeping good financial records at church.

White Oak Springs members who died during 1933: Mrs. Sarah Cole and Mrs. Ella Rainey. White Oak Springs members who died during 1934: Mrs. Elizabeth Cole. White Oak Springs members who died during 1936: Mrs. Nancy Wix and Mrs. George Cole. White Oak Springs members who died during 1937: Mrs. Florence Gamel, and Mrs. Martha Wix.

Nancy T. Wix (b. 1853–d. 1936) was married to Joseph H. Wix (b. 1852–d.1923). Both are buried in the church cemetery. Don Wix recalls that his father, J. Edwin Wix, shared that Joseph Hiram (J. H.) Wix and Nancy T. Wix were members at White Oak Springs Baptist Church. J. H. Wix and Zachariah Wix were brothers.

Rev. James A. Crabb

Pastor James A. Crabb[32] pastored White Oak Springs Baptist Church from 1939 to 1941.

On October 19, 1940, White Oak Springs Baptist Church ordained Ben Carter and Ralph Harris as deacons.

Gloria Caldwell Byrd wrote the following about Pastor James Crabb:

I remember this man and his wife, Irene. They lived across the road from Jeff (Byrd)'s house, which was my grandparents' house back then. My grandparents used the spring across the road before the (Buchanan) highway was paved. Well, this pastor kept a bucket at the spring and when he came to visit my grandparents he brought them a bucket of water. Then when he went home, he carried an empty bucket and left it at the spring until he came back. He once told about the cracks being so big in the floor of the old house and how bad the wind blew in through them.

My grandfather, W. A. Harris, was a deacon and very active in the church. He was the church clerk for many years too. After he gave it up, his son, my uncle Ralph, took the job. Uncle Ralph was also a deacon for many years. Some of the church records were at his house when it burned, and they lost the old church records. Uncle Ralph and Aunt Ruby were very close to the last two pastors, Marion Moon and James Crabb. They named their oldest son Marion and their youngest son James. Uncle Ralph and his family lived across the road from my house, but they

---

[32] The Mercer University Archives granted permission to use this photo.

eventually moved to Austell for him to work there, so they left White Oak for a closer church.

Deacon Ben Carter

Ben Carter was born in 1905 and passed away in 1973. His first name was Bennett, but he went by Ben. He married Effie Roberts. He accepted Christ as his Savior in 1929. He served as the chairman of the deacon board from 1963 until his death in 1973. The booklet "Deacons of White Oak Springs" says, "he loved his church. He was a Sunday School teacher for many years. He was a faithful member."

Ernest Gober had the following praise about Ben Carter:
- Ben Carter could get the best out of people.
- Ben Carter also had a big smile.
- Ben Carter always had a good word to say.
- Ben Carter never was negative.

Ben Carter and Rev. Paul Carter were brothers. Ben Carter served as the chairman of the deacons for 10 years. Ben and Paul's parents were Thomas M. Carter and Hettie Carter. Paul and Ben had two other brothers named John T. Carter and Calvin Carter. Jeff Byrd said that Ben Carter was the anchor deacon at church.

White Oak Springs Baptist Church members from 1939 through 1941 when James A. Crabb was pastor: Ester Baggett, Nora Lee Baggett, Tom Baggett, H. M. Brown, Owen Caldwell, Ben Carter, Mrs. Mary Francis Cole, T. J. Fuller, Ralph Harris, Myra Harris, Joe Morgan, Bessie Roberts, Dean Roberts, Elmer Roberts, Offord Hutcherson, and J. N. Wix.

Mrs. Ola Caldwell attended church at White Oak Springs. She was a faithful member, attendee, and pianist. Her husband's name was Homer. He was from a Methodist background, but in his later years was a member at White Oak Springs Baptist Church (from his obituary dated December 16, 1977).

Horse Hairs and Cake

Gloria Byrd told the story that her mother, Ola Harris Caldwell, and her grandmother, Mary Louise (Lou) Leatherwood, rode in a horse and buggy carriage to church one night in the 1920s. There was a special service at church that evening, so they made a big cake in the afternoon, put it in their carriage, and drove from their house to the church. They lived about a mile west of the church on Buchanan Highway. When they arrived at church and started to take the cake out of the buggy, they noticed that the cake was covered in horse hair. They pulled off all the hair they could see while outside. They took the cake inside and proceeded to discreetly remove the rest of the horse hair. Then they placed it on the table with the rest of the desserts and served it. No one noticed. No one complained about it either. That was just a part of life back in the good old days.

White Oak Springs members who died during 1939: Mrs. Lilla Wix, Mr. J. M. Lindsey, Mrs. Omie Lindsey. White Oak Springs members who died during 1940: Mrs. Nettie Bullock, and Mrs. Ella Cole. White Oak Springs members who died during 1941: Bro. Carl Hitchcock, Bro. Tasker Baxter, Mrs. Zilla Sinyard. Zilla was the wife of Jacob Sinyard, daughter of Haman Roberts and the mother of Addie Sinyard.

Rev. E. J. Cain

Rev. E. J. Cain pastored White Oak Springs Baptist Church from 1942 to 1946. He was born on October 30, 1901, and died on December 30, 1992. His tombstone states: "Just a sinner saved by grace." Gloria Byrd thinks that Pastor Cain's first name may have been Ernest. His wife was Jewel Cain. She was born January 6, 1903, and died on February 2, 1951. They both are buried in New Georgia Baptist Church Cemetery in Villa Rica, Georgia.

Gloria Byrd wrote the following about Pastor Cain: "My uncle Ralph [Harris] was close to this pastor. He was a very friendly pastor. He lived to be old, and his wife was in a nursing home before she died. He was very friendly when you saw him out, and he had lots of funerals. He had part in my mother's funeral."

White Oak Springs Baptist Church members from 1942 through 1946 when E. J. Cain was pastor: Aubrey Baggett, Lowell Baggett, Fae Baggett, Tom Baggett, H. M. Brown, Bennet Carter, Effie Carter, Ethel Cochran, T. J. Fuller, Etta Cole, Ralph Harris, D. E. Harris, T. J. Fuller, Bessie Roberts, Pauline Roberts, J. O. Wilson, Ruth Wilson, and J. N Wix.

White Oak Springs members who died during the year 1942: Mr. Carey Hitchcock, Mr. Will Ragan, and Mrs. Lizzy Fuller. White Oak Springs members who died during 1943: Deacon M. B. Roberts and Mr. D. G. Harris.

D. G. Harris is David G. Harris. He went by Dave. Dave married Alice Hitchcock. Gloria Caldwell Byrd said that when she was a young girl she liked Alice's name so much that she named her doll after Alice Hitchcock.

White Oak Springs members who died during the year 1944: Mrs. Oma Lois Coalson and Mrs. Lula Cola. White Oak Springs members who died during 1945: Bro. G. R. Roberts. White Oak Springs members who died during 1946: C. H. Arnold and Mrs. Lois Harris.

Rev. Herman H. Long

Rev. Herman H. Long pastored White Oak Springs Baptist Church from 1947 to 1956. When Herman Long became pastor, the one service a month was moved from the fourth Sunday to the third Sunday of the month.

Gloria Byrd wrote: "I should remember his wife's name, but I don't. They lived in Atlanta and he came by himself lots of times. They had, I believe, five or more children. This is the man who married Frank and I on May 26, 1956."

White Oak Springs Baptist Church members from 1947 through 1956 when Herbert H. Long was pastor: Tom Baggett, H. M. Brown, Claude Caldwell, B. A. Carter, Ben Carter, Hobart Chatman, Woodrow Clark, John Cole, W. Tim Cole, Ralph Harris, T. J. Fuller, Sim Roberts, J. O. Wilson, J. N. Wix, and Loring Wix.

On September 15, 1947, White Oak Springs Baptist Church ordained Charlie Cason as a deacon. In July 1951, the church ordained John T. Cole and Woodrow Clark as deacons.

The booklet "Deacons of White Oak Springs" gives the following on Charlie Cason:

Charlie Cason was ordained September 15, 1947.

He was born October 4, 1912. He has lived in Polk County for the past 48 years (in 1977). He married the former Norma Head. They have one son, two daughters, seven grandchildren. Brother Charlie is now retired, but he was in the gas station business before retirement.

Brother Charlie moved his membership here to White Oak in 1977 from Fairview Baptist Church of Rockmart, GA, where he [had been a] member for 30 years.

He enjoys his grandchildren, good gospel singing, and gardening. I asked Brother Charlie for a comment to describe Brother Larry (Davis). He said, "He's a good preacher. He really preaches the Word and he's a fine man."

Charlie Cason did not remain a deacon at White Oak Springs Baptist Church for many years. He moved his membership to a new church in 1979. Charlie may have returned to Fairview Baptist Church after he left White Oak Springs Baptist Church.

Deacon John Cole

Brother John Cole was born March 5, 1905. He was ordained a deacon at White Oak in July 1951. He married Josie Baxter. Brother Cole was able to serve the Lord as deacon at White Oak Springs for only a few short months because he passed away January 30, 1952. The booklet "Deacons of White Oak" states that he was a faithful member.

Deacon Woodrow Clark

Woodrow Clark served for many years as the maintenance man, caretaker, and handyman of the church. Praise the Lord for those that use their talents to keep the house of the Lord in good working order.

The booklet "Deacons of White Oak Springs" gives the following on Brother Clark:

Woodrow Clark is a deacon ordained July of 1951.

He was born December 13, 1913. He grew up in the area.

Forty-five years ago he took Annie Lou Gamel as his wife. They have one daughter, one son, and four grandchildren. He is still employed with Lockheed as a fireman.

In July of 1929, he was saved and joined this church. He has been a very faithful member. He served as secretary and treasurer from July 1951 through August of 1972. In the past he has taught the men's Bible class and presently teaches the Tom Fuller Adult Class.

He enjoys working around the church and cemetery. He also likes to garden, hunt, and fish.

Brother Woodrow is our oldest living deacon. I am sure he could tell us much about the Lord and His Word. I know of two things that will give a person spiritual wisdom: trusting and serving God. This Brother Woodrow has done for many years.

I asked Brother Woodrow to make a comment on our pastor. He looked at me as if in search of words to describe such a man and replied: "I don't know what to say except that he can't be beat and he's doing a great job." What more could one say?

White Oak Springs members who died during 1947: Deacon D. E. Harris and Mrs. Louella Henderson. White Oak Springs members who died during 1948: Deacon J. O. Wilson, Leonard Wix, John M. Cole, and Quiller Cole. White Oak Springs members who died during 1949: Charlie Cole, and Mrs. Ollie Harris.

From 1856 until 1953, White Oak Springs Baptist Church held services once a week. They usually preferred the fourth Sunday of the month, but the week of the month they met on could be changed to accommodate a preacher's schedule.

A New Way of Doing Church: 1947-63

"I was glad when they said unto me, Let us go into the house of the Lord."
—Psalm 122:1

The year 1953 marked a new chapter in the history of White Oak Springs Baptist Church. It was in this year that the church decided to start holding two preaching services a month rather than just one Sunday service. The church had been holding weekly Sunday School classes for the children since sometime in the 1910s or 1920s, but they had only one preaching service per month during those years. However, change was now on its way.

The church was very diligent to hold a business meeting each third Saturday. They would have the business meeting at church. Afterward, the men would go to the place about 100 yards down the access road to what is now Bureau of Land Management land. It is just southeast of the intersection of James Wix Road with White Oak Springs Church Road. They prayed there at least once a month.

Rev. Herman H. Long

Rev. Herman H. Long pastored White Oak Springs Baptist Church from 1947 until 1956. He served as pastor for longer than most did before him—over nine years. Some members recall that Pastor Long went by the name Herman, which may have been his middle name.

In 1953, when Rev. Herman Long was pastor, the church started meeting two weekends a month rather than one. They added the first Sunday of the month to the third Sunday of the month (which had been their regular meeting day).

In 1953, 1956, and 1957, Guy Gazaway served as the Sunday School superintendent. In 1954, Lowell Baggett filled in that year. The Sunday School enrollment that year was 114. By 1957, the Sunday School enrollment had grown to 135. The church was starting to grow. From 1958 until 1965, H. L. ("Red") Kinney served as the Sunday School superintendent, with the exception of 1960 when Ben Carter served, and in 1964 when R. S. Gazaway had those honors. T. W. Clark served as superintendent of the Sunday School in 1966.

Vernon Cole Gets Baptized
1955

Ernest Gober told the story about the morning Vernon Cole was baptized. Ernest said that on a Sunday morning, they "had one of those services that kind of got out of hand." At the end of a rather long service, maybe at the end of some protracted meetings, Vernon Cole came forward during the altar call. Vernon may have accepted Christ as his Savior that morning. After praying, Vernon got up and said to the pastor out loud for all the church to hear: "Pastor, I want to get baptized today!" Everyone loaded up in their cars, went to Lucious Baxter Lake, broke the ice so they could get in the water, and Vernon Cole was baptized that very chilly winter afternoon. Brother Vernon put into practice Acts 2:41: *"Then they that gladly received his word were baptized ... "*

Deacon Vernon Cole

Vernon Cole was born September 14, 1925, and passed away May 3, 1971. He married Betty Wix. He was ordained a deacon at White Oak on December 17, 1967. He accepted Christ as his Savior in 1955, when he probably was baptized. The booklet

"Deacons of White Oak Springs" states that Vernon was a most devoted and faithful member. He was a Sunday School teacher and a member of Brotherhood[33], and he also served on the mission board.

White Oak Springs Baptist Church members when Herbert H. Long was pastor: Fay Baggett, Lowell Baggett, Mrs. Ola Caldwell, Ben Carter, Hobart Chatman, Woodrow Clark, J. T. Cole, Nath. Cole, Ray Cole (Roy Cole?), Tim Cole, T. J. Fuller, Charles Gamel, Guy Gazaway, Ernest Gober, Gene Lipton (Lipscomb?), Sim Roberts, and J. N. Wix.

White Oak Springs members who died during the year 1953: H. M. Brown—deacon, and Miss Emma Hitchcock. White Oak Springs members who died during 1956: Gene Gamel, Brother G. O. Wilson.

Emma Cornelia Hitchcock was the daughter of John Matthew Hitchcock and Mary Ann Chambless. She never married. She was the granddaughter of John (b. 1805) and Mary Polly Hitchcock and also of Rev. James (b.1791) and Martha Roberts (b. 1798). Emma probably was a member of White Oak Springs Baptist Church all her life after she accepted Christ and was baptized.

Rev. Roy Goodson

Rev. Roy Goodson pastored White Oak Springs Baptist Church from 1957 until 1959. He is remembered by many members today.

---

[33] Brotherhood was the name for the men's ministry at churches.

Jeff Byrd said that "Pastor Roy Goodson was the hinge that took the church from being a small, old-time country church to a more modern one." In 1957, the church began to hold services once each week, instead of once a month like they did prior to 1953 or twice a month like they did from 1953 through 1956. It was during these years that the church membership began to climb as well.

In 1957, the church reported 20 baptisms, 20 members received by letter, and a membership of 284. In 1958, the church reported 29 baptisms and a membership of 303. In 1959, the church reported 24 baptisms, 21 members received by letter, and a membership of 324.

Deacon Kenneth Cohran recalls that when Rev. Roy Goodson was pastor, three lay preachers at church went to visit a man on Mulberry Rock Road. The man came out of the house with a huge butcher's knife and chased after them. The next week, those same three young men were out visiting other people, still telling them about the Lord.

Gloria Byrd wrote the following about Pastor Goodson: They lived in the new parsonage, so the new parsonage was built in the late 1950s. They had several boys, and his wife complained about the red mud and keeping the parsonage floor clean. I know he had granddad Harris' funeral in 1958."

Deacon H. L. "Red" Kinney

On June 5, 1957, White Oak Springs Baptist Church ordained H. L. Kinney as a deacon. Herbert "Red" Kinney was a deacon, and he worked with the youth at church.

The booklet "Deacons of White Oak Springs" gives the following on Brother Kinney:

Brother Kinney was ordained June 5, 1957.

Brother Kinney was born April 17, 1902. He worked in the grocery store business all his life, owning a store for seventeen years.

He married the former Ada Fields. Having no children of their own, they helped to rear three girls and one boy.

At the age of fourteen, Brother Kinney was saved and joined Mt. Creek Baptist Church where he was a member for many years.

In 1953, the Kinneys moved to Dallas. After visiting several churches in the area, Brother Kinney knew White Oak was the right church to bring his letter of membership. He served as Sunday School Superintendent for many, many years. Approximately forty-five people attended Sunday School at this time. He started the first bus ministry using his automobiles to bring people to our church.

He served God for many years. On May 6, 1977, Brother "Red" Kinney was called home to be with the Lord.

White Oak Springs Baptist Church members from 1957 until 1960 when Roy Goodson was pastor: J. T. Atchenson, Linda Baxter, Bobby Brooks, J. M. Brooks, Ben Carter, Darrel Carter, Mrs. Effie Carter, Paul Carter, Jr, Robert Carter, T. W. Clark, Jake Cole, Tim Cole, Bob Daughtery, Arnold Henderson, Lester Freeman, Chas. Gamel, Guy Gazaway, Ernest Gober, Reuben

Jackson, H. L. Kinney, Jake McDowell, Job Meadows (Jeb Meadows?), Wendell Phillips, Mrs. Bessie Roberts, Sim Roberts, and Jimmie Smith.

In 1958, White Oak Springs Baptist Church ordained Lincoln Cole as a deacon.

Deacon Lincoln Cole

Brother Lincoln Cole was born January 10, 1927, and he passed away May 19, 1972. He married Mildred Morris. Lincoln accepted Christ as his Savior in 1950. He served as Sunday School teacher, Sunday School Superintendent, and president of the Vacation Bible School. He also served as a visitation chairman at another church prior to attending White Oak. At White Oak, he served as chorister, Sunday School teacher, and bus driver in the bus ministry (information taken from "Deacons of White Oak Springs"). Sandra Wyatt said that Lincoln and Mildred Cole had been friends with her family for many years, and this was one of the reasons she and her family started attending this church.

White Oak Springs members who died during 1957: Mrs. Clara Clark. White Oak Springs members who died during 1958: Deacon W. A. Harris, Deacon J. M. Daniel, and Tom R. Bullock. White Oak Springs members who died during 1959: Mrs. Lex Roney, and Mr. Jimmie Smith.

White Oak Springs Baptist Church licensed Jim (J. M.) Brooks to preach during the year (1959).

Rev. Paul E. Carter

Rev. Paul E. Carter pastored White Oak Springs Baptist Church in 1960 and 1961. Paul Carter was born in 1911 and died in 1978. He is buried in Paulding Memorial Gardens. He and deacon Bennett (Ben) Carter were brothers.

Gloria Byrd wrote: "He and his wife were pastoring in 1961. The first Sunday I took Jeff to church, Pastor Paul took him up in the pulpit and introduced him to the congregation. The Carters had many descendants at White Oak."

White Oak Springs Baptist Church members in 1960 and 1961 when Paul Carter was pastor: Ben Carter, Darrell Carter, Mrs. Effie Carter, T. W. Clark, Curtis Cole, T. W. Clark, Kenneth Cohran, Guy Gazaway, Mrs. Mertha Gazaway, Ernest Gober, J. C. Hardy, Arnold Henderson, H. L. Kinney, Jab Meadows (Jeb Meadows?), Sim Roberts, and Robert Wehunt.

White Oak Springs Baptist Church licensed Brother Gene Lipscomb to preach during 1960. White Oak Springs Baptist Church had the following people listed as licensed preachers during 1961: Brother Gene Lipscomb, Curtis Cole, Jab Meadows, Darrel Carter, and Paul Carter, Jr.

White Oak Springs members who died during the year 1961: Mr. Milton Cole.

Rev. Gene Lipscomb was an ordained minister of this church in 1961.

Rev. Charles E. Williams

Rev. Charles E. Williams pastored White Oak Springs Baptist Church twice. The first time he pastored here was in 1962 and 1963. He is beloved by many still to this day. Many people were saved at White Oak Springs Baptist Church during his ministry. It was during his second tenure of ministry that the church reached its highest attendance levels and became known in Fundamental Baptist circles for its ministry and for its bus ministry.

On July 8, 1962, White Oak Springs Baptist Church ordained Kenneth Cohran and Ernest Gober as deacons.

Deacon Ernest Gober

Ernest Gober taught Sunday School for 25 years. He said he taught from the "little bitty ones" up to the 25-year-olds. He taught high school kids when his children were in high school. He also was a deacon at White Oak Springs for many years and served as church clerk for many decades.

The booklet "Deacons of White Oak Springs" gives the following on Brother Ernest Gober:

Ernest Gober is a deacon ordained July 8, 1962. He was born December 19, 1931. He has lived in Paulding County all of his life. He graduated from Hiram High School. Following graduation, he went to work for Simmons Mattress Company of Atlanta, GA. He still works there.

He married the former Carolyn Roberts on September 30, 1951. They had two sons. The first son was born in April 1955, however their first son was taken in an automotive wreck in January 1970.

Ernest was saved during a revival in July of 1951. He joined White Oak in July 1952 and was baptized in July 1952. He was elected church clerk in 1953. In April 1954, he left for two years in the army. Upon his return in 1956, he resumed the office of church clerk which he still holds. He has taught Sunday School since he joined the church. He has taught the juniors, the intermediates, young married class, and the Tim Cole class which he still teaches.

If you ask what he enjoys most, you will find that it is visiting the nursing home and the hospital.

He is a dedicated member, teacher, and deacon.

Ernest Gober passed away on February 21, 2017, and is buried in the White Oak Springs Cemetery. Even though he was unable to attend church very often during the last years of his life, due to his age and health, he still loved this church and supported its ministries.

White Oak Springs Baptist Church members in 1962 and 1963 when Charles E. Williams was pastor: Ben Carter, Darrel Carter, Paul Carter, Jr, Robert Carter, T. W. Clark, Kenneth Cohran, Curtis Cole, Lincoln Cole, Robert Cole, Guy Gazaway, Mrs. Mertha Gazaway, Ernest Gober, H. L. Kinney, Herb Kinney, Arthur Meadows, Mrs. Bessie Roberts, B. J. Roberts, and Charles E. Williams.

White Oak Springs members who died during 1962: Mrs. Temple Harris, Mr. Milt Cole, and Mr. Marion Baxter.

White Oak Springs Baptist Church had the following ordained deacons or preachers in their membership (1962): Gene Lipscomb, Mr. Kenneth Cohran, Mr. Guy Gazaway. The last two names were listed as "Mrs. Kenneth Cohran" and "Mrs. Guy Gazaway" in the Tallapoosa minutes.

Deacon Kenneth Cohran

Kenneth Cohran served as a deacon of the church for over 40 years. His wife, Caroline, was a very active bus captain when the church had one of the largest bus ministries in the state. Caroline would visit her bus route for hours each Saturday. She would go out on Sunday mornings and bring the children in. Through the years, she taught the 6- and 7-year-olds, the junior age class, and the young people. Caroline Cohran taught Sunday School for 48 years at White Oak Springs Baptist Church. She was an active member of White Oak Springs Baptist Church from the 1950s to the 2000s. Caroline Cohran is an example of faithfulness and dedication to the Lord. "She hath done what she could," and she did a very good job at it.

The booklet "Deacons of White Oak Springs" gives the following on Brother Kenneth Cohran:

> Kenneth Cohran is chairman of our deacons. He was ordained in 1962 and elected chairman of the deacons in 1973.

> He was born March 23, 1938; he graduated from Dallas High School in 1956. He lived in Paulding County for 22 years and in

Cobb County for the past 18 years. He married the former Caroline Rogers in December of 1956. They have one daughter, Denise.

Kenneth was saved and joined the church in July of 1952. In the past 26 years he has served White Oak in many ways. Assistant Sunday School Superintendent; a teacher for adult men and women; primary boys; he served five years as the treasurer; was in charge of the junior church and Youth Director for over a year; has served on all past building committees. Presently (1977) he is in charge of the devotion for church leaders on Sunday morning at 9:40; in charge of soul winning class on Thursday night, and has been our bus director since 1973. He also helps with the mechanical repairs on the buses.

Kenneth enjoys fishing and hunting when he finds time.

Ministers ordained at White Oak Springs during 1962: Arthur Meadows. Curtis Cole was ordained to preach in 1963. White Oak Springs Baptist Church had the following ordained preachers in their membership in 1963: Gene Lipscomb, Curtis Cole, and J. M. Brooks.

The following members were licensed preachers of the church in 1962: Darrel Carter, Curtis Cole, and Paul Carter, Jr.

White Oak Springs members who died during 1963: Mrs. Claudie Baggett, Deacon T. J. Fuller, and Mr. Aubrey Baggett.

Clara Mae Baggett has been a long-time member and is the secretary of the church. Her parents were Aubrey and Faye Baggett.

Deacon Thomas Jefferson Fuller

Mr. T. J. Fuller, who died in 1963, was a deacon at White Oak Springs. His full name is Thomas Jefferson Fuller, and his wife's name is S. Elizabeth (Lizzie) Fuller. They are both buried in the church cemetery. Mr. Fuller was ordained a deacon at this church on October 23, 1920. He served the Lord and this church as a deacon for 43 years.

The booklet "Deacons of White Oak Springs" gives the following on Brother T. J. Fuller:

T. J. Fuller is a deacon ordained October 23, 1920. He went by the name "Uncle Tom."

He was born on August 8, 1871, and he passed away on June 12, 1963. He married Lizzie Wix. He was a devoted member. He served his church well; kept the cemetery; reorganized Sunday School in 1947; and served as Sunday School Superintendent. He and Brother Wix were elected to visit and talk with members who did wrong, encouraging them to make it right with the Lord and with their church; promptly at 11 o'clock he would knock on the side of the church, indicating to everyone that services were to begin.

A New Sanctuary Is Built: 1964–67

"Let us rise up and build." —Nehemiah 2:18

Rev. George Barnett

Rev. George Barnett pastored White Oak Springs Baptist Church from September 1964 until February 18, 1967. It was during his tenure as pastor that the church voted to build a new modern sanctuary.

The church dedicated its new modern building on Sunday, October 2, 1966. Rev. Jerry Vines was one of the main speakers that day. Jerry Vines has been one of the influential leaders of the Southern Baptist Convention for the past 50 years. His church grew to be the third largest in the SBC and had a membership 23,000 people during its largest days.

Jerry Vines' website (www.jerryvines.com) states: "I was a pastor for over 60 years. I served twice as President of the Southern Baptist Convention, and for over 23 years as pastor of the internationally recognized First Baptist Church of Jacksonville, Florida."

Rev. Jerry Vines preached at White Oak Springs Baptist Church on several occasions. Jerry Vines and Charles Williams both were saved at Fullerville Baptist Church in Villa Rica, Georgia, when Pastor Horace Wilson was the pastor. Jerry Vines and Charles Williams were saved about the same time, were friends in the youth group, and were both called to preach about the same time. Jerry Vines is from Villa Rica.

In addition to hearing wonderful preaching from the pastors of White Oak Springs Baptist Church each Sunday, the church has been privileged through the years to have had many well-known pastors and evangelists preach at our church. Here is a partial list of some of the more renowned pastors and evangelists that have preached at this church:

Rev. Jerry Vines

Rev. Maze Jackson—evangelist

Dr. Bill Kelly from South Carolina.

John R. Rice from the Sword of the Lord

Dr. Walley Bee Bee—famous bus director

Rev. Lester Roloff —children's home director

Dr. Curtis Hudson from the Sword of the Lord

Dr. Ed Ballew—Evangelist and Rock of Ages Missions Director

Dr. James W. Crumpton—Founder of Maranatha Baptist Missions

(famous for his "Jesus" sermon on the names and titles of Jesus)

Dr. Ed F. Vallowe—Known for his books of prophecy and biblical numerology

Kenneth Cohran remembers Mel and Dottie Rutter, missions director for Maranatha Baptist Missions. Pastor Mel would come to church often. When he came, he would stay with Kenneth and his wife. Mel Rutter loved frog legs, so Caroline Cohran always cooked frog legs for him when he was in town. Rev. Robert Jenkins was a member of White Oak Springs Baptist Church, and he served as a missionary with Maranatha Baptist Missions for a time.

Precious Memories from the Past

When the church took down the old 1889 building after the 1966 building was constructed, Rev. Ed Wix got some wood from the old church, made some judges' gavels out of that wood, and gave them to about six people. The families that received the gavels were either deacons or maybe the building committee members. Also, someone in the Lindsey family commissioned an artisan to sculpt some praying hands out of some of the old wood from the 1889 sanctuary.

On December 12, 1967, White Oak Springs Baptist Church ordained Vernon Cole, Ray Cole, and Frank Byrd as deacons.

Deacon Frank Byrd

Frank Byrd was in the Korean War. He started dating his future wife, Gloria Caldwell, at that time and married her on May 26, 1956.

One day, Frank Byrd got up on Sunday morning before his wife and kids got up, and he went to little Buzzard's Roost (a rock cliff) behind his house. It was summer time. Buzzard's Roost is up on a high spot, and the church is across the way up on another high spot. Through the trees he could see the church and hear them singing that morning. While he was up there he said: "Frank Byrd, you better get your life straight." He rededicated his life to the Lord at that time (July 1964) and started attending White Oak Springs Baptist Church with his wife and children.

Frank Byrd exemplified Joshua 24:15 "...choose you this day whom ye will serve: but as for me and my house, we will serve the

LORD." He made a spiritual decision that day that changed the spiritual destiny of his family and grandchildren and hopefully many future generations still to come.

Frank Byrd was ordained a deacon at White Oak Springs Baptist Church on December 17, 1967. He was an auto repairman and a school bus driver for Paulding County. His son, Jeff, said that his father would paint all the church buses for White Oak Springs Church. Jeff would help him prep the buses for painting by placing the masking tape (painting tape) on the buses.

Frank Byrd was very active in the church when it was at its highest years of attendance. He taught Sunday classes. He served as Sunday School Superintendent for many years. He was the bus director when they were bringing in 500 children each week. He taught the junior boy's Sunday School class for many years. He was in charge of children's church as well. That was a big responsibility because so many children were coming to church on the church buses during those years. He taught the Bible lesson, played games with them, and did puppet shows. Frank was also on the "Group of Three," which was responsible for the cemetery.

The booklet "Deacons of White Oak Springs" gives the following on Brother Frank Byrd:

Frank Byrd is a deacon ordained December 10, 1967.

He was born August 26, 1936. At the age of 17 he was saved at Merritt's Avenue Baptist Church. Two years later, he married the former Gloria Caldwell. They have two daughters and one son.

He moved his membership to White Oak in 1957 after moving to Paulding County. He served 3 ½ years in the Air Force. In July 1964, he rededicated his life to the Lord.

In the past he has served as Sunday School Superintendent; assistant Sunday School Superintendent; Youth Choir Chorister; Youth Choir Director; on the board of trustees and finance for our new church in 1966; on the pulpit committee; a teacher for intermediates and juniors. He drove one of the first buses in 1969; bus driver for buses five and seven in 1975; bus captain and youth director in 1976. Presently, he is head of the Youth Church and assistant Sunday School Superintendent.

Brother Frank enjoys deer hunting very much; he also enjoys working. He has been employed by John Smith Company of Atlanta for 21 years.

Deacon Ray Cole

The booklet "Deacons of White Oak Springs" gives the following on Brother Ray Cole:

Ray Cole is a deacon ordained December 10, 1967.

He was born November 28, 1916. He grew up in this area and has maintained a farm all of his married life. For twenty-eight years he ran a dairy farm and for 15 years he raised broilers. He is now retired.

This July will be forty-three years since he took the former Lessie Hitchcock for his wife. They have one son and three grandchildren.

Brother Ray was saved and joined the church in 1937. However, there came a time of rededication in his life. He has served this church well for many years.

Outside the church, Brother Ray still gardens and especially enjoys fishing and his grandchildren. His wife said: "After 43 years I can say he is a good husband."

White Oak Springs Baptist Church members from 1964 through 1967 when George Barnett was pastor: Frank Byrd, Gloria Byrd, B. A. Carter, Ben Carter, Effie Carter, Robert Carter, Robert Coates (Robert Cole?), T. W. Clark, Cardine Cohran (Caroline Cohran), Kenneth Cohran, Betty Cole, Lincoln Cole, Robert Cole, Vernon Cole, Charles Gamel, Ernest Gober, H. L. Kinney, Mrs. Mertha Gazaway, R. S. Gazaway, Mrs. Bessie Roberts, Junior Weatherington, and James Wix.

In 1967, Raymond McLarty began to serve as the Sunday School superintendent, and he continued in that capacity until 1982. The following numbers show how the Sunday School grew while he filled this position. The bus ministry started in 1970, which also helped to increase the attendance and enrollment, and year after year Raymond faithfully served in this key leadership role.

Year	SS enrollment	SS Attendance
1970	- - -	- - -
1971	207	190
1972	352	293
1973	390	328
1974	430	321

1975	484	399
1976	520	469
1977	482	444
1978	528	451
1979	522	449
1980	746	468

VBS attendance in 1980 was 431

1981	516	397
1982	466	387

VBS attendance in 1982 was 367

Mrs. Mertha Lea Baxter Gazaway was a member of White Oak Springs Baptist Church. Her obituary was published in *The Atlanta Journal-Constitution* on June 12, 2007:

"(Mertha Gazaway) was the daughter of the late Charlie Gordon Baxter and the late Lottie Cole Baxter of Paulding County. She had four brothers and four sisters, whom preceded her in death. She was a dedicated and faithful member of White Oak Springs, Second Baptist of Dallas, and Corner Baptist Church from July 1925 until her death. She loved her church and attended regularly, as long as her health permitted… She was preceded in death Jan. 6, 1992 by her husband Robert Guy Gazaway, after 59 years of marriage.

White Oak Springs members who died during 1964: John Wix, Mrs. Thersey Cole, Mrs. Minnie Husley Green, Mrs. Daley Clark, and Mrs. Addie Sinyard. White Oak Springs members who died during 1966: Mr. Tim Cole, and Mrs. Hettie Carter.

White Oak Springs Baptist Church had the following ordained preachers in their membership in 1964: Gene Lipscomb, Curtis Cole, and J. M. Brooks. In 1966, the church had the following ordained preachers: Gene Lipscomb, Curtis Cole, and J. M. Brooks.

Rev. Grover Cook

Grover Cook pastored White Oak Springs Baptist Church from March 18, 1967, until August, 20, 1967. Gloria Byrd said that Grover Cook and his wife were great encouragers.

Our Most Recent Pastors: 1967 to date

"So they strengthened their hands for this good work."
—*Nehemiah 2:18*

Rev. Charles E. Williams

Rev. Charles Williams pastored White Oak Springs Baptist Church during his second term of service from August 20, 1967, until February 6, 1977. During the ten years he served as pastor, the church grew to average 500 to 600 weekly and over 1000 on special days.

"Rev. Charles Williams came back to White Oak in the late 1960s. Mrs. Jean was a great prayer warrior, and his daughter Becky was a great blessing to the church for many years with her piano playing and singing. Brother Charles was pastor when we sent out our first missionary, Brother Robert Jenkins, and when we started the bus ministry and children's church. He saw the church at its highest attendance and at the height of the bus ministry. I believe the highest recorded attendance was a few over 1,000. It was not uncommon in those days for the buses to bring in as many as 300 every Sunday" (Recollections of Mrs. Gloria Byrd).

1971 Membership List

In 1971, White Oak Springs Baptist Church printed up a church photo directory. In the back of the photo book, it gives a list of names that is much longer and more complete than the names listed with the photos of members and their families. The list looks like a membership list, but there might be a few names of family members that had their photo taken along with members of the church. Here is the list as it is printed in the back of the book.

Acklins, Gail

Acklins, Paul

Agan, A. V.

Agan, Lindal

Alford, Jean

Alford, Johnny

Ammonds, Mary Jane

Arnold, Dick

Austin, Brenda

Austin, Irma N.

Austin, James

Austin, Linda

Baggett, Barry

Baggett, Betty

Baggett, Billy

Baggett, Brenda

Baggett, Clara Mae

Baggett, Donna

Baggett, Edna Fae

Baggett, Glen

Baggett, Lowell

Baggett, Rudy

Baggett, Wayne

Bankstone, Bertha Nell

Bankstone, Danny Dean

Bankstone, James Hubert

Bankstone, Kent

Bankstone, Rock

Barber, Norma

Baxter, Brenda

Baxter, David

Baxter, Douglas

Baxter, Evelyn

Baxter, Jewel

Baxter, Jimmie Lynn

Baxter, Kimbal

Baxter, Leona

Baxter, Lottie

Baxter, Lola

Baxter, Lucious

Baxter, Marie

Baxter, Maybell

Baxter, Pete

Baxter, Randy

Baxter, Danny

Baxter, Sherry

Baxter, Tim

Baxter, Vealer

Baxter, Whitie

Bearden, Becky

Bearden, Jean

Bearden, Junior Neal

Bearden, Lavenna

Bice, Jay

Bice, Marvene

Bone, Eddie

Bone, Virginia

Boynton, Kenneth

Boynton, Kim

Boynton, Virginia	Camp, Joy
Bricken, Connie	Camp, Lynn
Brinson, Barbara Cason	Camp, Martha
Brown, Bessie	Carter, Ben
Brown, Marlene	Carter, Effie
Brown, Sharon	Carter, Chris
Bullock, Brenda K. Haggard	Carter, Gail
Burmely, Cathy Cohran	Carter, Jennifer
Butler, Lela	Carter, Paul Jr.
Butler, Lonnie	Carter, Robert
Butler, Richard	Carter, Roben
Byrd, Claude T.	Cason, Bertha Mae
Byrd, Frank,	Cason, Ernest
Byrd, Francine	Champman, Bill
Byrd, Glenda	Champman, Hobart
Byrd, Gloria	Champman, Ruby
Byrd, Jane	Clark, Annie Lou
Byrd, Joann	Clark, Celcia (Sis)
Byrd, Jeff	Clark, Georgia
Byrd, Kenneth and Brenda	Clark, Gertrude
	Clark, Irene
Caldwell, Claude	Clark, Marvin
Caldwell, Emma	Clark, Sammy
Caldwell, Homer	Clark, Tommy
Caldwell, Ola	Clark, Woodrow
Caldwell, Pete	Cochran, Caroline
Camp, Fannie Mae	Cochran, Denise
Camp, Al	Cochran, Elise
Camp, Elaine	Cochran, Fain
Camp, Joe	Cochran, Fred

Cochran, Gladys
Cochran, Glenda Cason
Cochran, Kenneth
Cochran, Louise
Cochran, Parks
Cochran, Ruth
Cochran, Tony
Cole, Alma
Cole, Annie Mae
Cole, Barbara
Cole, Bill
Cole, Becky
Cole, Betty
Cole, Boyd
Cole, Charles
Cole, Clifford
Cole, Curtis
Cole, Deloris
Cole, Dennie
Cole, Floy T.
Cole, Fonda
Cole, Francine
Cole, Gertrude
Cole, Hattie
Cole, Herman
Cole, Jane
Cole, Jimmy
Cole, Josie
Cole, Kansas
Cole, Larry

Cole, Larry, Jr
Cole, Kim
Cole, Landry
Cole, Lessie
Cole, Lizzie
Cole, Lola
Cole, Melisa
Cole, Mildred
Cole, Mollie
Cole, Oscar
Cole, Pearlie
Cole, Ray
Cole, Renford
Cole, Roger
Cole, Sammy
Cole, Shane
Cole, Tracy
Cole, Vanda
Collins, Annette
Collins, Ben
Collins, Kathy
Cooper, Amonda

Daniel, Ida
Daniel, Nellie
Day, Ezell
Day, Larry
Day, Lennie
Day, Margaret
Day, Pete

Day, Ronnie
Day, Ronnie
Day, Vanessa
Day, Veronica
Denton, Kay
Denton, Patricia
Dodd, Shar-main
Drummond, Anthony
Drummond, Pauline
Drummond, Robert
Duke, Wesley
Dutton, Ricky

Elrod, Angie
Elrod, Tammie
Eskew, Danny
Eskew, Sharon
Evans, Jaynell
Evans, T. C.
Everidge, Wayne

Farr, Oree
Ferguson, Bill
Ferguson, Butch
Ferguson, Ray
Ferguson, Sandy
Ferguson, Vickie
Fields, Edward
Fields, Frances
Fincher, Dickie

Fincher, Melinda
Fuller, Amy
Fuller, Berdie
Fuller, Betty Ann
Fuller, J. O.
Fuller, Jimmy
Fuller, Joyce
Furr, Angie Lee
Furr, Larry

Gamel, Clyde
Gamel, Glenda
Gamel, L. K.
Gamel, Mildred
Gamel, Rufus
Gamel, Snote
Garner, Foster
Gaylord, Glenda
George, Delilah
George, Dorothy
Gober, Carolyn
Gober, George E.
Goosby, Lucile
Gurley, Annie Mae
Gurley, Martha

Haggard, Debra Cole
Hale, Hattie
Hall, Jean
Hardy, Alta

Hardy, J. C.
Hardy, Randy
Harris, Bell
Harris, Clinton
Harris, Kenny
Harris, Linda
Harris, Myra
Harris, Ralph
Harris, Rudy
Hatcher, Ann
Hatcher, Carl
Hatcher, George
Hayes, Dura
Hayes, Joe I.
Hayes, Junior
Hembree, Margaret
Henderson, Aubry
Henderson, Jean
Henderson, Freddie
Henderson, Ola Mae
Henderson, Tony
Hicks, Aileen
Hicks, Barbara
Hitchcock, Bennett
Hitchcock, Carolyn
Hicks, Charlene
Hicks, Dennie
Hitchcock, Hallie
Hicks, J. B.
Hicks, J. C.

Hicks, Josie
Hitchcock, Keith
Hicks, Mack
Hicks, Marie
Hicks, Marvine
Hicks, Maudie
Hicks, Nancy
Hicks, O. K.
Hicks, Ola
Hitchcock, Ruby
Hicks, Sally
Hicks, Sue
Hicks, Treva Nell
Holder, Geraldine
Holder, Hollie
Holder, Keith
Holder, Sandra
Holland, Laura Hardy
Hollis, Burma
Hulsey, Alton
Hulsey, Bernice
Hulsey, Cliff
Hulsey, Debra
Hulsey, Mary
Hutchenson, Dovie

Jacobs, Jo
Jacobs, Walter
Jenkins, Ann
Jenkins, Luanne

Jenkins, Nancy
Jenkins, Robbie
Jenkins, Robert
Jenkins, Roger
Jones, Larry
Jordan, Landrum
Jordan, Marie
Jordan, Martha

Kelly, Linda
Kilpatrick, Charmane
Kilpatrick, Denman
Kinney, Ada
Kinney, H. L.
Kinney, Ross
Kirby, Annie Mae
Knight, Ruth
Koplin, Loretta
Kramer, Becky
Kramer, Frances
Kramer, Sonya
Kramer, William

Lane, William
Lanzo, Sammy
Lindsey, Ethel
Lindsey, Kelly
Lindsey, Linda
Lindsey, Marion
Lindsey, Paul

Lindsey, Phyllis
Lindsey, Spurgeon
Lipcomb, Frances
Locklear, Ann

Maner, Mary
Marsh, Mary Lou
Matthew, Bonnie
Matthew, Ollie
Matthews, Willie Mae
Maxwell, Julie
Mayberry, Debra
McDurmon, Carolyn
McDurmon, Robert
McLarty, Margie
McLarty, Raymond
McLarty, Rhonda
McMichen, Cleo
McMichen, John
McMichen, Lonnie
McMichen, Virginia
Meeks, Ricky
Moody, Amy Carolyn
Moody, Billy Rogers
Moody, Mary Frances
Moore, Linda Whitley
Morgan, Joe
Morris, Brenda
Morris, Irma Ruth Baggett
Morris, Vera Mae Cole

Morrow, Doris
Morrow, Randal
Murdock, Edward

Neal, Geneva
Neal, Ollie Lee
Newton, Debbie
Newton, Evelyn
Newton, Lynn
Newton, Timmy
Newton, Wayne

Overton, Pamela Cole

Pace, Lynn
Pace, Lynn
Palmer, Eddie
Palmer, Edward
Palmer, Shirley
Palmer, Bennie
Palmer, Denise
Palmer, Franklin
Palmer, Jackie
Parker, Randy
Perry, Michael
Phillips, Cynthia
Phillips, Martha
Phillips, Robert
Pinson, Berdie
Pitts, Etta Mae Baxter

Poss, Bill
Poss, Dot
Poss, Michael
Prater, Roger
Pruett, Claudia
Pruett, Donald
Pruett, Jane
Puckett, Earl

Radcliff, Brenda Holder
Radcliff, Inez
Radcliff, Jerry
Radcliff, Larry
Radcliff, Marvin
Ragan, Lewis
Raney, Lou Ann
Ray, Bobbie Jean
Ray, Charlotte
Ray, Henry
Ray, Jessie
Ray, Pattie
Ray, Rhonda
Ray, Ronnie
Ray, Thomas
Reese, Louise
Renfroe, Eunice
Roberts, B. J.
Roberts, Bessie
Roberts, Edna Fae Cole
Roberts, Elmer

Roberts, Ida

Roberts, Linda

Roberts, Myrtle

Roberts, Pauline

Roberts, Rebecca

Roberts, Sim

Roberts, Thelma

Roberts, W. B.

Rose, Dorothy

Rollins, David

Rollins, Diane

Rollins, Diane

Rollins, Jim

Ruff, Gary

Ruff, Lovona

Rutledge, Emma

Rutledge, Sandra

Sanders, Betty

Sanders, Harold

Scoggins, Myrtis

Shead, Mollie

Shirley, Irene

Shoemaker, Jewell Taylor

Silvey, Francene

Sinyard, Annie

Smith, Carroll

Smith, Diane

Smith, Leo

Smith, Pat

Still, Robin

Still, Sue

Stone, Grady

Tallent, Gary

Tallent, Linda

Tallent, Louise

Tallent, Tommie

Thompson, Connie

Thompson, Jane

Taylor, Minnie Lee

Upton, Wendell

Walker, Loretta Baxter

Walker, Richard

Watts, Dennis

Weather, Lynn

Weatherington, Herman

Weatherington, Joe

Weatherington, Junior

Weatherington, Lela

Weatherington, Margie

Weatherington, Nancy

Wehunt, Gregg

White, Bill

White, June

White, Katherine

White, Larry

White, Osara

White, Steve

Wigley, Lillian

Williams, Aline

Williams, Mark

Wilson, Annie

Wilson, Joyce

Wilson, Lillie

Wilson, Rebecca

Wilson, Randall

Wilson, Randy

Wilson, Ruth

Wilson, Vonnie

Winters, JoAnne

Winters, Linda

Winters, Tommy

Wisner, Debroah

Witcher, Theresa

Wix, Bennett

Wix, Georgia (oldest living member of the church)

Wix, Donnie

Wix, Gerald

Wix, James

Wix, Mildred

Wix, Leonard (Bud)

Wix, Sue

Wix, Alan

Wix, Grace

Wix, Lorong

Wix Luther

Wix, Lena

Wix, Ralph

Wix, Velma

Wix, Sandra

Wix, Wayne

Wood, Lois

Wood, Spurgeon

Woody, Earnest

Woody, Orlee

Wyatt, Eddie

Wyatt, Sandra

More About the Bus Ministry

Kenneth Cohran substituted for one of the bus captains one week. It was the first day of dove or quail season. He really wanted to go hunting, but he spent most of the day visiting the route. The Lord gave him 80 people that rode the route that day. He said that was a special blessing the Lord gave him for missing the first day of hunting season.

A bus captain looked sad one morning, and Kenneth Cohran asked him what was wrong. The bus captain said: "This is the only place in the world a person can bring 50 kids to church on the bus and only get fifth place." What he was saying was that at any other church, anyone who brought in 50 kids would usually be the bus captain that brought in the most number of children that day at that church. However, at White Oak Springs Baptist Church, when he brought in 50 children, he received only fifth place, because four other bus captains brought in much more than 50 on that day.

Brother Cohran shared a poignant memory from his bus ministry days: A little girl rode a bus from Corn Crib trailer park, a rough area in Douglasville. The young girl had cigarette burns up and down both arms. That little girl appreciated any attention, and she tried to stay close by Brother Cohran.

Caroline Cohran said that one special blessing was when Jene Williams's niece came and accepted Christ as her Savior. Jene Williams had been praying for her niece to be saved for a long time.

Kenneth Cohran recalled a time they went to Alabama to attend a bus conference. The leader showed them how to make "ooey sticks." They are also called gee-haw whimmy diddle sticks, magic propellers, and magic stick propellers. It is a stick with notches on it, with a propeller on the end. When one runs a stick across the notches, it makes the propeller turn. Kenneth Cohran made 500 of them for bus prizes for the kids.

A Rainy Night in Georgia

One night during VBS, "it came up a bad cloud" (bad thunderstorm), and the storm knocked a tree across the highway about the time they were to let the kids out. Kenneth Cohran said that many people needed to use that way to go home, so the men went down to get the tree out of the way. While they were working down on Buchanan Highway, the lights went out at church when all the kids were still in the building. Churches did not have emergency back-up exit lights then. The ladies in charge had 500 screaming, scared children they had to help exit the building without the help of the men or lights. The ladies had no idea where their men went off to.

Prayer Time

One day Pastor Charles Williams and Kenneth Cohran were up on the roof fixing something. A preacher friend came by and needed to talk to Pastor Williams. Pastor Williams descended the ladder, talked to the man, then they went into the church and started praying. Kenneth Cohran could hear them praying out loud when he was up on the roof just standing there waiting for the pastor to get back. He did not know if he should fix the problem (he was not very sure what it was) or just wait until the pastor came back. Eventually, after a very long time, the pastor remembered he had left someone on the roof and proceeded to finish the project he was working on.

Prayer Time in the Woods

Luke 18:1 states: "And he *[Jesus]* spake a parable unto them to this end, that men ought always to pray, and not to faint." The men of White Oak Springs would have a season of prayer on a Saturday afternoon before protracted meetings. They would go to a special place about 100 yards from the gate that goes in to the Bureau of Land Management (BLM) property near the corner of James Wix Road and Old White Oak Springs Cemetery Road. The gate is about 75 yards southeast of that intersection. About 100 yards past the BLM property gate, the rock-pile (see "Prayer Rocks" below) place of prayer is to the right (west), going into the woods.

About once a month, they prayed on Sunday afternoons before the evening service. They used this spot during the 1950s and continued to use it into the 1970s. It is not known why that spot was important, but it could have been used as a place of prayer before 1889 when the church was meeting at the other property.

Sometimes they would pray at the same spot on Friday and Saturday nights. They would start about 1½ to 2 hours before dark and pray until dark.

Most men would stand the entire time of prayer there in the woods. Sometimes they prayed for two hours or longer. James Wix did not want to stand the whole time, nor did he want to sit directly on the ground. So James would sit on an old discarded Radio Flyer wagon that had no tires on it. Even though he was only two or three inches off the ground, he turned that old wagon upside down and sat on it. Each week, the men wondered why he never looked under it to see if it had snakes, spiders, tigers, or something worse lurking beneath.

Prayer Rocks

The men started a little prayer rock pile. Men would take a little rock and leave it on the rock pile as they arrived each time. It grew to be about waist high. Wayside Baptist Church in Dallas, Georgia, has a prayer rock pile on the hill behind their church that was started a few years ago and is getting to be large. Dr. Billy Bell is currently the pastor of that church. Faith Baptist Temple in Powder Springs, where Pastor Tibbitts is the pastor, also uses prayer rocks (polished marble pieces).

It was common for the men to pray out loud (i.e. very loudly) when they prayed. Caroline Cohran said Mrs. Jene Williams was a prayer warrior and a shouter (one that shouted "Praise the Lord" in the church services). Effie Carter and Annie Lou Clark were also prayer warriors.

In the 1970s or early 1980s, the men would go to the spring across the street from the current church and pray before church services. Later they used a Sunday School classroom and prayed there before the services.

A Blast from the Past

On December 10, 2016, Kenneth Cohran took Pastor Keith Lee to show him the place where the men would meet to pray. They found the old place of prayer without any difficulty. They found the old prayer rocks scattered all over the ground and down the side of a little hill. Pastor Keith stepped on something covered in leaves. It was the little red Radio Flyer wagon that had no tires on it that James Wix would sit on during their prayer times. Pastor Keith picked it up and brought it back to show to the church on the service the next day. (Pastor Keith and Brother Kenneth Cohran very carefully checked to see if anything alive was under it. They did not find anything).

Remains of Red Radio Flyer Wagon

Found at the old place of prayer in December 2016 by Rev. Keith Lee and Kenneth Cohran

In September 1969, White Oak Springs Baptist Church ordained Bethel Noble as a deacon. On June 24, 1973, White Oak Springs Baptist Church ordained Ollie Matthews, Ralph Wix, and Dennis Barber, as deacons. On July 25, 1974, White Oak Springs Baptist Church ordained Jerry Godfrey as a deacon.

Deacon Bethel Noble

The booklet "Deacons of White Oak Springs" gives the following on Brother Bethel Noble:

Bethel Noble is a deacon ordained September of 1969.

He was born July 10, 1939; graduated from Etowah County High School in Attalla, Alabama, in 1957. In 1958 he married the former Shirley Wills. They have three children: Pam, Tim, and Lisa. They moved from Alabama to GA in 1967.

Bethel was saved in July of 1946. He joined the Second Baptist Church in Douglasville after their move in 1967. In 1973, he and his family moved their letters to White Oak. Since that time, he has worked in the bus ministry and served as assistant choir director. Now he serves as organist, a member of the missions committee; chairman of our new activity building project; teaches the young adult Sunday School class. This class set a record of 102 attendance in Sunday School. His concern for the young people of this church is obvious. I believe all the young people have a very special love and appreciation for Bethel and all he does in our church.

Bethel truly enjoys fishing and hunting, and most will agree when Bethel states that "he is an all around good guy."

Deacon Ollie Matthews

The booklet "Deacons of White Oak Springs" gives the following on Brother Ollie Matthews:

Ollie Matthew is a deacon ordained June 24, 1973.

He was born March 1943. He grew up in Paulding County and graduated from Dallas High School in 1961. He married the former Bonnie Palmer. They have two sons: Brian and Keith. He and Sammy Cole have their own plumbing business.

In the past Ollie taught the Junior Boys Sunday School class; also, he served on the pulpit committee.

Presently he serves as: Assistant Sunday School Superintendent; Assistant Choir leader; chorister for the children's church; and chorister for the Sunday School; and he is also the assistant clerk for our church. He really likes working in the children's church, and it shows.

Outside the church, he enjoys coon hunting and deer hunting. It has been said that Ollie doesn't care for fishing, but he has to take the boys anyway.

Deacon Ralph Wix

The booklet "Deacons of White Oak Springs" gives the following on Brother Ralph Wix:

Brother Ralph Wix was ordained a deacon June 24, 1973.

Brother Ralph was born October 18, 1920. He married the former Lena Kelley. They have one daughter, Jean, and one son, James.

Brother Ralph served this church in many ways. He served as the men's Sunday School teacher from 1965 to 1976; the mission treasurer from 1969 to 1976. He also served as the treasurer of the Brotherhood from 1966 to 1973.

Brother Ralph was saved in 1944. For many years he served God to the fullest of his ability. On October 13, 1976, God called Brother Ralph home to heaven.

Deacon Jerry Godfrey

The booklet "Deacons of White Oak Springs" gives the following on Brother Jerry Godfrey:

Jerry Godfrey is a deacon ordained March 25, 1974.

Jerry was born October 24, 1944. Jerry graduated from Pickens County High School in 1962. He married the former Bobbie Brown. They have been married for 15 years and have two sons, Colin and Gregg; also, they are rearing Bobbie's younger sister,

Lynn. He served in the Navy from August of 1962 until March of 1966.

Brother Jerry was saved in July of 1962. In 1968 he moved to Paulding County; and in 1975 he and his family moved their letters to White Oak from Macedonia. Here he has taught the Primary boys in Sunday School. Presently he teaches the Intermediate boys; is a bus driver; a devoted mechanic for our buses, and is assistant leader in the Junior Children's Church.

Outside church, Jerry enjoys hunting, golf, and most of all tennis.

White Oak Springs Baptist Church members from 1967 through 1976 when Charles E. Williams was pastor: Clara Mae Baggett, Robbie Ballinger, Mrs. Sherri Ballanger, Becky Bearden, Jay Leonard Bice (from his obituary), Francine Byrd, Frank Byrd, Gloria Byrd, Ben Carter, Effie Carter, Robert Carter (lives on Carter Road), George Clark, Woodrow Clark, Caroline Cohran, Kenneth Cohran, Bill Cole, Boyd Cole, Lincoln Cole, Ray Cole, Sammy Cole, Vernon Cole, W. T. Clark, Edna Fennell, Hurbert Fincher, Robert Jenkins, Mrs. Dorothy Fuller, Jerry Godfrey, Ernest Gober, Jean Henderson, Mrs. Robert Jenkins, Dan Kramer, Kerry Lindsey, Raymond McLarty, Danny Moody, Shirley Moody, Bethel Noble, Bessie Roberts, Pauline Roberts, Mrs. Sandra Skinner, Will Sorrells, Junior Weatherington, Kenneth Weatherington, Nancy Weatherington, James Westbrook, Jean Williams, James Wix, and Ralph Wix.

White Oak Springs members who died during 1967: Estelle Gamel, Cleveland Cole, and Dean Roberts.

White Oak Springs members who died during 1968: Mr. H. L. Cole, Mr. R. T. Carter, Mrs. Louise White, Mrs. Annie Byrd, and Mrs. Rosie Cole.

White Oak Springs members who died during 1969: Tom Carter, and Mrs. Minnie Baxter. White Oak Springs members who died during 1970: Mrs. Debra Thompson Evans, Mr. George Edward Gober, Mr. Terry Meeks, and Mr. Ralph Cole.

Thomas M. Carter

Tom Carter was born in 1881 and died in 1969. Tom and his wife, Hettie, are buried in the church cemetery. Tom attended White Oak Springs Baptist Church his whole life. He first started attending the little log frame church at the old property. He was present when the second church was built in 1889 and attended there most of his life, until October 1966 when the newest church was built. Two of his sons were Ben and Paul Carter. They were also longtime members of White Oak Springs.

White Oak Springs members who died during 1971: Vernon Cole (deacon), W. L. Cole, and Fred Clark.

White Oak Springs members who died during 1972: Mrs. Kansas Cole, Deacon L. O. Cole, Mrs. Emma Caldwell, and Mrs. Jackie Wehunt.

White Oak Springs members who died during 1973: Bro. Lucious Baxter, Bro. B. A. Carter (chairman of the deacons), Marvin Clark,

Sister Claudia Cole, Brother Herman Cole, Sister Ida Roberts, and Sister Theresa Witcher.

White Oak Springs members who died during 1974: Clifford Cole, Mrs. Dura Harris, Mrs. Leona Cole, Mrs. Pearlie Cole, and Mr. Claud Burt, Sr.

White Oak Springs members who died during 1975: Mr. Bufford Ivey.

White Oak Springs members who died during 1976: Rufas Gamel, Miss Debra Hicks, and Mr. R. L. Rice.

The following members were licensed preachers of the church in 1968: Robert Jenkins, Leonard Wix, Bill Poss, T. C. Evans, and Paul Carter. The following members were licensed preachers of the church in 1970: Robert Jenkins and Leonard Wix.

White Oak Springs Baptist Church had the following ordained preachers in their membership in 1967: Curtis Cole.

White Oak Springs Baptist Church had the following ordained preachers in their membership in 1968: Curtis Cole and Robert Jenkins.

White Oak Springs Baptist Church had the following ordained preachers in their membership in 1969: Curtis Cole and J. M. Brooks.

White Oak Springs Baptist Church had the following ordained preachers in their membership in 1970: Curtis Cole and Willis Herman Weatherington.

White Oak Springs Baptist Church had the following ordained preachers listed in their membership in 1971: Curtis Cole, Robert Jenkins, Leonard Wix, Joe Camp, and Kerry Lindsey.

White Oak Springs Baptist Church ministers listed in their membership in 1972: Curtis Cole, Robert Jenkins, Leonard Wix, Joe Camp, Dan Kramer, Harold Sanders, Willis Weatherington, Kerry Lindsey, and T.C. Evans.

White Oak Springs Baptist Church had the following ministers listed in their membership in 1973: Curtis Cole, Robert Jenkins, Leonard Wix, Joe Camp, Dan Kramer, Harold Sanders, Willis Weatherington, and Kerry Lindsey.

White Oak Springs Baptist Church ministers listed in their membership in 1974: Curtis Cole, and Robert Jenkins (missionary to West Indies).

In 1975, they had the following ministers listed in their membership: Kenny Byrd, Joe Camp, Curtis Cole, Robert Jenkins (missionary to West Indies), Horace Fennell, Hurbert Fincher, Lonnie McMichen, Danny Moody, and Levoy Whitton.

In 1976, they had the following ministers listed: Kenny Byrd, Curtis Cole, Robert Jenkins (missionary to West Indies), Hurbert Fincher, Horace Fennell, and Kerry Lindsey.

Jay Leonard Bice

Jay Leonard Bice (b. 1941–d. 2009) was baptized by Rev. Charles Williams. In 1973 he was ordained for the ministry by White Oak Springs Baptist Church. His wife was Marvene Farr Bice. During his lifetime he pastored the following churches: Callie Harbin Baptist Church in Villa Rica, Georgia; Second Baptist Church in Boaz, Alabama; Victory Baptist Church in Dallas, Georgia; and Antioch Baptist Church in Whitesburg, Georgia.[34]

More about Jay Bice and the White Oak Springs Baptist Church Bus Ministry

The church has a photocopy of an undated article from *The Southern Baptist Journey*. It was published in the October/November edition of either 1975 or 1976. It is titled: "One Man Begins a Revolution." Here is the article in its entirety.

One Man Begins a Revolution
By Bill Powell

"But I am only one. What can I do?"

The White Oak Springs Baptist Church is located on rural route 4, Dallas, GA. They're out in the country, 5 ½ miles from the nearest town. There are very few houses anywhere near the church.

They enrolled 201 and averaged less than 100 in attendance in Sunday School in 1970. They also had an old rundown bus with

---

[34]http://www.jones-wynn.com/obituaries/RevJayLeonard-Bice-1042/#!/FamilyTreePage. Accessed December 30, 2016.

a dead battery, flat slick tires, dirty seats, and cobwebs on the inside.

And they had a new convert, Jay Bice, who had been saved two or three months. He wanted permission to fix up the old bus and use it to bring people to church. They explained to him that this had been tried several times before without success.

He still wanted to try it and they let him. He brought between 25-30 the first Sunday. Then 45 on the second Sunday. Then he and pastor Charles Williams attended a bus conference and the revolution was underway.

Bice began asking for more buses. They bought him more buses and promised to give him as many as he could fill.

After he filled five buses the church told him to stop—they had no more room to put them. Every corner of every room was filled.

They built a children's building in 1974 containing 12 classrooms and a children's church auditorium. And started buying more buses.

I visited the church last Wednesday night. Its out in the country, but full of people. Chairs were in the aisles, I found a chair by a side window at the front.

Last Sunday they had 497 riders on their eight bus routes. That's an average of 62 riders per bus for that country church. And it rained all night Saturday and all day Sunday.

The pastor's wife helps Gail Wright on her bus route that goes near my home on a lonely country road. They would leave the church about 8:00 and rush to get back by 10:00. They had 83 on their route in all that rain last Sunday.

Sandra Wyatt moved into the century club last Sunday. She had 115 riders on her country bus route in the all-day rain.

They passed the 600 mark in their Sunday School attendance in 1974. They had 663 attending Sunday School last February when they dedicated their new children's building. They had 678 on their round-up day last fall.

Their membership has grown from about 250 to 600 in these five years. Their income has increased from $20,618 in 1970 to $73,253 for 1975. They (gave) $31,358 to missions in 1975.

They had 142 people saved during two months this year.

God called Jay Bice to preach. White Oak Springs ordained him in 1973. He is now the pastor of Callie Harbin Baptist Church in Villa Rica, GA.

Kenneth Cohran, the chairman of the deacons, is now the Bus Director. Dickie Fincher, a youth minister, is the minister of Youth and the director of children's worship services.

Charles Williams has been pastor of this country church for 13 years. "We give all the praise and glory to God," he explained. "We have wonderful workers in our church."

The rest of the article invites people to a Church Bus Evangelism Clinic and Children's Worship Conference that following January 26-27. Conference speakers' names are listed and prices are given (end of article).

Bus Captain Sandra Wyatt—27 Years of Faithful Service

Sandra Wyatt started attending White Oak Springs Baptist Church after Jay Bice made contact with her family through the bus ministry of White Oak Springs Baptist Church. Sandra stated she came by car the first Sunday with her children and then started riding the bus. Deacon Lincoln Cole and his wife, Mildred, had been friends with Sandra and her family for many years and had invited them many times to church.

Sandra said that she started helping Jay and Marvene Bice and Larry and Margaret Day on the bus route and became friends with both of these families. This was bus one, and it picked up children in the Villa Rica area. After a few years, they purchased a second bus. Henry and Charlotte Ray helped her on Route Two. Ray was the driver. Sandra recalls that Mark and Marie Dockery also were bus captains for some years.

Sandra said that when Jay Bice was called to pastor at a different church, Kenneth Cohran became the bus director. When Larry gave up his bus route, Sandra took over the route and served as a bus captain for 27 years. Her route picked up children from the Villa Rica and New Georgia communities. She recalls that one Sunday she had 113 children come on her bus route to church. Sandra also taught Sunday School for many years, but she had to choose between being a Sunday School teacher or a bus captain, because the bus would arrive late to church many times due to delays.

Fruit That Remains of Her Ministry Until This Day

Three children that rode her bus later served the Lord in other ministries. The first bus rider Sandra mentioned was Cathy Still. Cathy rode Sandra's bus and later married Jeff Byrd. Jeff's father worked in the bus and children's ministries at church. Rev. Jeff Byrd, along with his wife, Cathy, served as pastor of Gateway Baptist Church for over 18 years.

Sandra's son Eddie Wyatt later became the pastor of Happy Valley Baptist Church in Villa Rica. He has been serving as pastor at that church for the past 24 years. May the Lord bless him for his faithfulness.

Timmy Newton was another child that rode Sandra's bus to church. Timmy was from a family of eight. Later, he became the bus director at Victory Baptist Church in North Augusta, South Carolina. Years later, Tim Newton invited Sandra Wyatt to come speak to his bus workers and bus kids, and he told them that Sandra was the one that God had used in his life to bring him to the Lord.

Rev. Charles Edgar Williams

Obituary for Rev. Charles Edgar Williams.

Brother Charles Edgar Williams, 88, of Villa Rica, GA passed away Friday, August 1, 2014 at Tanner Medical Center in Carrollton. A native of Villa Rica, he was born May 16, 1926, the son of the late Mr. Homer Lee Williams and the late Mrs. Sara Frances Browning Williams. He served honorably in the United States Navy from 1944–1947. He married Martha Jean Smith on January 18, 1947, in New, GA. After receiving the call to preach, Brother Williams went on to serve the Lord for over 60 years as a pastor. Over the years, he has served in the following churches: New Georgia Baptist Church, Harmony Grove Baptist Church, Mt. Carmel Baptist Church, White Oaks Springs Baptist Church, Abilene Baptist Church, Calvary Baptist Church, Second Baptist Church of Riverdale, Callie Harbin Baptist Church, and Lighthouse Missionary Baptist Church. He served as President of Windward Island Mission, served on the Board of Directors for Rock of Ages Mission for over 30 years, and was a moderator for Preacher's Fellowship for over 20 years. He was strong in his Faith, was devoted to the Lord, and loved his family dearly. He was a member of Callie Harbin Baptist Church.

In addition to his parents, he was preceded in death by his wife, Martha Jean Smith Williams; and sisters, Oree Parks and Pauline Drummond.

He is survived by three daughters and sons-in-law, Becky and Junior Bearden of Dallas, Robin and Tim Brown of Marietta, and Lisa and Terry Thomas of Eatonton; one son and daughter-in-law, Steve and Terre Williams of Dallas; eleven grandchildren; fourteen great-grandchildren; several nieces and nephews.

The family will receive friends at Jones-Wynn Funeral Home in Villa Rica, Sunday, August 3, 2014, from 2:00 PM until 9:00 PM.[35]

---

[35](http://www.jones-wynn.com/obituaries/Charles-Williams-16/#!/Obituary

Interim Roy Stanford

Roy Stanford served as the interim pastor from May 18, 1977, to June 26, 1977. Gloria Byrd said that "Roy, and his wife, Estelle, was the interim pastor when daddy was sick and passed away. He was good to visit us and bring us food."

Caroline Cohran said the church had 1,000 for Easter the last year Rev. Charles Williams was the pastor there. The next year, Rev. Larry Davis could not believe they had 800 for VBS.

Rev. Larry G. Davis

Larry G. Davis served as pastor of the church from June 26, 1977, until March 14, 1979. He and his wife had three children. Rev. Davis was pastor at White Oak Springs when the booklet "Deacons of White Oak Springs" was produced that recorded firsthand information on the deacons of White Oak at that time.

The booklet "Deacons of White Oak Springs" gives the following biography on Pastor Davis.

How proud we are to have such a great man as our pastor!!!

Brother Larry was reared in Cedartown, Ga. He graduated from Cedartown High School and attended Berry College in Rome.

He married the former Juanita Jones, and they have three children: Barry, Kaye, and Traci.

Brother Larry was saved in 1948. He was called to preach in 1954. In 1956 he was ordained to preach and began pastoring at the Dugdown Church in Haralson County. Since then, he has pastored the Wimberly Hill Church, Cedartown, GA, the

Fairview Baptist Church in Rockmart, GA, and the East Rome Church in Rome, GA. Brother Larry came to White Oak in June 1977 from Mount Carmel Baptist church in Ft. Payne, Alabama. He served Mt Carmel for four years.

Brother Larry has a visible love for our Lord and our church. He is dedicated to his calling from God to preach the Word. He has an earnest desire to see souls saved.

Outside the church, Brother Larry enjoys a game of tennis; camping; and a round or two of golf. He really enjoys chewing gum; and he receives such joy from making people laugh.

Thank God for such a pastor!

While the booklet the "Deacons of White Oak Springs Baptist Church" was being compiled, the author of that booklet also asked each of the deacons to give a short comment or praise for their at that time: Pastor Larry E. Davis. Almost all of these comments were made on the spur of the moment between services or while the deacons were on their way to some other responsibility.

"He's God called, God sent, and he is not one man's pastor, but the pastor of all." - Ernest Gober

"He's ideal, willing, co-operative, very understanding, and he will work." – Kenneth Cohran.

"He's a very unusual person." - Brother Frank Byrd.

"He's the best I've ever seen as a man, as preacher, and as a leader." - Ray Cole

"He's a good man and good preacher." As stated by Ollie Matthews.

"He's an overall good leader; he preaches the Gospel, and he is burdened for the lost, which is really what counts." - Jerry Godfrey

White Oak Springs Baptist Church members in 1977 and 1978 when Larry G. Davis was pastor: Clara Mae Baggett, Becky Bearden, Effie Carter, Robert Carter, Charles W. Cole, Sammy Cole, Larry Davis, Ernest Gober, Caroline Cohran, Kenneth Cohran, Ollie Matthews, Raymond McLarty, Bessie Roberts, Sandra Skinner, Junior Weatherington, and Nancy Weatherington.

White Oak Springs members who died during 1977: Mrs. Isabel Harris, Mrs. O. K. Hicks, Mrs. Burma Hollis, Deacon H. L. Kinney, and Deacon Ralph Wix.

White Oak Springs Baptist Church ministers listed in its membership in 1977: Kenny Byrd, Curtis Cole, Jack Fambrough, Robert Jenkins, Kerry Lindsey, Horace Fennell, and Wayne Wix.

White Oak Springs members who died during the year of 1978: Mrs. Clyde Gamel, Mrs. Bessie Brown, Homer Caldwell, Miss Geneva Neal, Mrs. Lottie Baxter, Mr. Emmett Henderson, Peter Day, Mrs. Mary Maner, Mrs. Lois Ann Rainey, Willie Wilson.

White Oak Springs Baptist Church had the following ministers listed in its membership in 1978: Curtis Cole, Roy Stanford, Jack

Fambrough, Joseph Fields, Kerry Lindsey, Wayne Wix, Stanley Speegle.

1977 Membership List

In 1977, White Oak Springs Baptist Church printed another church photo directory. This book states it is a membership directory and in the back gives the following membership list. Since this list was a photo directory, there may be some young children who are listed as members or spouses listed as members who were not members. They had their photo taken with their family and their name appears in the list.

Abercrombie, Cindy

Abercrombie, Elaine

Abercrombie, Vickey

Acklins, Melvin

Acklins, Glenda

Acklins, Randy

Alford, Sammy

Ammonds, Mary Jane

Arnold, Dick

Austin, Brenda

Austin, Betty

Austin, James

Austin, Linda

Baggett, Barry

Baggett, Bell

Baggett, Betty

Baggett, Billy

Baggett, Clara Mae

Baggett, Donna

Baggett, Edna Fae

Baggett, Glen

Baggett, Lowell

Baggett, Rudy

Bankstone, Danny Dean

Bankstone, Rocky

Baxter, Brenda

Barnett, Connie

Baxter, Danny

Baxter, Douglas

Baxter, Evelyn

Baxter, Jewel

Baxter, Jimmie Lynn

Baxter, Junior

Baxter, Kimbal

Baxter, Lola

Baxter, Lois
Baxter, Maybell
Baxter, Pete
Baxter, Sherry
Baxter, Stefanie
Baxter, Randy
Baxter, Tim
Baxter, Vealer
Baxter, Whittic
Bearden, Becky
Bearden, Jean
Bearden, Lavenna
Bearden, Junior Neal
Blackmon, Rebecca Lynn
Bone, Eddie
Boynton, Virginia
Bricken, Connie
Brown, Bessie
Bullock, Linda
Burmely, Cathy Cohran
Butler, Leia
Butler, Lonnie
Butler, Richard
Byrd, Brenda
Byrd, Claude T.
Byrd, Jane
Byrd, Jr.
Byrd, Frank
Byrd, Glenda
Byrd, Gloria

Byrd, Jeff
Byrd, Joann
Byrd, Kenneth

Caldwell, Claude
Caldwell, Homer
Caldwell, Ola
Caldwell, Melissa
Caldwell, Pete
Camp, Fannie Mae
Camp, Al
Camp, Lynn
Camp, Martha
Cason, Bertha Mae
Cason, Ernest
Carson, Charlie
Carson, Nora
Carson, Kathy
Carter, Ben
Carter, Effie
Carter, Chris
Carter, Gail
Carter, Janet
Carter, Jennifer
Carter, Jill
Carter, Paul Jr.
Carter, Robert
Chappel, Debbie
Chappel, Kay
Clark, Annie Lou

Clark, Celcia (Sis)
Clark, Sammy
Clark, Sue
Clark, Tommy
Clark, Woodrow
Cochran, Glenda Cason
Cochran, Gladys
Cochran, Parks
Cochran, Ruth
Cochran, Tony
Cohran, Caroline
Cohran, Kenneth
Cole, Alma
Cole, Annie Mae
Cole, Bill
Cole, Francine
Cole, Boyd
Cole, Jane
Cole, Barbara
Cole, Becky
Cole, Curtis
Cole, Deanie
Cole, Dennie
Cole, Deloris
Cole, Ficy T.
Cole, Fonda
Cole, Frances
Cole, Hattie
Cole, Jimmy
Cole, Larry

Cole, Larry, Jr
Cole, Lessie
Cole, Lizzie
Cole, Oscar
Cole, Ray
Cole, Roger
Cole, Sammy
Cole, Shane
Cole, Tracy
Cole, Vonda
Cole, Wendy
Cook, Larry
Cooper, Amonda

Daniel, Ida
Daniel, Nellie
Daniels, Annette
Darbry, Angie
Davis, Barry
Davis, Clara
Davis, Darlene
Davis, Donnie
Davis, Juanita
Davis, Kaye
Davis, Jimmy
Davis, Larry
Davis, Traci
Day, Larry
Day, Lennie
Day, Margaret

Day, Pete

Day, Ronnie

Day, Tammy

Day, Vanessa

Day, Veronica

Dockery, Annette

Dockery, Mark

Dockery, Marie

Dockery, Randy

Dockery, Rhoda

Denton, Kay

Denton, Patricia

Dodd, Shar-main

Drummond, Anthony

Drummond, Pauline

Drummond, Robert

Dudley, John

Duke, Wesley

Dyer, JoAnn

Dykes, Mildred

Edwards, Tony

Ellis, Debbie

Ellis, Jeanette

Elrod, Angie

Elrod, Tammie

Eskey, Danny

Eskey, Sharon

Evans, Ruth

Everidge, Wayne

Fairchild, Sheila

Farr, Oree

Ferguson, Bill

Ferguson, Butch

Ferguson, Ray

Ferguson, Sandy

Ferguson, Vickie

Fields, Edward

Fields, Felix

Fields, Lorene

Finnell, Edna

Finnell, Horace

Finnell, Judy

Finnell, Gloria

Freeman, Sue

Freeman, Susan

Fuller, Amy

Fuller, Berdie

Fuller, Betty Ann

Fuller, J. O.

Fuller, Jimmy

Fuller, Joyce

Furr, Angie Lee

Furr, Larry

Garnett, Joe

Gamel, Clyde

Gamel, Glenda

Gamel, L. K.

Gamel, Mildred

Gamel, Snote	Harness, Steve
Garnel, Foster	Harness, Stoney
Garner, Randy	Hart, Faye
Garner, Treva	Hart, Jim
Gaylord, Glenda	Hayes, Joe I.
George, Delilah	Hayes, Junior
Gober, Carolyn	Hembree, Margaret
Gober, George E.	Henderson, Bessie
Gober, Steve	Henderson, Freddie
Gravette, Pauline	Henderson, Jean
Grimsley, Frank	Henderson, Jane
Gurley, Annie Mae	Henderson, Lois
Gurley, Martha	Henderson, Ola Mae
	Henderson, Robert
Haggard, Debra Cole	Henderson, Tony
Hall, Emma Jean	Hicks, Aileen
Hardy, Alta	Hicks, Barbara
Hardy, David	Hicks, Charlene
Hardy, Gerald	Hicks, Dennie
Hardy, Mary	Hicks, Frankie
Hardy, J. C.	Hicks, J. B.
Hardy, Randy	Hicks, J. C.
Harris, Clinton	Hicks, Josie
Harris, Kenny	Hicks, Kathy
Harris, Linda	Hicks, Mack
Harris, Myra	Hicks, Marie
Harris, Ralph	Hicks, Marvine,
Harris, Rudy	Hicks, Maudie
Harness, Cassie	Hicks, Nancy
Harness, Shirley	Hicks, Natalie

Hicks, Ola
Hicks, Sally
Hitchcock, Bennett
Hitchcock, Carolyn
Hitchcock, Keith
Hitchcock, Ruby
Holcomb, Jerry
Holcomb, Martha
Holder, Geraldine
Holder, Phylis
Holder, Sandra
Holland, Laura Hardy
Holmes, Cheyeene
Holmes, Denise
Holmes, Edna
Hollis, Lillie
Holt, Rayburn
Hulsey, Alton
Hulsey, Bernice
Hulsey, Cliff
Husley, Lillie
Hulsey, Mary
Hutchenson, Dovie
Hurst, LuAnne

Ivery, Cecil
Ivery, David
Ivery, Edna
Ivey, Jackie
Ivery, Randy

Jenkins, Ann
Jenkins, Nancy
Jenkins, Ricky
Jenkins, Robert
Jennings, Becky
Jones, Larry
Jones, Myrtle
Johns, Lillie Mae
Johnson, Lisa
Jordan, Ines

Kaplin, Loretta
Kinney, Ada
Kinney, Ross
Kirby, Annie Mae

Lane, William
Lang, Karen
Lanzo, Sammy
Lewis, Glen
Lewis, Wayne
Lindsey, Ethel
Lindsey, Davis
Lindsey, Kelly
Lindsey, Linda
Lindsey, Marion
Lindsey, Paul
Lindsey, Phyllis
Lindsey, Raymond
Lindsey, Susan

Lindsey, Traci
Lipcomb, Frances
Loudermilk, Jenny
Lummer, Kim

Mammenga, JoAnn Wix
Maner, Mary
Massey, Carolyn
Massey, Glenda
Matthew, Bonnie
Matthew, Bryan
Matthew, Keith
Matthew, Ollie
Matthews, Willie Mae
McClendon, Betty
McCullough, Minnie Lee
McGurt, Ann
McLarty, Cynthia
McLarty, Margie
McLaty, Paula
McLarty, Raymond
McLarty, Rhonda
McMichen, Cleo
McMichen, John
McMichen, Lonnie
McMichen, Virginia
Meeks, Ricky
Miles, Jimmy
Moody, Billy Rogers
Moody, Charlie

Moody, Franklin
Moody, Janice
Moody, Loretta
Moody, Mary Frances
Moody, Ricky
Moore, Linda Whitley
Morgan, Joe
Morris, Vera Mae Cole
Morrow, Randal

Neal, Geneva
Neal, Ollie Lee

Newton, Albert
Newton, Lynn
Noble, Bethel
Noble, Lisa
Noble, Shirley
Noble, Tim

Overton, Pamala Cole
Owens, Terry

Pace, Jesse
Padgett, Diane
Padgett, Robin
Palmer, Eddie
Palmer, Edward
Palmer, Jeff
Palmer, Shirley

Parker, Jackie

Parsons, Bertie

Parsons, Gary

Perry, Michael

Pilgrim, Pete

Pinson, Berdie

Pitts, Chris

Pitts, Etta Mae Baxter

Ploof, Eddie

Pollard, Sandra

Poss, Bill

Poss, Dot

Poss, Michael

Prater, Roger

Pruett, Teresa

Puckett, Earl

Radcliff, Brenda

Radcliff, Holder

Radcliff, Larry

Radcliff, Inez

Radcliff, Jerry

Radcliff, Marvin

Ragsdale, Robin

Ray, Bobbie Jean

Ray, Carolyn

Ray, Jessie

Renfroe, Eunice

Roberts, B. J.

Roberts, Bessie

Roberts, Edna Fae Cole

Roberts, Lois

Roberts, Pauline

Roberts, Rebecca

Roberts, Thelma

Roberts, W. B.

Robertson, Carroll

Rollins, David

Rollins, Diane

Rollins, Jim

Rollins, Russell

Rollins, Steve

Ruff, Gary

Ruff, Lovona

Shead, Keith

Shead, Mollie

Shores, Rodney

Shores, Shelia

Shoemaker, Jewell Taylor

Singleton, Doris

Skinner, Amelia

Skinner, Danny

Skinner, Sandra

Smith, Carroll

Smith, Diane

Smith, Leo

Stanford, Estelle

Stanford, Roy

Swafford, Steve Darrel

Swafford, Danny Eugene
Still, Cathy
Still, Robin
Still, Sue

Tallent, Gary
Tallent, Linda
Tallent, Louise
Tallent, Tommie
Tant, Brenda
Tant, Curtis
Tant, Dale
Tant, Eddie
Tant, Travis
Tant, Zora
Thomas, Charlotte
Thomas, DeWayne
Thompson, Connie
Thompson, Jane
Thompson, Richard
Thompson, Tommy
Tomlin, Diane
Turner, Charlotte
Turner, Jackie
Turner, Mary

Upton, Bobbie
Upton, David
Upton, June
Upton, Lora Lee

Upton, Patti
Upton, Robert
Upton, Tony
Upton, Wendell

Vaughn, Cheryl
Vaughn, Janice
Verner, Betty
Verner, Jack
Verner, Melody

Walker, Loretta Baxter
Walker, Richard
Watts, Dennis
Waters, Carolyn
Weatherington, Herman
Weatherington, Margie
Weatherington, Joe
Weatherington, Junior
Weatherington, Nancy
Weaver, Patricia
Wehunt, Gregg
White, Bill
White, June
White, Katherine
White, Osara
White, Steve
Wigley, Lillian
Williams, Sherry
Williams, Steve

Williams, Tracy
Wilson, Annie
Wilson, Joyce
Wilson, Allen
Wilson, Becky
Wilson, Billy
Wilson, Lillie
Wilson, Randy
Wilson, Rodney
Wilson, Vonnie
Winters, JoAnne
Winters, Linda
Winters, Tommy
Wisnener, Debroah
Wisener, Shirley Pace
Wix, Diane
Wix, Donnie
Wix, Georgia
Wix, Gerald
Wix, James
Wix, Mildred

Wix, Lena
Wix, Leonard (Bud)
Wix, Sue
Wix, Luther
Wix, Velma
Wood, Lois
Wood, Spurgeon
Woods, Roy E.
Woods, Tommy
Woods, Wanda
Woody, Earnest
Woody, Lee
Womack, Elizabeth
Womack, Sue
Workman, Judy
Wright, Gail
Wright, James
Wright, Letitia
Wyatt, Eddie
Wyatt, Sandra

Interim Clarence Harris

Clarence Harris served as interim pastor of the church about six months from March 14, 1979 until September 12, 1979.

Rev. Druey Tierce

Rev. Druey H. Tierce pastored White Oak Springs Baptist Church from September 12, 1979, to June 2, 1982. Pastor Tierce was born April 20, 1927 and died in May 14, 2005. His wife's name was

Toni C. Tierce. He was born in Alabama. He pastored many churches in Georgia and Alabama. He spent most of his life in Cherokee County, Alabama (information from his obituary).

Jeff Byrd related that one time, either Pastor John Robinson or Pastor Druey Tierce was preaching on marriage. At the end of the service, the pastor called all the marriage couples down front to renew their marriage vows. Woodrow Clark, who was treasurer at the time, said: "I done did that once, and it cured me."

White Oak Springs Baptist Church members from 1979 to 1981 when Druey Tierce was pastor: Douglas Baxter, Becky Bearden, Robert Carter, T. W. Clark, Kenneth Cohran, Annie Lou Clark, Wanda Clark, Woodrow Clark, Charles Cole, Charles W. Cole, Mildred Cole, Renford Cole, Robert Cole, Sammy Cole, Edna Fennell, Horace Fennell, Charles Gober, Ernest Gober, Tony Henderson, Raymond McLarty, and Sandra Skinner.

White Oak Springs members who died during 1979: Lizzy Cole, Dovie Hutcheson, and Georgia Wix. White Oak Springs members who died during the year 1980: Mr. Shane Cole, Mr. Bennett Hitchcock. White Oak Springs members who died during 1981: Alma Cole, Richard Thompson, and William White.

White Oak Springs Baptist Church ministers listed in its membership in 1979: Kenny Byrd, Curtis Cole, Jack Fambrough, Horace Fennell, Joseph Fields, Kerry Lindsey, Stanley Speegle, Roy Stanford, and Wayne Wix. White Oak Springs Baptist Church ministers listed in its membership in 1980: Kenny Byrd, Joe Camp, Curtis Cole, Jack Fambrough, Horace Fennell, Kerry Lindsey,

Stanley Speegle, and Roy Stanford. White Oak Springs Baptist Church ministers listed in its membership in 1981: Kenny Byrd, Joe Camp, Curtis Cole, Ernie Dodd, Jack Fambrough, Horace Fennell, Joseph Fields, Kerry Lindsey, Stanley Speegle, and Roy Stanford.

Rev. Fred J. Watts

Fred Watts (aka Junior) pastored White Oak Springs Baptist Church from September 15, 1982 until November 6, 1983. His wife's name was Betty. Gloria Byrd remembers that they were great workers and encouragers in the church. They once cooked lunch for all the bus workers at their house.

White Oak Springs Baptist Church members in 1982 when Fred J. Watts was pastor: Becky Bearden, Frank and Gloria Byrd, Jeff and Cathy Byrd, Robert Carter, Wanda Clark, Kenneth Cohran, Charles W. Cole, Renford Cole, Ernest Gober, Woodrow and Annie Clark, Raymond and Margie McLarity, Raymond McLarty, and Tommy and Louise Tallent.

White Oak Springs members who died during 1982: Mrs. Hettie Fuller, J. D. Dotson, and Vonnie Cole Wilson.

White Oak Springs Baptist Church ministers listed in its membership in 1982: Joe Camp, Curtis Cole, Jack Fambrough, Horace Fennell, Joseph Fields, and Kerry Lindsey.

Rev. John Robinson

Rev. John Robinson pastored White Oak Springs Baptist Church from November 6, 1983, until February 17, 1985.

Rev. Ken Martin

Ken Martin pastored White Oak Springs Baptist Church from May 19, 1985, until December 14, 1985. Pastor Martin graduated from the University of Alabama. He played football for the school when Bear Bryant was the football coach. Gloria Byrd said that "Pastor Ken and his wife, Barbara, had four daughters. They helped out in the youth ministry. He is now the successful pastor of Grace Baptist Church and School."

The last year that Tallapoosa Baptist Association received reports from White Oak Springs Baptist Church was 1985. When we asked Ernest Gober why the church left the SBC, he said the "Southern Baptist Convention was supporting some things we did not believe in." Another member addressing the same subject said that Pastor John Robinson sent a request to the Tallapoosa Baptist Association not to include his name in the Tallapoosa Baptist Association minutes. At the next yearly associational meeting, it was moved to dismiss White Oak Springs Baptist Church from the county association.

The church started supporting missionaries in 1970. They took on three or four missionaries when they got started.

Rev. Earl Partain

Pastor Earl Partain pastored White Oak Springs Baptist Church for eight years from February 19, 1986, until November 16, 1994. Brother Partain was saved at Hyde's Chapel Baptist Church in Conyers, Georgia, in 1952. He was licensed to preach at that church on November 5, 1967, and ordained at the same church on May 23, 1971.

Gloria Byrd recalls: "Brother Earl and his wife, Becky, had two girls and two boys. Brother Earl was a great country preacher who preached the old-time gospel. Sister Becky was one of the sweetest, talented, and hardest working pastor's wives we ever had. She was killed in a tragic car accident. Their son Earl Jr. is a preacher, and the other son, Carl, is an evangelist and singer."

1987 Membership List

In 1987, White Oak Springs Baptist Church printed another church photo directory. This book lists the following leaders of the church in 1987:

Earl Partain—Pastor

Jimmy Davis—Youth Church Pastor

Jeff Byrd—Junior Church Pastor

Junior Bearden—Sunday School Director

Louise Tallent—Church Secretary

Delores Cole—Church Secretary

Robin Carter—Choir Director

Francine Smith—Organist

Carl Partain—Guitarist

Kenneth Cohran—Chairman of the Deacons

Ernest Gober—Church Clerk

Faye Hart—Ladies Director

Raymond McLarty—Missions Chairman

Robert Lee—Bus Director

Roger and Delores Cole—Youth Directors

Frank and Gloria Byrd—Senior Citizens Directors

Junior Bearden—Tape Ministry

The following are the names listed in the back of this 1987 photo directory. Most of these are believed to be members. However, since this was a photo directory, some of the names included in this list could be children or spouses of a family member that was a member of White Oak Springs Baptist.

Abercrombie, Cindy   Abercrombie, Vickie

Ackerman, Denise

Allen, Gene

Allen, Andrew

Allen, Dusty

Allen, Joanna

Allen, Ralph

Ammonds, Mary Ann

Arnold, Dick

Austin, Betty

Austin, Brenda

Austin, James

Austin, Linda

Austin, Michelle

Austin, Sherry

Bankston, Danny

Baggett, Ashley

Baggett, Barry

Baggett, Betty

Baggett, Billy

Baggett, Clara Mae

Baggett, Fae

Baggett, Frankie

Baggett, Glen

Baggett, Jessie

Baggett, Kerrie

Baggett, Lowell

Baggett, Rudy

Bankstone, Rocky

Barber, Dennis

Barber, Jenny

Barber, Kathy

Barber, Travis

Barnett, Connie

Bates, Charlene

Bates, Dana

Baxter, Betty (née McClendon)

Baxter, David

Baxter, Earlon F.

Baxter, Jewel

Baxter, Kimbal

Baxter, Levena

Baxter, Lola

Baxter, Maybelle

Baxter, Randy

Baxter, Tim

Baxter, Vealer

Bearden, Becky

Bearden, Chris

Bearden, Jamie

Bearden, Jason

Bearden, Junior

Bearden, Keith

Bearden, Rhonda

Bearden, Tammy Lee

Blair, Mildred

Blair, Wanda

Bone, Eddie

Bowen, Essie Powell

Breedlove, Teresa

Bricken, Connie
Brookshire, Candance
Brown, Michael
Bullock, Linda
Butler, Richard
Butler, Lonnie
Byrd, Angie
Byrd, Claude T.
Byrd, Jane
Byrd, Frank
Byrd, Gloria
Byrd, Kenny

Callahan, D. C.
Caldwell, Pete
Camp, Chester
Camp, Fannie
Camp, Lynn
Camp, Martha
Carroll, Brandy
Carroll, Brian
Carroll, Denise
Carroll, Joey
Carroll, Tonya
Carson, Kathy
Carter, Joann
Carter, Amanda
Carter, Brittany
Carter, Caleb
Carter, Denise

Carter, Roben
Cason, Bertha Mae
Cason, Ernest
Chepwood, Valarie
Clark, Annie Lou
Clark, Celcia
Clark, Randy
Clark, Rhonda
Clark, Sue
Clark, Thomas L.
Clark, Toni
Clark, Woodrow
Clifton, Connie
Cohran, Aaron
Cohran, Amber
Cohran, Caroline
Cohran, Gladys
Cohran, Heather
Cohran, Kathy
Cohran, Kenneth
Cohran, Parks
Cohran, Tony
Cole, Annie Mae
Cole, Barbara
Cole, Boyd
Cole, Claude
Cole, Curtis
Cole, Dana
Cole, Deloris
Cole, Floyd

Cole, Fonda

Cole, Frances

Cole, Hattie

Cole, Jane

Cole, Joy

Cole, Larry

Cole, Landry

Cole, Lessie

Cole, Mary

Cole, Mattie

Cole, Ray

Cole, Renford

Cole, Roger

Cook, Larry

Cooper, Amanda

Criswell, Diane

Croker, Candy

Crowe, Joey

Culver, Lynn

Daniel, Annette

Daniel, Ida

Daniel, Nellie

Darbry, Angie

Davis, April

Davis, Clara

Davis, Darlene

Davis, David

Davis, Donnie

Davis, Jerry

Davis, Margaret

Davis, Jimmy

Davis, Loy

Davis, Lisa

Davis, Loy

Davis, Lynn

Davis, Martha

Davis, Teresa

Deems, Gordon

Deems, Tonya

Denton, Kay

Dudley, David

Denton, Patricia

Dockery, Annette

Dockery, Mark

Dockery, Marie

Dockery, Randy

Dodd, Shar-main

Dudley, Lloyd

Dudley, Elaine

Dudley, Renee

Duke, Wesley

Dunn, Becky

Dunn, Leann

Dycus, David

Dyer Michael

Dykes, Michael

Dykes, Anthony

Dykes, Craig

Dykes, Mildred

Edwards, Tony
Ellis, Becky
Ellis, Debbie
England, Joan
England, Stephanie
Estes, Bonnie
Eskey, Danny
Eskey, Sharon
Ethenridge, Cynthia
Ethenridge, Marie
Ethenridge, Wayne
Evans, Ruth
Evans, Tammy

Fairchild, Sheila
Ferguson, Bill
Ferguson, Butch
Ferguson, Edith
Ferguson, Ray
Ferrell, Adam
Ferrell, Dixie
Ferrell, Doug
Ferrell, Ginny
Ferrell, Michael
Ferrell, Richard
Fields, Edward
Fields, Jeanette
Fields, Jobia
Fields, Joy
Fields, Kathy

Fowler, Dan
Fowler, Shirley
Freeman, Chad
Freeman, Chris
Freeman, Florine
Freeman, Rosa
Freeman, Susan
Fuller, Amy
Fuller, Berdie
Fuller, Betty Ann
Fuller, Dorothy
Fuller, J. O.
Fuller, Jimmy
Fuller, Joyce
Fuller, Minnie Lee

Gamel, L. K.
Gamel, Mildred
Gamel, Snote
Gamel, Sylvia
Garner, Randy
Garner, Treva
Garnett, Ann
Gaylord, Glenda
George, Delilah
Glass, Felicia
Gober, Ernest
Gober, Carolyn
Gober, Steve
Godfrey, Christy

Godfrey, Colin
Godfrey, Connie
Godfrey, Greg
Godfrey, Jerry
Gravette, Jeff
Gravette, Kelly
Gravette, Randall
Gravette, Wendy
Green, Becky
Green, Laynette
Green, Missy
Griffith, Christi
Griffith, Dianne
Grimsley, Frank
Gurley, Annie Mae

Hackney, Teresa
Hagan, Andy
Haggard, Debra
Hall, Emma Jean
Hanna, Cindy
Hardy, Alta
Hardy, J. C.
Hardy, Randy
Harness, Cassie
Harris, Kenny
Harris, Linda
Harris, Myra
Harris, Ralph
Harris, Rudy

Harris, Shirley
Hart, Faye
Hart, James
Hayes, Joe
Hayes, Junior
Hembree, Margaret
Henderson, Bessie
Henderson, Jane
Henderson, Jean
Henderson, Lois
Henderson, Ola Mae
Henderson, Robert
Henderson, Tracy
Hicks, Aileen
Hicks, Aileen
Hicks, Barbara
Hicks, Debra
Hicks, Frankie
Hicks, John
Hicks, Josie
Hicks, Kathy
Hicks, Mack
Hicks, Marvene
Hicks, Maudie
Hicks, Ola
Hitchcock, Carolyn
Hitchcock, Keith
Hitchcock, Paula
Hitchcock, Ruby
Hoffman, Curt

Holcomb, Geraldine

Holcomb, Jerry

Holcomb, Martha

Holder, Phyllis

Holder, Sandra

Holland, Laura

Hollis, Lillie

Hollis, Lynn

Holmes, Edna

Hopkins, Sharon

Horton, Sue

Hudgins, Pat

Hulsey, Alton

Hulsey, Cliff

Husley, Lillie

Husley, Mary Bernice

Hurst, Lou Anne

Huston, Angie

Ivey, Cecil

Ivey, Cindy

Ivey, David

Ivey, Edith

Ivey, Randy

Jackson, Hattie

Johns, Lillie Mae

Johnson, Lisa

Jenkins, Ann

Jones, John

Jones, Larry

Jones, Myrtle

Jordan, Inez Sue

Kaplan, Loretta

Key, Sherry

Kirby, Annie

Kirkland, Jeff

Koss, Kinney

Lacy, Sharron

Lane, William

Lang, Karen

Lanzo, Sammy

Ledford, Robin

Lewis, Cindy

Lewis, Glen

Lewis, Wayne

Lindsey, Ethel

Lindsey, Linda

Lindsey, Marion

Lindsey, Paul

Lindsey, Raymond

Lindsey, Susan

Locklear, Barbara

Locklear, Beverly

Locklear, Kathy

Locklear, Stacy

Locklear, Dana

Locklear, Gene

Locklear, Jeff
Locklear, Michael
Locklear, Randy
Locklear, Wayne
Loudermilk, Jenny

Mammenga, J. T.
Mammenga, JoAnn Wix
Mammenga, Marsha
Mammenga, Michael
Mammenga, Terry
Mammenga, Tina
Massey, Glenda
Massey, Randy
Matthews, Bryan
Matthews, Keith
Matthews, Ollie
Matthews, Willie Mae
Mauldin, Brian
Mauldin, Wendy
McClendon, Betty (Baxter)
McDuemon, Christy
McDuemon, Luanne
McElroy, Cindy
McGurt, Ann
McKiney, Paula
McLarty, Cynthia
McLarty, Paula
McLarty Margie
McLarty, Raymond

McMichen, Virginia
Meeks, Randy
Mitchel, Josie
Moody, Billy Rodgers
Moody, Denise
Moody, Franklin
Moody, Janice
Moody, Loretta
Moody, Mary Frances
Moody, Ricky
Moore, Linda
Morgan, Joe
Morris, Pam
Morris, Vera Mae
Morrow, Randal
Moss, Martha

Newton, Albert
Noble, Angie
Noble, Bethel
Noble, Heather
Noble, Lisa
Noble, Mitch
Noble, Shirley
Noble, Tim

O'Brian, Sharon
Overton, Pamala Cole
Owens, Terry

Pace, Dennis

Pace, Jesse James

Pace, Rex

Padgett, Diane

Padgett, Robin

Parker, Jackie

Parks, John

Parks, Oree

Partain, Becky

Partain, Carl

Partain, Earl

Patterson, Steve

Perry, Michael

Peter, Michelle

Pitts, Chris

Ploof, Eddie

Pollard, Sandra

Poss, Bill

Poss, Dot

Poss, Michael

Prater, Roger

Pruett, Claudia

Pruett, Deidra

Pruett, Donald

Pruett, Jennifer

Pruett, Teresa

Puckett, Earl

Pugh, Brenda

Ragsdale, Dale

Ragsdale, Elaine

Ragsdale, Jana

Ragsdale, Robin

Ragsdale, Sara

Rakestraw, Jeremy

Rakestraw, Jimmie Lynn

Rakestraw, Ricky

Ray, Dianne

Ray, Kelly

Renfroe, Eunice

Rentz, Peter

Reynolds, Margaret

Riggs, Joan

Roberts, B. J.

Roberts, Bessie

Roberts, Edna Fae

Roberts, Lois

Roberts, Pauline

Roberts, Thelma

Robertson, Carroll

Robertson, Mary

Rollins, Diane

Rollins, Glenda

Rollins, Jim

Rollins, Russell

Rollins, Steve

Ruff, Linda Ann

Saladrigas, Joyce

Sanders, Carmen Lee

Scott, Margaret
Shead, Keith
Shead, Mollie
Shoemaker, Jewell
Shores, Rodney
Shores, Shelia
Singleton, Doris
Skinner, Geanene
Smith, Angie
Smith, Beth
Smith, Carroll
Smith, Dennie
Smith, Diane
Smith, Francine
Smith, Laura
Smith, Leo
Smith, Lynn
Sorrel, Emma
Speck, Byron
Speck, Gilbert
Speck, Kathy
Speck, Melody (Melony?)
Speck, Stephanie
Speegle, Stanley
Sprayberry, Jamie
Sprayberry, Michelle
Stanford, Estelle
Stanford, Roy
Still, Robin
Still, Sue

Swafford, Danny
Swafford, Steve

Tallent, Louise
Tallent, Tommie
Tant, Brenda
Tant, Dale
Tant, Glenda
Tant, Travis
Tant, Wayne
Tapley, Corry
Tapley, Judy
Tapley, Sanford
Tapley, Tonya
Thomas, Charlotte
Thomas, Dewayne
Thomas, Jane
Thomason, Connie
Thompson, Rita
Thompson, Tabitha
Thompson, Timmy
Thompson, Toby
Thompson, Todd
Townsend, Wayne
Tumlin, Dianne
Turner, Charlotte
Turner, Jackie
Turner, Jamie
Turner, Marty

Upton, Bobbie
Upton, David
Upton, J. R.
Upton, June
Upton, Lora Lee
Upton, Patti
Upton, Tony
Upton, Wendell

Vaughn, Jamie
Vaughn, Janice
Vaughn, Lamar
Vaughn, Melissa
Vaughn, Tammy
Verner, Betty
Verner, Melody

Walker, Angie
Walker, Cathy
Walker, Loretta
Walker, Richard
Walker, Sharon
Wall, Sharon
Wash, Carey
Waters, Carolyn
Waters, Denise
Watts, Dennis
Weatherington, Herman
Weatherington, Joe
Weatherington, Junior

Weatherington, Nancy
Weatherington, Margie
Weaver, Rachel
Weaver, Tommy
Webb, Sharon
Wentz, Jamie
Wentz, Janice
Wentz, Marion
White, June
White, Katherine
White, Larry
White, Osara
White, Steve
Whitely, Sherrie
Whitely, Vicky
Wigley, Lillian
Williams, Anita
Williams, Amber
Williams, Joshua
Williams, Micah
Williams, Steve
Williams, Terry
Willoughby, Cristina
Willoughby, Rhonda
Willoughby, Tony
Wilson, Annie
Wilson, Allen
Wilson, Becky
Wilson, Billy
Wilson, Carol

Wilson, Joshua

Wilson, Joyce

Wilson, Lillie

Wilson, Karen

Wilson, Mark

Wilson, Randall

Wilson, Rodney

Winters, Carol

Winters, JoAnne

Winters, Linda

Winters, Tommy

Wisener, Deborah

Wisener, Lucy

Wisener, Shirley

Wix, Allan

Wix, Anne

Wix, Diane

Wix, Donnie

Wix, Eddie

Wix, James

Wix, Lena

Wix, Mildred

Weldon, Mark

Wood, Spurgeon

Woods, Dick

Woods, Joe

Woods, Tommy

Woods, Wanda

Woody, Earnest

Woody, Ora Lee

Womack, Judy

Wyatt, Angie

Wyatt, Ashleigh

Wyatt, Eddie

Wyatt, Sandra

Wyatt, Pam

Youngblood, Sonja

In 1993 the church produced another photo directory. This was the second one the church produced while Earl Partain was pastor. Pages two, three, and four list the following leaders of the church:

Brother Earl Partain—Pastor
Jeff Byrd—Junior Church Pastor
Timmy Thompson—Youth Church Pastor
Kenneth Cohran—Chairman of the Deacons and Sunday School Director
Ernest Gober—Church Clerk

Roben Carter—Choir Director

Carl Partain—Assistant Choir Director

Becky Bearden—Church Pianist

Mike Ross—Assistant Church Pianist

Terry Williams—Junior Church Pianist

Louise Tallent—Church Secretary

Junior Bearden—Tape Ministry and Sound Director

Raymond McLarty—Missions Chairman

Frank and Gloria Byrd—Senior Citizens Directors

Robert and Lisa Lee—Church Custodians

Diane Camp—Ladies Special Director

Loy Davis—Bus Mechanic

Larry Roberson—Assistant Bus Mechanic

This 1993 book also had a "family roster" in the back of the book and these are the names listed in that family membership list:

Abercrombie, Cindy	Arnold, Dick
Abercrombie, Crystal	Austin, James
Abercrombie, Elaine	Austin, Linda
Abercrombie, Vickie	Avant, Rhonda (Spruill)
Ackerman, Denise	
Akins, Glenda	Baggett, Barry
Akins, Randy	Baggett, Betty
Allen, Andrew	Baggett, Billy
Allen, Joanna	Baggett, Clara Mae
Allen, John	Baggett, Fae
Allen, Ralph	Baggett, Glen
Ammonds, Mary Ann	Baggett, Jessie
Anthony, Donna E.	Baggett, Lowell

Baggett, Rudy

Bankstone, Danny

Barber, Dennis

Barber, Jeanette

Barker, Kathy

Barker, Robert

Barrett, Connie

Bates, Charlene

Baxter, Betty

Baxter, Danny

Baxter, Jewel

Baxter, Junior

Baxter, Lola

Baxter, Maybelle

Baxter, Pete

Bearden, Becky

Bearden, Chris

Bearden, Jason

Bearden, Junior

Bearden, Lavenna

Bearden, Tammy Lee

Beyers, Tonya

Biggers, Karen

Blackmon, Rebecca Lynn

Blair, Wanda

Bowen, Eddie

Bowen, Heather

Bowen, Regina

Bowen, Robby

Bowen, Essie Powell

Bragg, Lynn

Bricken, Connie

Brookshire, Candace

Brown, Lynn

Brown, Michael

Brown, Mildred

Buckner, Lynda

Bullock, Linda

Butler, Richard

Burney, Cathy

Burney, April

Bush, Benjamin

Bush, Bonnia

Bush, Norman

Bush, Randy

Bush, Roger

Byrd, Cathy

Byrd, Claude

Byrd, Frank

Byrd, Gloria

Byrd, Jeff

Caldwell, Pete

Callahan, D. C.

Camp, Diane

Camp, Harold

Camp, Joe

Camp, Martha

Carroll, Tonya

Carson, Kathy

Carson, Janet

Carter, Amanda

Carter, Denise

Carter, Joann

Carter, Roben

Cason, Bertha Mae

Chepwood, Valarie

Childers, Diane

Clark, Celelia

Clark, Kimberly

Clark, Thomas L.

Clark, Woodrow

Clifton, Connie

Cohran, Amber

Cohran, Anthony

Cohran, Caroline

Cohran, Gladys

Cohran, Glenda Cason

Cohran, Kathy

Cohran, Kenneth

Cohran, Parks

Cole, Barbara

Cole, Bill

Cole, Boyd

Cole, Cathy Allen

Cole, Christy

Cole, Curtis

Cole, Dana

Cole, Deloris

Cole, Floy T.

Cole, Fonda

Cole, Frances

Cole, Jimmy

Cole, Jodie

Cole, JoAnn

Cole, Joel

Cole, Joy

Cole, Kelli (Moore)

Cole, Kristi (Payne)

Cole, Larry

Cole, Lessie

Cole, Mary

Cole, Peggy

Cole, Ray

Cole, Renford

Cole, Roger

Cole, Roy

Cole, Rusty

Cole, Vonda

Cole, Wendy

Collins, Annette

Copeland, Shirley

Copeland, Wayne

Criswell, Billy

Criswell, Diane

Criswell, Linda Fay

Criswell, Sherry

Croker, Candy

Culver, Lynn

Cummings, Denise

Daniel, Annette
Darbry, Angie
Davis, Daphne
Davis, Darlene
Davis, David
Davis, Donnie
Davis, Jerry
Davis, Jimmy
Day, Lennie
Davis, Lisa
Davis, Loy
Davis, Mary
Davis, Martha
Day, Ronnie
Deems, Ann
Deems, Gordon
Denton, Kay
Denton, Patricia
Dockery, Annette
Dockery, Randy
Dodd, Shar-Main
Dodson, Alene
Dudley, Elaine
Dudley, John
Dudley, Lloyd
Duke, Wesley
Dunn, Becky
Dunn, Leeann
Duvall, Thomas Lee Jr.
Dycus, David

Dyer Michael
Dykes, Anthony
Dykes, Mildred

Earwood, Donna
Earwood, Joel
Edwards, Tony
Ellis, Becky
Ellis, Debbie
Ellis, Janette
Elrod, Chris
Elrod, Tammy
England, Joan
Eskey, Danny
Eskey, Sharon
Estes, Bonnie
Ethenridge, Cynthia
Ethenridge, Marie
Ethenridge, Wayne
Evans, Ruth
Evans, Wayne

Fairchild, Sheila
Farr, Pam
Farr, Randy
Ferguson, Bill
Ferguson, Butch
Ferguson, Edith
Ferrell, Adam

Ferrell, Christy

Fields, Cathy

Fields, Edward

Fowler, Dan

Fowler, Shirley

Freeman, Chad

Freeman, Chris

Freeman, Florine

Freeman, Rosa

Freeman, Susan

Fristad, Amanda

Fristad, Candi

Fristad, Jim

Fristad, Rhonda

Fuller, Amy

Fuller, Betty Ann

Fuller, Dorothy

Fuller, J. O.

Fuller, Jimmy

Fuller, Joyce

Gamel, L. K.

Gamel, Mildred

Garner, Randy

Garner, Treva

Garnett, Ann

Gault, John

Gaylord, Glenda

George, Delilah

Glass, Felecia

Gober, Carolyn

Gober, Ernest

Gober, Steve

Godfrey, Bobbi

Godfrey, Colin

Godfrey, Greg

Gravette, Jeff

Gravette, Kelly

Gravette, Pauline

Gravette, Wendy

Green, Laynette

Gregory, Tony

Grimsley, Frank

Gulledge, Dusty

Gurley, Annie Mae

Hackney, Teresa

Hagan, Andy

Haggard, Debra Cole

Hall, Emma Jean

Haney, Tabitha

Hannah, Cindy

Hardy, Alta

Hardy, Elaine

Hardy, J. C.

Hardy, Randy

Harness, Cassie

Harris, Kenny

Harris, Linda

Harris, Myra

Harris, Shirley

Hart, Faye

Hayes, Joe

Hayes, Junior

Heath, Debra Payne

Hembree, Margaret

Henderson, Bessie

Henderson, Freddy

Henderson, Jean

Henderson, Lois

Henderson, Robert

Henderson, Tracy

Hicks, Barbara

Hicks, Debra E.

Hicks, Josie

Hicks, Kathy

Hicks, Kim

Hicks, Mack

Hicks, Marie

Hicks, Marvene

Hicks, Maudie

Hicks, Ola

Hicks, Sally

Hill, Luanne

Hill, Stephen

Hitchcock, Carolyn

Hitchcock, Keith

Hitchcock, Paula

Hitchcock, Ruby

Hoffman, Curt

Holcomb, Jerry

Holcomb, Geraldine

Holcomb, Martha

Holder, Phyllis

Holder, Sandra

Holland, Laura Hardy

Hollis, Lillie

Holmes, Edna

Holt, Alene

Holt, Rayburn

Holt, Ronald

Hopkins, Sharon

Horton, Sue

Hudgins, Patricia

Hulsey, Alton

Hulsey, Cliff

Husley, Lillie

Husley, Mary

Hurst, Lou Anne (Louanne)

Israel, Sue

Ivey, Cecil

Ivey, Cindy

Ivey, David

Ivey, Edith

Ivey, Randy

Jackson, Hattie

Johns, Lillie Mae

Johnson, Lisa

Jones, John
Jones, Larry
Jordan, Inez Sue
Kaplan, Loretta
Key, Sherry
Kinney, Ross
Kirkland, Jeff

Lacy, Sharron
Lane, William
Lang, Karen
Lanzo, Angie
Lanzo, Sammy
Lee, Elaine
Lee, Jean
Lee, Jessica
Lee, Lisa
Lee, Robert
Lewis, Cindy
Lewis, Glen
Lewis, Wayne
Lindsey, Ethel
Lindsey, Linda
Lindsey, Marion
Lindsey, Paul
Lindsey, Susan
Lindsey, Raymond
Lipscomb, Frances
Locklear, Cathy
Locklear, Dana

Locklear, Gene
Locklear, Jeff
Locklear, Michael
Locklear, Randy
Locklear, Stacy
Locklear, Wayne
Loudermilk, Jenny

Mammenga, JoAnn
Massey, Carolyn
Matthews, Bryan
Matthews, Keith
Matthews, Kelly
Mauldin, Brian
McDaniel, Tabitha
McDaniel, Tracy
Mcelroy, Cindy
McGurt, Ann
McKenzy, Paula
McKenzy, David
McKenzy, Melissa
McLarty, Margie
McLarty, Raymond
McMichen, Virginia
Meeks, Ricky (Randy)
Mitchel, Chris
Moody, Billy Rodgers
Moody, Charlie
Moody, Franklin
Moody, Janice

Moody, Ricky
Moore, Linda Whitley
Morgan, Joe
Morris, Pam
Morris, Randall
Morris, Vera Mae
Moss, Martha
Myers, Brenda

Newton, Albert
Noble, Angie
Noble, Bethel
Noble, Shirley
Noble, Tim

Owens, Sandy

Pace, Dennis
Pace, Jessie James
Padgett, Diane
Padgett, Robin
Palmer, Ed
Palmer, Jeff
Palmer, Shirley
Parker, Jackie
Parks, Oree
Partain, Angie
Partain, Becky
Partain, Carl
Partain, Earl

Pawley, Jackie
Pawley, Mark
Perry, Michael
Peter, Michelle
Pilgrim, Pete
Pinson, Donna
Pitts, Chris
Ploof, Eddie
Pollard, Sandra
Poss, Bill
Poss, Dot
Poss, Michael
Powers, Laura
Prater, Roger
Pruett, Claudia
Pruett, Dee Dee
Pruett, Deidra
Pruett, Donald
Pruett, Jennifer
Pruett, Max
Pruett, Penny
Pruett, Teresa
Puckett, Earl
Pugh, Brenda

Queen, Barbara
Queen, Larry

Radcliff, Brenda Holder
Ragsdale, Dale

Ragsdale, Jana

Ragsdale, Sara

Rakestraw, Angelia

Rakestraw, Jeremy

Rakestraw, Jimmie Lynn

Rakestraw, Ricky

Reynolds, Margaret

Robertson, Dianne

Robertson, Larry

Roberts, Bessie

Roberts, Edna Fae Cole

Roberts, Lois

Roberts, Sally

Roberts, Thelma

Robertson, Carroll

Robertson, Pam Wyatt

Robinson, Annabelle

Robinson, Henry

Robinson, Colinca

Robinson, Cindy

Robinson, Doug

Rogers, Anita

Rollins, David

Rollins, Diane

Rollins, Glenda

Rollins, Jim

Ross, Michael

Ross, Rhonda

Rollins, Russell

Rollins, Teresa

Ruff, Linda Ann

Sabinas, John Lee

Saladridgas, Joyce

Sanders, Carmen Lee

Scott, Dean

Scott, Margaret

Shanks, Joe

Shead, Keith

Shead, Mollie

Shoemaker, Jewell

Shores, Rodney

Shores, Shelia

Simpson, Rick

Simpson, Sheryl

Skinner, Geanene

Smith, Angie

Smith, Carroll

Smith, Diane

Smith, Laura

Smith, Lynn

Sorrells, Emma

Sprayberry, Jamie

Sprayberry, Michelle

Stanford, Estelle

Stanford, Roy

Swafford, Danny Eugene

Swafford, Steve Darrell

Tallent, Jeff

Tallent, Louise
Tallent, Shae
Tallent, Tabitha
Tallent, Tommie
Tant, Dale
Tant, Glenda
Tant, Joan
Tant, Travis
Tant, Wayne
Tapley, Corry
Tapley, Judy
Tapley, Sanford
Taylor, Hollis
Taylor, June
Teal, Angie
Teal, Debbi
Teal, Tony
Thomas, Charlotte
Thomas, Dewayne
Thomason, Jane
Thomason, Rita
Thomason, Timmy
Tibbits, Anna
Tibbits, Cody
Tibbits, Mary
Tibbits, Randy
Touchton, Linda
Touchton, Raymond
Townsend, Wayne
Tumlin, Dianne

Turner, Charlotte
Turner, Jackie
Turner, Jamie
Turner, Marty
Turner, Linda
Turner, Lisa
Turner, Rainey
Turner, Richard
Turner, Todd
Tyre, Sue

Upton, David
Upton, J. R.
Upton, June
Upton, Lora Lee
Upton, Samantha
Upton, Sandra
Upton, Wendell

Vaughn, Jamie
Vaughn, Janice
Vaughn, Lamar
Vaughn, Melissa
Vaughn, Tammy
Verner, Betty
Verner, Melody
Voyles, Scott
Voyles, Stacy

Walker, Cathy

Walker, Loretta
Walker, Richard
Walker, Sharon
Wall, Sharon
Wallace, David
Wallace, Jessica
Wallace, Shirley
Wash, Gary
Waters, Betty
Waters, Denise
Weatherington, Herman
Weatherington, Joe
Weatherington, Junior
Weatherington, Margie
Weaver, Rachel
Weaver, Tommy
Webb, Sharon
Weldon, Mark
Wentz, Jamie
Wentz, Janice
White, June
White, Larry
White, Katherine
White, Osara
White, Penny
White, Steve
Whitely, Sherrie
Whitely, Vicky
Wigley, Lillian
Williams, Anita Neal

Williams, Amber
Williams, Joshua
Williams, Micah
Williams, Steve
Williams, Terry
Willoughby, Brandi
Willoughby, Hollie
Willoughby, Rhonda
Willoughby, Wesley
Wilson, Allen
Wilson, Billy
Wilson, Joshua
Wilson, Joyce
Wilson, Karen
Wilson, Lillie
Wilson, Mark
Wilson, Randall
Wilson, Rodney
Wilson, Sherrie
Wines, Kathleen Denise
Wingers, Linda
Winters, Gregory
Winters, JoAnne
Wintz, Marion
Wix, Anne
Wix, Donnie
Wix, Eddie
Wix, Gina
Wix, James
Wix, Jennifer

Wix, Lena

Wix, Mildred

Wix, Roger

Womack, Elizabeth

Woods, Tommy

Woody, Earnest

Woody, Ora Lee

Workman, Judy

Wyatt, Angie

Wyatt, Eddie

Wyatt, Sandra

Youngblood, Sonja

Rev. Willard Toney

Rev. Willard Toney pastored White Oak Springs Baptist Church from November 30, 1994, until June 14, 1995. Gloria Byrd said of his ministry: "He did not pastor this church for very long."

Rev. Johnny Simpson

Rev. Johnny Simpson pastored White Oak Springs Baptist Church from September 13, 1995, until October 2007.

Gloria Byrd shared the following about Pastor Johnny Simpson's ministry:

"His wife was Sister Brenda, and they had three children. Sister Brenda was a hard working pastor's wife. All their children were also hard workers and very involved in the church. Their daughters were: Sondra and family; Rhonda; and their son Rick, along with his wife, Sheryl, and their two children. Brother Rick's son was saved at the age of nine at White Oak Springs and called to preach by age 11. When Brother Johnny left White Oak, we voted his grandson, Chris, in as our new, very young pastor."

In September 2001, Pastor Johnny Simpson was holding a missions conference. They started on Sunday with missionary presentations in both services that day and on Monday evening. On Tuesday, September 11, 2001, the Twin Towers at the World Trade Center were attacked and then fell. Services were held that evening, but the mission conference was suspended since so much uncertainty was in the air. All domestic airline flights were suspended for about two weeks, and the only planes in the air were military fighter jets.

In 1998, the church produced another photo directory. Johnny Simpson was the pastor when this photo directory was produced.

Pastor Simpson wrote the following dedication in the 1998 photo book.

> A lot of changes have occurred since White Oak Springs was established in 1856. However, there is one thing that remains the same, our love for the Lord, and our desire to please him, both in our worship and in our work. White Oak Springs has a rich past for which I am thankful. However, I am more excited about our future than I am the past. This directory is dedicated to those who make up the membership, and who are involved in the ministry. I am thankful to be the pastor of these wonderful people.

Pages two and three of the 1998 directory lists the following leaders of the church:

Brother Johnny Simpson—Pastor

Roger Wix—Junior Church Pastor

Toby Thompson—Youth Church Pastor

Roben Carter—Choir Director

Louise Tallent—Church Secretary

Shae Tallent—Sunday School Director

Becky Bearden—Church Pianist

Kenneth Cohran—Chairman of the Deacons

Max Pruett—Bus Director

Steve Williams—Missions Chairman

Carl and Angie Partain—Youth Directors

Terry Williams—Junior Church Pianists

Frank and Gloria Byrd—Senior Citizens Directors

Ernest Gober—Church Clerk

Larry Robertson—Bus Mechanic

Junior Bearden—Tape Ministry and Sound Director

This 1998 book also listed the following names in the "our Church Directory" section in the back of the book:

Abercrombie, Cindy	Allen, Ralph, and Joanna
Abercrombie, Crystal	Ammonds, Mary Ann
Abercrombie, Elaine	Austin, Darcile
Abercrombie, Vickie	Arnold, Dick
Ackerman, Denise	Arnold, Jana
Akins, Glenda	Austin, James
Akins, Paula	Austin, Linda
Akins, Randy	
Alford, Sammy	Baggett, Barry
Allen, Cathy	Baggett, Betty
Allen, John	Baggett, Billy

Baggett, Clara Mae

Baggett, Donna

Baggett, Jessie

Baggett, Lowell

Bankstone, Danny

Barber, Dennis

Barber, Jeanette

Barrett, Connie

Bates, Charlene

Baxter, Alan

Baxter, Betty

Baxter, Danny

Baxter, Junior

Baxter, Lola

Baxter, Maybelle

Baxter, Pete

Baxter, Teresa

Bearden, Becky

Bearden, Junior

Bearden, Lavenna

Bearden, Tammy

Beyers, Tonya

Biggers, Karen

Blackmon, Rebecca

Bowen, Eddie

Bowen, Regina

Bowen, Robert

Bowen, Essie

Brackett, Marcy

Brown, Lynn

Brown, Michael

Brown, Mildred

Brumley, Cathy

Burnley, April

Bush, Benjamin

Bush, Norman

Bush, Randy

Bush, Roger

Byrd, Claude

Byrd, Frank

Byrd, Gloria

Byrd, Jane

Caldwell, Pete

Callahan, D. C.

Camp, Al

Camp, Fannie

Camp, Evelyn

Camp, Joe

Camp, Lynn

Camp, Martha

Carroll, Tonya

Carson, Kathy

Carter, Amanda

Carter, Britney

Carter, Caleb

Carter, Denise

Carter, Roben

Cason, Bertha

Cason, Glenda

Chepwood, Valarie
Childers, Diane
Clark, Celelia
Clark, Sue
Clay, Shelby
Cohran, Anthony
Cohran, Kathy
Cohran, Caroline
Cohran, Kenneth
Cohran, Parks
Cohran, Ruth
Cole, Boyd
Cole, Barbara
Cole, Curtis
Cole, Dana
Cole, Deloris
Cole, Floy T.
Cole, Fonda.
Cole, Frances
Cole, Jimmy
Cole, JoAnn
Cole, Joel
Cole, Joy
Cole, Larry
Cole, Lessie
Cole, Mary
Cole, Peggy
Cole, Ray
Cole, Renford
Cole, Roger

Cole, Rusty
Cole, Wendy
Collins, Annette
Collins, Kaylie
Cooper, Tracy
Copeland, Shirley
Copeland, Wanda
Copeland, Wayne
Criswell, Billy
Criswell, Diane
Criswell, Linda
Criswell, Sherry
Croker, Candy
Culver, Lynn

Daniel, Annette
Darbry, Angie
Davis, Darlene
Davis, Donnie
Davis, Jerry
Davis, Jimmy
Davis, Loy
Davis, Mary
Davis, Martha
Day, Lennie
Day, Ronnie
Deems, Gordon
Denton, Kay
Denton, Patricia
Dockery, Annette

Dockery, Randy

Dodd, Mary

Dodson, Alene

Dudley, Elaine

Dudley, John

Dudley, Llyod

Duke, Wesley

Dunn, Becky

Dunn, Leeann

Duvall, Thomas Jr.

Dycus, David

Dyer Michael

Dykes, Anthony

Dykes, Mildred

Earwood, Donna

Earwood, Joel

Edwards, Tony

Ellis, Becky

Ellis, Debbie

Ellis, Janette

Elrod, Tammy

England, Joan

Eskey, Danny

Eskey, Sharon

Estes, Bonnie

Ethenridge, Cynthia

Evans, Ruth

Everidge, Wayne

Fairchild, Sheila

Farr, Pam

Farr, Randy

Ferguson, Butch

Ferguson, Edith

Ferguson, Ray

Ferrell, Adam

Ferrell, Christy

Fields, Cathy

Fowler, Dan

Fowler, Shirley

Freeman, Chad

Freeman, Chris

Freeman, Rosa

Freeman, Susan

Fristad, Amanda

Fristad, Candi

Fristad, Jim

Fristad, Jimmy

Fristad, Rhonda

Fuller, Amy

Fuller, Betty

Fuller, Dorothy

Fuller, J. O.

Fuller, Jimmy

Fuller, Joyce

Ganues, Jackson

Ganues, Yelenne

Garner, Randy

Garner, Treva

Garnett, Ann

Gault, John

George, Delilah

Glass, Felecia

Gober, George

Gober, Steve

Godfrey, Bobbi

Godfrey, Colin

Gravette, Jeff

Gravette, Kelly

Gravette, Pauline

Gravette, Wendy

Gray, Joann

Green, Laynette

Gregory, Tony

Grimsley, Frank

Gulledge, Dusty

Gurley, Annie Mae

Hackney, Teresa

Hagan, Andy

Haney, Tabitha

Hannah, Cindy

Hardy, Elaine

Hardy, Randy

Hardy, Scott

Harness, Cassie

Harris, Kenny

Harris, Linda

Harris, Myra

Harris, Shirley

Hart, Faye

Hatcher, Anne

Hayes, Joe

Hayes, Junior

Heath, Debra

Henderson, Bessie

Henderson, Freddy

Henderson, Lois

Henderson, Robert

Henderson, Traci

Herington, Sandra Jo

Hicks, Kim

Hicks, Barbara

Hicks, Debra E.

Hicks, Denice

Hicks, Kathy

Hicks, Mack

Hicks, Nancy

Hicks, Natalie

Hicks, Marie

Hicks, Marvene

Hicks, Maudie

Hicks, Sally

Hitchcock, Carolyn

Hitchcock, Keith

Hitchcock, Ruby

Hoffman, Curt

Holcomb, Jerry

Holcomb, Martha

Holcomb, Geraldine

Holder, Phyllis

Holder, Sandra

Holland, Laura

Hollis, Darrell

Holmes, Edna

Holt, Rayburn

Hopkins, Sharon

Horton, Sue

Hudgins, Patricia

Hulsey, Cliff

Hulsey, Mary

Husley, Lillie

Israel, Sue

Ivey, Cecil

Ivey, Cindy

Ivey, David

Ivey, Edith

Ivey, Jackie

Ivey, Randy

Jackson, Hattie

Johns, Lillie Mae

Johnson, Lisa

Johnston, Ann

Johnston, Roy

Johnston, Rita

Johnston, Tim

Jones, John

Jones, Larry

Jordan, Inez Sue

Kaplan, Loretta

Key, Sherry

Kinney, Ross

Kirkland, Jeff

Lacy, Sharron

Lane, William

Lang, Karen

Lanzo, Angie

Lanzo, Sammy

Ledford, Robert

Lee, Elaine

Lee, Jean

Lewis, Cindy

Lewis, Glen

Lewis, Wayne

Lindsey, Ethel

Lindsey, Linda

Lindsey, Marion

Lindsey, Raymond

Lindsey, Susan

Lipscomb, Frances

Locklear, Beverly

Locklear, Cathy

Locklear, Dana

Locklear, Gene

Locklear, Jeff

Locklear, Michael

Locklear, Randy

Locklear, Stacy

Locklear, Wayne

Loudermilk, Jenny

Mammenga, JoAnn

Massey, Carolyn

Matthews, Bryan

Matthews, Keith

Matthews, Kelly

Mauldin, Brian

McDaniel, Tabitha

McDaniel, Tracy

Mcelroy, Cindy

McGurt, Ann

McKenzy, David

McKenzy, Melissa

McKenzy, Paula

McLarty, Margie

McLarty, Raymond

McMichen, Virginia

Meeks, Ricky (Randy)

Michael, Chris

Moody, Billy Rodgers

Moody, Charlie

Moody, Franklin

Moody, Janice

Moody, Joanna

Moody, John

Moody, Ricky

Moore, Linda Whitley

Morgan, Debra

Morris, Pam

Morris, Randall

Morris, Vera Mae

Moss, Martha

Myers, Brenda

Newton, Albert

Owens, Sandy

Pace, Dennis

Pace, Jessie

Padgett, Dianne

Padgett, Robin

Palmer, Ed

Palmer, Jeff

Palmer, Shirley

Parker, Jackie

Parks, Oree

Partain, Angie

Partain, Carl

Perry, Michael

Peters, Michelle

Pitts, Chris

Ploof, Eddie

Pollard, Sandra

Powers, Laura
Prater, Roger
Pruett, Claudia
Pruett, Deidra
Pruett, Donald
Pruett, Jennifer
Pruett, Max
Pruett, Penny
Pruett, Teresa
Pugh, Brenda

Radcliff, Brenda
Rakestraw, Angelia
Rakestraw, Jimmie
Rakestraw, Ricky
Reynolds, Margaret
Riggs, Joann
Robertson, Dianne
Robertson, Larry
Roberts, Bessie
Roberts, Edna Fae
Roberts, Lois
Roberts, Thelma
Robertson, Carroll
Robinson, Cindy
Robinson, Colinca
Robinson, Doug
Robinson, Henry
Rogers, Anita
Rollins, David

Rollins, Glenda
Ruff, Linda Ann

Sabinas, John Lee
Saladridgas, Joyce
Sanders, Carmen
Scott, Dean
Scott, Margaret
Shanks, Joe
Shead, Keith
Shead, Mollie
Sheets, Charles
Sheets, Lisa
Shoemaker, Jewell
Shores, Rodney
Shores, Sheila
Simpson, Sheryl
Simpson, Rick
Skinner, Geanene
Smith, Angie
Smith, Carroll
Smith, Diane
Smith, Laura
Smith, Lynn
Sorrells, Emma
Sprayberry, Jamie
Sprayberry, Michelle
Spruill, Rhonda
Stanford, Estelle
Swafford, Danny

Swafford, Steve

Tallent, Louise
Tallent, Shae
Tallent, Tabitha
Tallent, Tommie
Tant, Dale
Tant, Joan
Tant, Travis
Tapley, Corry
Tapley, Judy
Tapley, Sanford
Tapley, Tonya
Taylor, Hollis
Taylor, June
Thomas, Charlotte
Thomas, Dewayne
Thomason, Jane
Thomason, Rita
Thompson, Larrin
Thomason, Timmy
Thompson, Toby
Tibbits, Anna
Tibbits, Cody
Tibbits, Emily
Tibbits, Mary
Tibbits, Randy
Touchton, Linda
Touchton, Raymond
Townsend, Wayne

Tumlin, Dianne
Turner, Charlotte
Turner, Jackie
Turner, Jamie
Turner, Linda
Turner, Lisa
Turner, Marty
Turner, Rainey
Turner, Richard

Upton, David
Upton, J. R.
Upton, June
Upton, Lora Lee
Upton, Samantha
Upton, Sandra
Upton, Stephanie
Upton, Wendell

Vaughn, Jamie
Vaughn, Janice
Vaughn, Lamar
Vaughn, Melissa
Vaughn, Tammy
Verner, Betty
Verner, Melody

Walker, Cathy
Walker, Loretta
Walker, Richard

Walker, Sharon
Wall, Sharon
Wallace, Shirley
Wash, Cary
Waters, Betty
Waters, Susan
Weatherington, Herman
Weatherington, Joe
Weatherington, Junior
Weatherington, Margie
Weaver, Rachel
Weaver, Tommy
Webb, Sharon
Wentz, Jamie
Wentz, Janice
White, June
White, Katherine
White, Larry
White, Osara
White, Penny
White, Steve
Whitely, Sherrie
Whitely, Vicky
Wigley, Lillian
Williams, Joshua
Williams, Sherie
Williams, Steve
Williams, Terry
Willoughby, Brandi
Willoughby, Carla

Willoughby, Cory
Willoughby, Hollie
Willoughby, Wesley
Wilson, Allen
Wilson, Billy
Wilson, Karen
Wilson, Lillie
Wilson, Mark
Wilson, Randall
Wilson, Rodney
Wines, Kathleen Denise
Winters, Gregory
Winters, JoAnne
Wintz, Marion
Wisner, Joyce
Wix, Anne
Wix, Donnie
Wix, Gina
Wix, Eddie
Wix, James
Wix, Jennifer
Wix, Lena
Wix, Mildred
Wix, Roger
Womack, Elizabeth
Woods, Tommy
Woody, Ora Lee
Workman, Judy
Wyatt, Angie
Wyatt, Eddie

Youngblood, Sonja

Effie Estell C. Ricks Stanford died July 22, 2004. Her obituary was published in the *Dallas New Era,* on Thursday, July 29, 2004.

> Mrs. Effie Estell Camp Ricks Stanford, 90 of Temple, GA, passed away in her sleep after a long struggle with Alzheimer's on Thursday, July 22, 2004 at WellStar Paulding Hospital. She was born November 7, 1913 in Douglas County, GA, the daughter of the late William T. Camp and the late Mrs. Ella Veal Camp. She was a member of White Oak Springs Baptist Church in Dallas and was a retired seamstress with Hubbard Manufacturing Company.

Members of White Oak Springs who passed away in 2004. The following is from his obituary published in the *The Atlanta Journal-Constitution* on October 3, 2004.

> Mr. Osara Jackson White, age 80, of Dallas, GA passed away on Saturday, October 2, 2004. He was born on December 16, 1923 in Carroll Co., to the late Andrew and Lula White. He was a member of White Oak Springs Baptist Church and was an Army veteran of World War II. He was retired from General Motors.

Randall "Randy" W. Garner was a member of White Oak Springs Baptist Church. His obituary was published in the April 25, 2005, *Dallas New Era:*

> Mr. Randall 'Randy' Wayne Garner, of Winston, GA, passed away Monday, April 25, 2005. He was born on January 27, 1955, son of Gerrill Garner and Mrs. Mary Jo Yearty Garner.

He married Treva Hicks on September 26, 1976, at White Oak Springs Baptist Church in Dallas. He was a retired construction coordinator from Atlanta Gas Company following 24 years of service. He was a member of White Oak Springs Baptist Church in Dallas. Randy was a person who displayed the core values of honesty and integrity and was a hard worker.

James Edward Wix was a member of White Oak Springs Church. His obituary was published June 9, 2005, in the *Dallas New Era.* His obituary states he was 80 years old and that he was a current member at White Oak Springs Baptist Church. He was born December 31, 1924, and died on May 30, 2005. His parents were Zach and Velma Wix. His wife was Mildred Miller Wix.

Danny Baxter was a member of White Oak Springs Baptist Church. His obituary was published in the June 16, 2005, *Dallas New Era.* His obituary states he was 47 years old and that he was a member at White Oak Springs Baptist Church. His wife's name was Emily "Kelly" Baxter. Danny was the son of Jimmy Baxter and Loretta Croker Baxter.

Mrs. Frances E. Cole

The following was published in the *Dallas New Era* on Thursday, March 23, 2006.

Mrs. Frances E. Cole, age 77, of Dallas, GA, passed away March 16, 2006 at WellStar Paulding Subacute in Dallas.

Mrs. Cole was born July 15, 1928, in Cleveland, Tennessee, daughter of the late James Blanco Wooden and the late Cordie Guffey Wooden. She was a member of White Oak Springs Baptist Church for many years and also a Homemaker.

In addition to her parents, James and Cordie Wooden, she was preceded in death by her husband, Mr. Fred Norman Cole, who passed away October 18, 1993; infant daughter, Gloria Jane Cole, who passed away in 1950, and three sisters, Betty Horner, Helen Rucker ,and Mildred Jordan.

Mrs. Irma Ruth (Knight) Evans was a member of White Oak Springs Baptist Church. Her obituary was published in The *Dallas New Era* on August 24, 2006:

Mrs. Irma Ruth (Knight) Evans of Marietta, GA, age 80, passed away August 15, 2006 at her residence.

Mrs. Evans was born August 2, 1926 in Paulding County, GA daughter of the late William Tim and Alma Cole. She was a member of White Oak Springs Baptist Church and owned a Grocery Store. ... In addition to her parents, William and Alma Cole, she was preceded in death by her husband, Mr. John C. Knight, who passed away in 1962; a sister, Mrs. Lola Frances Baxter and brothers, Mr. J. Ray Cole, Mr. Herman Cole and Mr. Ralph Cole.

Mrs. Marvene Roberts Hicks was a member of White Oak Springs Baptist Church. Her obituary was published in *The Atlanta Journal-Constitution* on February 9, 2008:

Mrs. Marvene Roberts Hicks, 87, of Winston, GA passed away February 7, 2008 at Wellstar Paulding Nursing Center. She was born October 8, 1920 in Dallas, GA, the daughter of the late Mr. Tyre Roberts and the late Mrs. Ida Fields Roberts. She was a member of White Oak Springs Baptist Church in Dallas, GA. She was a homemaker. She was known as "Nannie" to those who knew her. She enjoyed reading, sewing, cooking and gardening.

In addition to her parents, she was preceded in death by her husband, John Columbus "J. C." Hicks; daughter, Dianne Rollins; sons-in-law, Randall Garner and James Rollins; sister, Sallie Roberts Hicks; brothers, W.B. Roberts, Alva Roberts, and L.T. Roberts.

She is survived by her daughter, Treva Hicks Garner of Winston; grandchildren, Kristina Wright and Steve Rollins; great-grandchild, Violet Nash; brother, Cleveland Roberts of Hiram; sisters-in-law, Thelma Roberts of Temple, Jean Roberts Pettway and her husband, Steve of Acworth, and Louise Roberts of Hiram; several nieces, nephews, great-nieces, and great-nephews.

Rev. Chris Simpson

Rev. Chris Simpson pastored White Oak Springs Baptist Church from March 9, 2008, until 2013. Today (2018), Rev. Chris Simpson is pastoring Walter's Grove Baptist Church in Lexington, North Carolina. Pastor Chris and his wife have three lovely daughters and one son.

Brother Chris is a fifth-generation preacher. His wife is Heather. They both grew up in our church and have two children: Hayleigh and Weston. They are both hard working. Brother Chris and Sister Heather are both very talented. Brother Chris plays the piano. He and his wife, Heather, both sing. Brother Chris is very encouraging and motivating, and he has a great burden for the potential God has shown him for our church. He is wise beyond his years and is doing a great job pastoring this church that has already had so many great pastors down through the years (written by Gloria Byrd in about 2010).

Members of White Oak Springs who passed away in 2008. The following is from her obituary posted at meaningfulfunerals.net.

Edith Marie Ross Ferguson (October 20, 1921–October 14, 2008), age 86, … passed away Tuesday, October 14th… She was a member of the White Oak Springs Baptist Church in Paulding County, GA.[36]

---

[36] http://www.akinsfuneralhome.com/obituary/278517

Edith Marie Ross Ferguson's daughter and son-in-law were also members of White Oak Springs Baptist Church. They were Mark and Marie Dockery of Douglasville, Georgia.

Members of White Oak Springs who passed away in 2009. The following is from his obituary posted at findagrave.com.[37]

> William "Owen" Roberts, age 56, of Buchanan, GA, passed away on Thursday, June 18, 2009. He was born in Paulding County, May 6, 1953, the son of the late, W. B. & Thelma Roberts. Mr. Roberts enjoyed life and was a very caring person. His favorite song was "Don't Worry Be Happy." He was a member of White Oak Springs Baptist Church.

Members of White Oak Springs who passed away in 2011:

The following is from Albert Dewey Copeland's obituary posted at findagrave.com.

> Mr. Albert Dewey Copeland, age 80 of Dallas, GA, passed away after a brief illness on Saturday, October 1, 2011. ... Mr. Copeland was born on May 19, 1931, at Sand Mountain, Alabama, to loving parents Dewey Albert Copeland and Willie Mae Lancaster Copeland. Mr. Copeland was a retired heavy equipment operator for Aiken Grading Company. Mr. Copeland enjoyed walking and nature. Mr. Copeland was a member of White Oak Springs Baptist Church.[38]

---

[37] http://paulding.com/forum/topic/212732-william-owen-roberts/#entry2805481
[38] http://www.jeffeberhartfuneralhome.com/obituaries/Albert-Dewey-Copeland-484029/#!/Obituary

Members of White Oak Springs who passed away in 2012:

Mollie Roberts Shead died on December 18, 2012. She was the oldest member at White Oak Springs Baptist Church. Her obituary was published online at J. Collins Funeral Home's website (jcollinsfuneralhome.com):

> Mrs. Mollie Roberts Shead, age 90 of Dallas, died Tuesday, December 18, 2012, at her residence.
>
> Mrs. Shead was born September 16, 1922, in Paulding County, the daughter of the late George Cole and Minnie Hulsey Cole. … She was a devoted member of White Oak Springs Missionary Baptist Church where she was currently the oldest member.
>
> In addition to her parents, she was preceded in death by her first husband, Hugh M. Roberts, 6 grandchildren and 4 great grandchildren.[39]

Rev. Robert Jenkins was a member of White Oak Springs Baptist Church for most, if not all, of his saved life. The following is from his obituary published in the *Natchez Daily Tribune* on Dec. 9, 2012.

> Rev. Robert William Jenkins, age 76, of Natchez, Miss., formerly of Cartersville, died in Natchez Monday following a courageous battle with cancer. He was born in Ohatchee, AL., July 18,1936, a son of the late Boyd Lee Jenkins and Ovie Lee Tidwell Jenkins, moving to Cartersville at the age of 14. Prior

---

[39] http://www.jcollinsfuneralhome.com/memsol.cgi?user_id=847955

to being called to the Gospel ministry at White Oak Springs Baptist Church, he was a well-known contractor in Cartersville and Dallas. He first served for eight years as a missionary to the Island of Dominica in the West Indies. While there, Mrs. Jenkins' cousin and husband, Margaret and Parnick Jennings, Sr. served 3 weeks as lay missionaries. He then joined the Maranatha Baptist Mission in Natchez, serving 27 years, overseeing the building of Maranatha Haven. Brother Jenkins was called as Executive Director of Baptist Pioneer Mission, overseeing the building of their three story headquarters. Returning to Natchez, he and Brother Johnny Welborn formed Warrenton Baptist Mission Agency, and Robert oversaw the erection of their Mission Building. ... Surviving is his wife of 59 years, who served by his side in ministry, Nancy Pinson Jenkins, also, formerly of Cartersville...

Pastor Keith A. Lee

Pastor Keith A. Lee was born and raised in Atlanta, Georgia. He graduated in 1985 from Morrow High School in Morrow, Georgia. On December 2, 1990, Pastor Lee was saved at Peoples Baptist Church in Morrow, Georgia. He was called to preach in 1992 at the annual Peoples Baptist Church Campmeeting and ordained for the ministry on December 6, 1998, at Fellowship Baptist Church in Cumming, Georgia.

Prior to pastoring at White Oak Springs, Brother Lee served as pastor of the Fellowship Baptist Church, located in Cumming, Georgia, for just over 10 years. His first pastorate was at University Baptist Church in Brookhaven, Georgia, from 2000 to 2002. Brother Lee has worked in many ministries, including law enforcement chaplain, youth pastor, adult and youth Sunday School teacher, bus director and musician. Pastor Lee has been serving at White Oak Springs Baptist Church, Dallas, Georgia, since June 2013.

Pastor Lee has been married to Amanda J. Lee (Sanford) since July 29, 1988. The Lees have three girls (Megan, Kara, and McKenzie) and one boy (Matthew). Megan is married to Heath Snelgrove. Kara and McKenzie are currently attending a Christian college. Matthew is living at home and being homeschooled.

Pastor Lee's wife, Amanda, has a true servant's heart. She faithfully serves her family and church. Amanda is known for her cooking and her gift of hospitality. She works tirelessly in the church's nursery. Pastor Lee acknowledges she is an asset to the family and a benefit to the ministry.

Pastor Lee's vision is for White Oak Springs Baptist Church to be the pillar and ground of the truth in Dallas, Georgia. Pastor Lee is committed to preaching the Gospel and teaching sound Bible doctrine. Pastor Lee desires to disciple believers and to encourage people in their walk with the Lord.

Members of White Oak Springs who passed away in 2015:

The following is from Shelby Jean Clay's obituary posted at www.jhoytthomas.com:

> Shelby Jean Clay, 73, of Villa Rica, died September 21, 2015. She was born in Villa Rica on December 29, 1941, the daughter of the late Ancy J. Williams and the late Ona Pearl Morrow. She lived her entire lifetime in this area and worked for many years at the Villa Rica Hosiery Mills. She devoted her life, love and time to her children, grandchildren, and great grandchildren and to her Christian faith and church. She was a member of White Oak Springs Baptist Church in Dallas and attended the adult Sunday School class.[40]

Mrs. Gloria Byrd was a long-time member of White Oak Springs Baptist Church. Her husband was Deacon Frank Byrd. She and her family were very active members and leaders of White Oak Springs Baptist Church during the 1970s. Many years ago, Gloria

---

[40] http://www.jhoytthomas.com/memsol.cgi?user_id=1659438

Byrd wrote a three-page "History of White Oak Springs Pastors as Remembered by Gloria Caldwell Byrd." Her written memories of each pastor and ministry are included in the text of this book. She did a wonderful service in preserving some of the history of the church. Due credit was attributed to her in each case when her "History of White Oak Springs Pastors" was used.

In the early summer of 2017, Rev. Jeff Byrd was sent a first draft of the manuscript of this book. He was reading the manuscript for historical accuracy. Brother Byrd read the whole manuscript of this book to his mother, Gloria, over the course of a few weeks. He would read to her some each day when she was most alert. The suggestions she gave have been incorporated into this final version.

As this final version was being sent to the proofreader, this author came across her obituary.

Obituary for Mrs. Gloria Byrd

Mrs. Gloria Joan Byrd, age 81, of Dallas, Georgia, passed away Saturday, September 16, 2017, at Wellstar Tranquility at Cobb.

Mrs. Byrd was born December 11, 1935, in Paulding County to Mr. and Mrs. Homer Marcus (Ola Grace Harris) Caldwell. She was married to Mr. Gene Franklin Byrd. Mrs. Gloria was a homemaker.

Mrs. Byrd is survived by: Children, Mr. and Mrs. Dennie (Francine) Smith; Mr. and Mrs. Ralph (Jo Ann) Allen; Rev. and Mrs. Jeff (Cathy) Byrd; Grandchildren; Beth Smith, Andrew and Amanda Allen, Jonathan and Althea Byrd, Cainan and Heather Byrd, Marcus and Angela Byrd; Great-Grandchildren; Eli and Ansley Allen, Silas Byrd, Hannah Byrd, Hadassah Byrd and Hadley Byrd.

Mrs. Byrd was preceded in death by: Husband, Mr. Gene Franklin Byrd; Parents, Mr. and Mrs. Homer Marcus (Ola Grace Harris) Caldwell; Brother, Mr. Owen Caldwell; Brother, Mr. Pete Caldwell.

Services for Mrs. Gloria Byrd will be held on Tuesday, September 19, 2017, 1:00 P.M. at Benson Funeral Home Chapel. Rev. Earl Partain will officiate. Interment will follow at White Oak Springs Baptist Church Cemetery.

Pallbearers will be: Andrew Allen, Cainan Byrd, Marcus Byrd, Ralph Allen, Dennie Smith, Eli Allen, Silas Byrd and Ben Tyre.[41]

(From left to right) Bro. Chris Simpson, Bro. Earl Partain, Bro. Johnny Simpson, Bro. Keith Lee
c. 2015

---

[41] http://www.bensonfuneralhome.net/obituaries/Mrs-Gloria-Joan-Byrd?obId=2554239#/obituaryInfo

Plans for the Future

"Looking unto Jesus the author and finisher of our faith; who for the joy that was set before him endured the cross, despising the shame, and is set down at the right hand of the throne of God." —Hebrews 12:2

Our vision for White Oak Springs Baptist Church is to continue to please God by our love, obedience, service, and giving.

In Acts 2:43–47, God gives us a snapshot of a church that is actively pleasing Him. White Oak Springs' plans for the future are to fulfill God's plan of reaching our community by

1. Continuing to Preach the Word of God   Acts 2:38-40
2. Continuing to Obey God's Commands (baptism) Acts 2:41
3. Continuing in Doctrine   Acts 2:42a
4. Continuing in Fellowship   Acts 2:42b
5. Continuing in Breaking of bread   Acts 2:42c
6. Continuing in Prayers   Acts 2:42d
7. Continuing in Worship   Acts 2:46
8. Continuing in Praising God   Acts 2:47a
9. Continuing in Soul Winning   Acts 2:47b

God has truly blessed White Oak Springs Baptist Church during the last 162 years. However, I believe that, with God's help and our continued obedience to Him and His word, the best years of ministry for White Oak Springs Baptist Church are still yet to come.

Section Three

Our Appendixes

Appendix One

White Oak Springs Baptist Church

(From the *Challenger* newsletter from the Concord-Tallapoosa
Baptist Association, November 1966)

We constituted in 1856 in a church about a mile southeast of the present building. They worshipped there until 1889 and then moved to the present location. In 1963, the church started the basement of the new building for extra Sunday School rooms. In the early spring of 1966, the church voted to build the new church building.

Pastors who have pastored the church are: Rev. Jasper Smith, Rev. Ogel, Rev. Gilland, Rev. Jenkins, Rev. D. Wortham, Rev. M. F. Waddell, Rev. Jesse Hitchcock, Rev. Marks, Rev. Davis, Rev. Will Womack, Rev. Fred Wigley, Rev. Marion Moore, Rev. James Crabb, Rev. Ernest Cain, Rev. Herman Long, Rev. Roy Goodson, Rev. Paul Carter, Rev. Charles Williams, Rev. George Barnett.

We are grateful for this upward vision, inward searching, and outward response and service of a people, who have a mind to work, which is often the case, when true dedication follows a personal encounter with God. The day of dedication, October 2, was truly a great one for White Oak Springs Baptist Church. Recognition was given to former pastors, visitors, contractors and builder, building committee: R. G. Gazaway, Kenneth Cohran, and Ray Cole; trustees & finance committee: Ben Carter, T.W. Clark, and Frank Byrd; organizational leaders: S.S. Superintendent: Ray McClarity; Brotherhood Pres.: Kenneth Cohran; W.M.U. Pres.:

Mrs. Mertha Gazaway; Treasurer: T. W. Clark; and church clerk: George E. Gober. Rev. Charles Williams, former pastor preached the Dedication Sermon, and Rev. Jerry Vines: Missions of the Church.

Thanks to God for this fine dedicated pastor, who loves people, his Lord, his church, and the preaching of the gospel of Jesus Christ. Congratulations to all for a fine job well done.

From the monthly newsletter, *Challenger*, November 1966, pages 1 and 2.

Appendix Two

History of White Oak Springs Baptist Church
By Jeff Byrd
c. 1987

The White Oak Springs Baptist Church began under a small group of White Oaks in 1856, when a group of Spirit-led people met to worship and praise God. Being settlers in the area and with the Cherokee Indians still scattered throughout the land, they reserved a low, marshlike parcel of land about two miles southeast of the church's present location to worship their God, bury their dead, and teach their children. A small building was built, and a church was born.

The name White Oak Church was chosen as a memorial for the White Oak that shaded them before a church was constructed.

As time passed, the marshlike land became less ideal for a meeting place, and in 1889 a new building was constructed on higher ground at the present location. The addition of "Springs" was added to the name of the church at this time. For almost 80 years, the log-frame building was renovated, repaired, and reconditioned to serve the needs of its members. However, in 1963, the growth of the church and the dilapidation of the building proved the need for new construction. A basement for a new church was built, and the next three years were spent building a new sanctuary. At long last, on October 2, 1966, the church held their first service in the present building.

A bus ministry was started in 1970. As the need arose and as God provided, additions have been added to the facility. A children's church for children ages 3 to 11 was held during the adults' Sunday School, and then the children had Sunday School while the adults had worship services. In 1974 a sanctuary for the children and additional Sunday School rooms were started and then completed in 1975. In 1976 the children had outgrown their space and a second children's church was started.

At the present, the White Oak Springs Missionary Baptist Church consists of the sanctuary, which can seat approximately 450 comfortably, a wing with two children's churches, approximately 15 Sunday School rooms, a spacious four-bedroom parsonage, a bus maintenance garage, an official gymnasium, and undeveloped space for future use.

The small frame fellowship building was built in April 1968. On April 8, 1985, during the 6:30 pm service, the building caught fire and was completely destroyed. A new, large fellowship building was completed in 1987.

Appendix Three

**History of White Oak Springs Baptist Church
with an additional paragraph added in the 2000s
By Jeff Byrd with additional notes by others**

The White Oak Springs Baptist Church began under a small group of White Oaks in 1856 when a group of Spirit-led people met to worship and praise God. Being settlers in the area and with the Cherokee Indians still scattered throughout the land, they reserved a low marshlike parcel of land about two miles southeast of the church's present location to worship their God, bury their dead, and teach their children. A small building was built, and a church was born.

The name White Oak Church was chosen as a memorial for the White Oak that shaded them before a church was constructed.

As time passed, the marshlike land became less ideal for a meeting place, and in 1889 a new building on higher ground was constructed at the present location. The addition of "Springs" was added to the name of the church at this time. For almost 80 years the log-frame building was renovated, repaired, and reconditioned to serve the needs of its members. However, in 1963, the growth of the church and the dilapidation of the building proved the need for new construction. A basement for a new church was built, and the next three years were spent building a new sanctuary. At long last, on October 2, 1966, the church held their first service in the present building.

A bus ministry was started in 1970. As the need arose and as God provided, additions have been added to the facility. A children's church for children ages 3 to 11 was held during the adults' Sunday School, and then the children had Sunday School while the adults had worship services. In 1974 a sanctuary for the children and additional Sunday School rooms were started and then completed in 1975. In 1976 the children had outgrown their space, and a second children's church was started.

At the present, the White Oak Springs Missionary Baptist Church consists of the sanctuary, which can seat approximately 450 comfortably, a wing with two children's churches, approximately 15 Sunday School rooms, a spacious four-bedroom parsonage, a bus maintenance garage, and official gymnasium, and undeveloped space for future use.

The small frame fellowship building was built in April 1968. On April 8, 1985, during the 6:30 pm service, the building caught fire and completely destroyed. A new, large fellowship building was completed in 1987.

On February 16, 2000, additional land near the parsonage was purchased for future use. On March 13, 2003, approximately 3.3 acres on the Buchanan Highway, along with a dwelling, were also purchased for future use.

Handwritten addition: May 2006—voted to start a Christian School in August 2006. Voted to hire pastor's assistant.

Appendix Four
Youth Sanctuary Dedication
White Oak Springs Baptist Church
Route 4
Dallas, Georgia

The White Oak Springs Baptist Church was constituted in 1856. This building was located about a mile southeast of the present building. They worshipped there until 1889 and then moved to the present location. In 1963 the basement of the present church was built and used for Sunday School rooms. In 1974, the church voted to build a new youth sanctuary and additional Sunday School rooms.

Below are the names of men who have pastored this church:[42] Rev. Jasper Smith, Rev. Ogel, Rev. Gilland, Rev. Jenkins, Rev. D. Wortham, Rev. M. F. Waddell, Rev. Jesse Hitchcock. Rev. Marks, Rev. Davis, Rev. Will Womack, Rev. Fred Wigley, Rev. Marion Moore, Rev. James Crabb, Rev. Ernest Cain, Rev. Herman Long, Rev. Roy Goodson, Rev. Paul Carter, Rev. Charles Williams, Rev. George Barnett.

February 2, 1975

---

[42] The names listed are the same names listed in the 1966 *Challenger* Newsletter.

Photo of the Old White Oak Springs Cemetery
November 2015

Appendix Five

Old White Oak Springs Baptist Church Cemetery

It is believed that the Old White Oak Springs Baptist Church Cemetery has over 100 graves, but in 1977 only four people were recorded as having tombstones. The four people with tombstones at the old cemetery in 1977 were: Hamon Roberts (1799–1882); Nancy Roberts (1826–1900); Mary J. Hitchcock (1845–1892); and Cumi Hitchcock (1869–1883). In 1947, someone placed a tombstone for Jesse Leatherwood. In the 1980s or 1990s, someone placed a tombstone for Thomas Postell.

Hamon Roberts and Nancy Roberts

Hamon Roberts (1799–1882) and Nancy Roberts (1826–1900) are considered founding members of White Oak Springs Baptist Church. They are buried in the old cemetery and have their own tombstones. Hamon was the brother of Rev. James Roberts, both of them are founders of White Oak Springs Baptist Church.

Mary J. Hitchcock

Mary J. Hitchcock, according to Jesse Hitchcock's Confederate Veterans' pension death benefit, states that Mary Jane Toler was born on January 17, 1845, in Bibb County, Alabama, and died on June 10, 1892. Mary was the daughter of William Charles Toler and Elizabeth Creel. She married Jesse Hitchcock on May 12, 1861. They had 11 children, 9 of whom were still alive in 1911. Her tombstone is in the Old White Oak Springs Cemetery.

Talithia Cumi Hitchcock

Cumi Hitchcock was the daughter of Jesse William Hitchcock and Mary J. Toler. Her name means little woman or daughter. She died at the age of 14 in the prime of her youth. The following is the newspaper article from the *Paulding New Era* published on March 13, 1885.

.

Paulding New Era
13 Mar 1885

A Shocking Accident. One of the most heart wrenching accidents which we were ever called upon to chronicle, occurred on the plantation of Squire Jesse Hitchcock, in Pumpkinvine district, last Monday evening. A new ground was being burned off, and the family were watching the fire to keep it from doing any mischief. At one point it followed up the dry leaves and sedge till it reached the fence. Cuma, the fourteen year old daughter of Squire Hitchcock, observed it and started to climb over the fence to arrest its progress. When she was on the fence the flames leaped up and caught her skirts. When she realized that her clothing was on fire she became panic stricken and ran screaming towards the house.

Her mother and sister Lee, aged sixteen, ran to her assistance, and succeeded in stripping the burning garments from her, but in doing so had their hands and arms badly burned. She was taken to the house and Dr. W. C. Connally sent for. When the doctor arrived he found that the condition of Cuma was very critical, at least two-thirds of the surface of her whole body being burned to a crisp, and that the right hand of Lee was so badly burned that it would be deformed if not entirely lost, while Mrs. Hitchcock's hands were painfully burned. He dressed the burns, and administered all the known remedies to relieve the pain. Cuma lingered in great pain till Wednesday evening, when death came to her relief. The others are doing as well as could be expected.

Richard J. Carter

Richard J. Carter served in the Civil War and was mortally wounded at the Battle of Vicksburg, Mississippi, on September 13, 1863. According to his pension papers, he was sent home and died six weeks later. Richard J. Carter married Judith (Judy) Adair on January 8, 1858, in Paulding County, Georgia.[43]

John B. Pace and Nancy Camp Pace

Mr. John B. Pace (1775–1857) and wife, Nancy Camp Pace, are buried in the Old White Oak Springs Baptist Church Cemetery according to their descendants. Their descendants posted the following information on the website findagrave.com. "She and her husband, John B. Pace were pioneer settlers of Cobb County, Georgia. In March 1833—The first general elections in Cobb County, Georgia, were held at their home."[44]

John Thomas Todd and Martha Lucinda Wilson Todd

John Thomas Todd (May 1800–April 12, 1860) and wife, Martha Lucinda Wilson Todd (1814–1898), are buried in the Old White Oak Springs Baptist Church Cemetery according to their

---

[43] Confederate Veterans and Widow Pensions, Paulding County, Georgia, p. 65.

[44] https://www.findagrave.com/cgi-bin/fg.cgi?page=gr&GRid=46469422

descendants. The posted information about this is on findagrave.com.[45]

Thomas T. Postell

Descendants of Thomas P. Postell have placed a tombstone in the Old White Oak Springs Baptist Church Cemetery. It lists the names of his wives from his three marriages. Thomas was born in 1802 and died in 1884. The names of his wives were Mary "Polly" Stuart, Lucinda Brock, and Nancy Brock. The names of his 14 children are also listed. The descendants of Thomas T. Postell know that he was buried at this cemetery, and it is appreciated that they honored his memory by placing a grave marker for him. His third wife, Lucinda Brock, was born in 1810 and died in 1864.

Jessie Leatherwood

Jessie Leatherwood has a tombstone that was placed in the cemetery in 1947 by Annie. A Jesse Leatherwood is listed in the 1880 Federal Mortality Schedule for Paulding County, Georgia. He died in October 1879. It lists that he was 58 years old at the time of his death. Therefore, he was born in about 1821. The 1870 Paulding County, Georgia Census lists Jesse Leatherwood (age 50) and his wife, Mary.

Thomas Moody and Retincy Hill Moody

Thomas Moody died in 1864 and is buried in the Old White Oak Springs Cemetery. His wife, Retincy Hill Moody, passed away 20 years later in 1884. Her obituary states she was buried in the old

---

[45]https://www.findagrave.com/cgibin/fg.cgi?page=gr&GScid=2195543&GRid=67008536&

church cemetery. It is said that the Moody tombstone was stolen from the old cemetery by vandals, found later, and then placed in the new cemetery for better protection. Their tombstones are located beside their daughter's gave: Sophronia Moody Wilson.

Isaac Wix and Missouri E. Wix

In the 1860 Paulding County, Georgia Census, Isaac Wix and his wife, Missouri E. Wix, are listed as living beside many of the founding members of White Oak Springs Baptist Church. Don Wix recalls that his father, Rev. J. Edwin Wix, stated that both Isaac and Missouri Wix were buried in the Old White Oak Springs Cemetery near one of the few graves that still have markers in that cemetery. The 1860 census states that Isaac Wix (spelled Weeks) was born about 1815. His wife, Missouri E., was born about 1825. They were not listed in the 1880 Paulding County, Georgia Census, and they are believed to have passed away before that.

Pr. Roy Goodson Baptizing in Lake
c1958

Photo used with permission from Lori English

Appendix Six

First Families Connected with
White Oak Springs Baptist Church,
New White Oak Springs Baptist Church Cemetery,
Those born before 1900

The following is a list of people buried in the White Oak Springs Church Cemeteries (both old and new) who were born before 1900. The people who are buried in the cemetery are some of the first families that attended White Oak Springs Baptist Church. All of them are either pioneers or children of the pioneers who were the first families, not only of White Oak Springs Baptist Church, but also of Paulding County. Due to the church minutes and records being lost in fires, the church does not have a complete list of members. We know many of those buried had a connection to White Oak Springs Baptist Church. Many of those buried in the two cemeteries probably were members and attended the church. Some could have even been deacons, song leaders, lay preachers, etc., but the church does not have any information that says they were actual members or had any connection at all to the church.

The old cemetery has over 100 graves, but we only have 15 names of those buried there. Over 90 percent of the family names listed here had children, grandchildren, and great-grandchildren that were active members and leaders of this church. We suspect many of these people were also active members and participants in the church. White Oak Springs knows they are there, appreciates what they did, and wishes to acknowledge them in this way. Husband and wife are together when possible.

Baxter

Baxter, C. Gordon	1885–1955—deacon
Leona Baxter	1885–1974
Baxter, Marion A.	1891–1962
Minnie S. Cason Baxter	1887–1967

Bradley

Bradley, C. B.	1862–1928
Edith Bradley	1867–1928

Cason

Minnie S. Cason, wife of Marion Baxter 1887–1967

Brown

Brown, Henry M.	1892–1953
Brown, J. Homer	1888–1919
G. Louvenia Head Brown	1884–1966

Carter

Carter, John T.	1886–1966
Carter, Richard T.	1881–1968
Mary Emma Wix Carter	1880–1947

Clark

Clark, William E.	1868–1947
Annie Cole Clark	1870–1947

Clark, Samuel	1839–1930
Celicie Moody Clark	1839–1928
Clark, W. L.	1874–1903
Clark, William M.	1843–1926

Cole

Cole, George W.	1886–1957
Minnie Cole	1891–1964
Cole, John Marion	1882–1948
Georgia Cole	1881–1936
Cole, Radar E.	1881–1918
Cole, James N.	1872–1951
Cole, G. W.	1849–1908
Mary Louisa Cole Hudson	1853–1922
Cole, Charlie A.	1878–1948
Cole, John W.	1862–1943
Martha C. Cole	1865–1909
Cole, Henry R.	1852–1938
Elizabeth Moody Cole	1858–1952
Cole, Whittic	1854–1926

Jane B. Cole   1856–1927

Cole, William T.   1875–1960
   Thersey Hitchcock Cole   1881–1963

Cole, Milton   1883–1961
   Janie Estelle Cole   1886–1964

Cole, Sallie (wife of M. B. Roberts)   1868–1919

Cole, Sarah   1848–1933

Cole, Walter R.   1887–1955
   Mary McBrayer Cole no dates
   Winnie Maner Cole   1891–1956

Cole, W. Tim   1887–1966

Cole, Henry L.   1896–1968
   Pearl Cason Cole   1903–1974

Cole, Samuel Melvin   1882–1954
   Kansas Langford Cole   1887–1973

Fuller

Fuller, Thomas Jefferson   1871–1963
   Sarah Elizabeth Wix Fuller   1873–1943

Harper

Harper, Mary Alice   1874–1907

Harris

Harris, William Jackson	1841–1909
Mary Ann Harris	
Harris, W. Alonzo	1869–1958
Mary Louise Harris	1872–1946
Harris, David	1871–1943
Mary A. Harris	1877–1957
Harris, Arnold W.	1895–1929
Harris, John D.	1882–1952
Tempie Rainey Harris	1888–1961
Harris, Erving	1878–1946
Meedie Lindsey Harris	1880–1922

Hitchcock

Hitchcock, Cary B.	1886–1942
Flossie Bell Hitchcock	1890–1943
Hitchcock, John	1847–1923
Mary A. Hitchcock	1847–1897
Hitchcock, Jesse (Rev.)	1836–1911
Mary Jane Toler	1845–1892
Judy Hitchcock Toler	No marker

Howard

Howard, Lucius F.   1880–1952

Lindsey

Lindsey, James M.   1884–1939
  Omie Roberts   1892–1939

Maner

Maner, George (Elder/Pastor)   1856–1962

Maner, William   1896–1942

Maner, Roland   1898–1956

Moody

Moody, Thomas   1811–1864
  Retincy H. Moody   1820–1884

Moody, Celicia (Clark)   1839–1928

Moody, Saphronia (Wilson)   1850–1896

Rainey

Rainey, P. Miluner   1864–1904
  Texaner Cole Rainey   1866–no date

Rainey, Robert Andrew   1892–1971
  Katie Fuller Rainey   1897–1943

Rainey, Jasper   No marker

Ove Hitchcock Rainey   No marker

Roberts

Roberts, George R.   1887–1945
 Birma E. Cole   1889–1951

Robert, M. B. (Moses Barto) 1862–1963
 Sallie Cole Roberts 1868–1919

Roberts, Hamon J.   1894–1936

Roberts, Hamon   1799–1882
 Nancy Roberts   1826–1900

Roberts, Cumi   1869–1885

Scott

Scott, George E.   1878–1965
 Vinnie R. Scott   1889–1970

Sinyard

Sinyard, Jacob   1853–1910
 Zellie Roberts Sinyard No marker

Wilson

Wilson, John Oliver   1883–1948

Wilson, George W.   1850–1896
 Saphronia Moody Wilson 1857–1893

Wilson, Harvey   1875–1929
   Dora Harper Wilson   1878–1922

Wix

Wix, Charlie   1895–1945
   Emma Butler Wix   1895–1976

Wix, I. L.V.   1883–1897

Wix, Isaac   1815–after 1860/before 1880
   Missouri E. Wix   1825–after 1860/before 1880

Wix, Joseph   1852–1923
   Nancy Wix   1853–1936

Wix, John N.   1877–1963

Wix, William T.   1874–1932
   Lillian M. Fuller Wix   1882–1939

Wix, Zachariah   1855–1892
   Josephine C. Hitchcock Wix 1860–1950

Appendix Seven

Note: This was written about 1977 and was included in the "Deacons of White Oak Springs" booklet. It is presented as is with no updates to this document except for the information on G. W. Cole.

Deacons Ordained by White Oak Springs Baptist Church

Ordained on June 23, 1888 (from his obituary published in 1908)
G. W. Cole (aka "Doc" Cole)

Ordained on July 24, 1908
H. H. Kemp
Moses Barto Roberts   b. 9-22-1826   d. 4-18-1943

Ordained on June 26, 1915
W. A. Harris   b. 1-22-1869   d. 2-11-1958
Walter Cole   b. 11-15-1858   d. 10-31-1970

Ordained on October 23, 1920
T. J. Fuller   b. 8-8-1871   d. 6-12-1963
J. M. Daniel   b. 8-7-1871   d. 12-12-1957

Ordained on October 22, 1927
D. E. Harris   b. 12-26-1876   d. 12-21-1946
J. O. Wilson   b. 4-12-1883   d. 3-6-1948
C. Gordon Baxter   b. 5-21-1986   d. 3-13-1955
J. N. Wix   b. 9-4-1877   d. 11-12-1963

Ordained on October 22, 1936
H. M. Brown   b. 11-15-1892   d. 9-19-1953

Ordained on October 19, 1940
Ben Carter   b. 6-26-1905   d. 7-1-1973
Ralph Harris   b. 9-8-1907   d.

Ordained on September 15, 1947
Charlie Cason   b. 10-4-1912   d.

Ordained on July 1951
John T. Cole   b. 3-5-1906   d. 1-30-1952
Woodrow Clark   b. 12-13-1913   d.

Ordained on June 5, 1957
H. L. Kinney   b. 4-12-1902   d.5-6-1977

Ordained in 1958
Lincoln Cole   b. 1-10-1927   d. 5-19-1972

Ordained July 8, 1962
Kenneth Cohran   b. 3-23-1923   d.5-19-1977
Ernest Gober   b. 12-19-1931   d.

Ordained on December 12, 1967
Vernon Cole   b. 9-14-1925   d. 5-3-1971
Ray Cole   b. 11-28-1916   d.
Frank Byrd   b. 8-26-1916   d.

Ordained September 1969
Bethel Noble   b. 7-10-1939   d.

Ordained on June 24, 1973
Ollie Matthews   b. 3-19-1943
Ralph Wix   b. 10-18-1939   d. 10-13-1973
Dennis Barber
Ordained on 7-25-1974
Jerry Godfrey   b. 10-24-1944

Also Ordained
Dale Ragsdale
Junior Bearden
Tommy Tallent
Robin Carter

Appendix Eight

Sunday School Superintendents of
White Oak Springs Baptist Church
1917–1982

The following people served as the Sunday School superintendents of this church. Other people also served as Sunday School directors after 1983, but the church does not have a complete list of names and dates that other people served.

Year	Name
1917-19	G. W. Cole
- - -	
1927-32	T. J. Fuller
1933	Ralph Harris
1934	Ralph Harris
1935	Ralph Harris
1936	Ralph Harris
1937	Ralph Harris
1938	T. J. Fuller
1939	T. J. Fuller
1940	T. J. Fuller
1941	Ralph Harris
- - -	
1947	T. J. Fuller
- - -	
1953	Guy Gazaway
1954	Lowell Baggett
- - -	

1956   Guy Gazaway

1957   Guy Gazaway

1958   H. L. Kinney

1959   H. L. Kinney

1960   Ben Carter

1961   H. L. Kinney

1962   H. L. Kinney

1963   H. L. Kinney

1964   R. S. Gazaway

1965   H. L. Kinney

1966   T. W. Clark

1967-1982+   Raymond McLarty

Appendix Nine

Men Ordained to Pastor from White Oak Springs Baptist Church. Please note: this list is incomplete.

Rev. Jay Leonard Bice

Rev. J. M. Brooks

Rev. Jeff Byrd

Rev. Darrel Carter

Rev. Randy Clark

Rev. Curtis Cole

Rev. Bob Daughtery

Rev. Dickey Fincher

Rev. Jimmy Green

Rev. Robert Jenkins

Rev. Gene Lipscomb

Rev. Chris Simpson

Rev. Ronnie Tibbits

Rev. Eddie Wyatt

Rev. Jab (Jeb) Meadows

Rev. Shae Tallent

Rev. Bud Wix

Rev. Ed Wix (J. Edwin Wix)

Appendix Ten

Rev. Jasper Smith

White Oak Springs Baptist Church's oral history states that Rev. Jasper Smith and Rev. Jesse Hitchcock were pastors of their church. However, research of the 1856 to 1982 Tallapoosa Baptist Association minutes shows no listing that these men ever pastored at White Oak Springs. The church has a complete list of their pastors from 1860 until the present (2018). Neither of these men's names were listed as ever pastoring a church in the Tallapoosa Association minutes. Minutes from adjoining sister associations were not checked.

The 1933 *A History of Paulding County* book states that White Oak Springs Baptist Church was founded in 1856 and that Jasper Smith was its first pastor. Historical records confirm that the church was founded in 1856. Those same historical records reveal the names of its pastors in the fall of each year from 1856 to 1985.

Historians state that *a short pencil is better than a long memory.* That means that something written is better than someone's foggy memory many years later. There had to be a reason that someone stated sometime or another that Rev. Jasper Smith was the first pastor of this church. There are only three possibilities to answer that statement: that information was correct, incorrect, or partially correct.

Rev. Jasper Smith (born 1866)

Jeff Byrd said that in the 1980s, some people said that the Rev. Jasper Smith who had pastored White Oak Springs Baptist Church was buried at New Georgia Baptist Church Cemetery. A search was made and his tombstone was found.

Rev. Jasper C. Smith was born on April 1, 1866, and died on June 13, 1941. He was the son of F. M. Smith. Jasper C. Smith is listed along with his parents, F. M. and Virginia Smith, in the 1870 and 1880 censuses. In both of those censuses, Jasper is listed as "Jasper C. Smith." The name used on his tombstone was Jasper C. Smith.

Jasper married Lula *"Luella"* Linsey *(Lindsey)* Smith on October 24, 1886. Lula was born on February 22, 1868, and died January 18, 1938. They are both buried at the New Georgia Baptist Cemetery in Paulding County, Georgia.

Lula Lindsey's parents, according to the 1880 Paulding County, Georgia Census, were most likely M. Lindsey (age 40), and Catherine (age 33). The children listed with M. Lindsey and Catherine were: Luella (13), Sarah (11), John (10), William (7), George L. (5), and Patsy. This Lindsey family was living beside Craven Harris and many of the founders of this church. This Jasper C. Smith did have a connection to the church, and later on he was a Baptist pastor.

In the 1920 Paulding County Census, Jasper C. Smith and Luella Smith had the following children: Lottie (age 15), Menbrey (age 13), Willie (age 7), Bennie (age 5).

Since members of White Oak Springs Baptist Church in 1933 named a Jasper Smith as their founding pastor, and then others identified that pastor as the Jasper C. Smith (born 1866 and died 1941) as that pastor, there may be one explanation for the confusion. The Jasper C. Smith (b. 1866–d. 1941) identified in 1933 as the founder of the church (80 years after the church was founded) was the son of Rev. F. M. Smith, who was pastoring the church in 1866 when Jasper Smith was born. However, that was nine years after the church was founded. That Smith family did have a connection to the early days of the church, but it was the father not the son. The father was one of the early pastors of this church, but not the first pastor.

Jasper C. Smith (born 1845)

In the 1860 Paulding County, Georgia Census, a B. H. Smith (age 49), wife Mary (age 47), and children Jasper (age 15), Newton (age 15), Emily (age 14), David (age 10), Frances (age 9), Nancy A (age 7), and Ann (age 6) are listed. That family was living close to many of the family members of White Oak Springs.

In the 1870 Carroll County, Georgia Census, a Jasper L. Smith (age 30), wife Narcissa (29), son Jasper C. (age 7), Posey N. (age 3), and daughter Arminda (6 months). In the 1880 Census, Cains district near White Oak Springs, in Paulding County, Georgia listed the same family with everyone 10 years older.

In the 1860 Paulding County, Georgia Census there is a John M. Smith (age 64), his wife Nancy (age 60) and son Jasper (age 21) listed. This Jasper Smith was born in 1839.

This is the information about Jasper Smith that was found researching for this book. Hopefully this information will be useful to other researchers in the future.

Appendix Eleven
Rev. J. A. Smith (born 1806)

Extensive research was also done to find information on J. A. Smith, who pastored some churches in Paulding County, Georgia, in the 1850s, 1860s, and 1870s. It was thought that this J. A. Smith could be the Jasper Smith listed as the founding pastor of White Oak Springs. He was not the pastor but was an active pastor in the Tallapoosa Baptist Association for many years, and since such extensive research was done to figure out who he was, his information is being presented to help others doing research.

The Tallapoosa Baptist Association minutes stated that J. A. Smith lived in Rivertown, in Campbell (now Fulton) County, Georgia. Rev. J. A. Smith was very active pastoring many Baptist churches in the Tallapoosa Baptist Association. As he aged, he stayed closer and closer to his home base in Campbell County, Georgia. He lived just south of Douglas County on the Fulton County side of the Chattahoochee River in Rivertown, Georgia.

He pastored Providence Baptist Church for several years. In the 1872 Fairburn Baptist Association minutes, he is listed as John A. Smith. In the 1873 Fairburn Baptist Association minutes, he is listed as J. A. Smith. In 1880 and 1881, he was pastoring the Enon Baptist Church in the Fairburn Baptist Association. The 1881 Fairburn Baptist Association minutes state that Rev. J. A. Smith had died during the past 12 months and that he had been the pastor of Enon at the time of his death.

J. A. Smith is buried in the Pineywood Baptist Church Cemetery in Rico, Fulton County, Georgia.

Here is his information: J. A. Smith is the Rev. John Augustine Smith. His tombstone reads that he was born on February 3, 1806, (in Mecklenburg County, Virginia). He died on June 23, 1881 (in Fulton County, Georgia). His descendants report that he first married Lavinia Cooper on December 27, 1832, and then Susan Ann Cooper on July 12, 1868.

In the 1850 Campbell County, Georgia Census, p. 803, he is listed with his family:

J. A. Smith, age 43 (born in VA); and wife Lavinia, age 40 (born in SC). Their children were: Elizabeth (age 16); Jas. C. (14); Henry H. (12); Sarah M. (11); Benj. J. (9); Lucy E. (7); Jno. K. (5); and Armanda L. (3).

John A. Smith (J. A.) never pastored White Oak Springs Baptist Church. This J. A. Smith is also not Jasper Smith. Neither one of these two men are listed in the Tallapoosa Baptist Association minutes (1886-1985) in connection with White Oak Springs Baptist Church.

A short pencil is better than a long memory, because sometimes peoples' recollections 80 years after the fact are not 100 percent accurate.

Appendix Twelve
Intriguing Mystery Membership List

The following list is intriguing. It was found in the loose history papers of White Oak Springs Baptist Church. There is no title or explanation of this list. It looks like a membership list, but some of these people died before others were born. Jacob Sinyard was born in 1843 and died in 1910. Lincoln Cole was born in 1927 and died in 1972. Many people that were known to be prominent members of the church are not listed. Many pastors of the church are listed.

Whoever worked on this list may have been trying to compile a list of former members and pastors sometime after the church membership lists were lost in a fire. The person that worked on this list spent a lot of time on it, alphabetized it, and used impeccable penmanship. It is an important list of names connected to White Oak Springs Baptist Church. The exact purpose of the list is not known; however, the names listed here were probably members at White Oak Springs Baptist Church sometime during their lifetime This author speculates that the list could have been written in the late 1930s or early 1940s, or about 1966 when the new church sanctuary was being built.

Note: The asterisks that follow certain names were added by this author and are people who have pastored this church.

1. (Mr.) M. R. Adair (L)
2. Tom A. Baggett
3. Birdie Baxter
4. C. Gordon Baxter
5. Dewey Baxter
6. C. B. Baxter
7. Clindon Baxter
8. Henry Brown

9. Tom Brown
10. Bennett Bullock
11. T. R. Bullock
12. Ben Carter
13. R. T. Carter
14. W. M. Clark
15. Babe Cole
16. Connie Cole
17. Doc Cole (G. W. Cole)
18. G. C. Cole
19. H. L. Cole
20. Homer Cole
21. J. M. Cole
22. J. Robert Cole
23. J. W. Cole
24. Jake Cole
25. John Cole
26. Lincoln Cole
27. Nathan Cole
28. Quilla Cole (Quiller)
29. Rannie Cole
30. Vernon Cole
31. W. T. Cole
32. Wafford Cole
33. Z. C. Cole
34. C. B. Cooper
36. John M. Daniel
37. J. H. Davis*
38. George Dayal
39. W. A. Dodd

40. Dossey Fuller
41. Oliver Fuller
42. Tom J. Fuller
43. Ware Fuller
44. Clifton Gamel
45. J. C. Gamel
46. Snowden Gamel
47. J. J. Gazaway
48. Rev. Gilland*
49. Hiram Harper
50. D. Erwin Harris
51. D. G. Harris
52. W. Alonzo Harris
53. Aubrey Henderson
54. C. B. Hitchcock
55. Jesse Hitchcock
56. John Hitchcock
57. W. T. Hollis
58. E. A. Hopkins
59. Rev. Jenkins*
60. J. A. Jenkins
61. Andrew Kemp
62. H. Hendred Kemp
63. H. L. (Red) Kinney
64. J. H. Lester
65. W. A. Leatherwood
66. James Lindsey
67. H. H. Long
68. Marion B. Moon*
69. Joe C. Morgan

70. Rev. H. T. R. Marks*
71. John Harrison Ogle*
72. Robert L. Ogle
73. Warner Osborne
74. Louis Ragan
75. W. L. Ragan
76. Jasper Rainey
77. Peek Rainey
78. R. A. Rainey
79. George Roberts
80. H. J. Roberts
81. M. Bart Roberts
82. Sim Roberts
83. Tyre Roberts
84. Jacob Sinyard
85. Will Sinyard
86. J. C. Smith
87. Jasper Smith
88. Rev. M. F. Waddell*
89. G. Fred Wigley*
90. H. R. Wilson
91. J. O. Wilson
92. Oscar Wilson
93. Ben Wix
94. John N. Wix
95. Luther Wix
96. Ralph Wix
97. Silas Wix
98. J. Will Womack*
99. Rev. D. Wortham*

Baptism of Vernon Cole and Ernest Cason
By Rev. Roy Goodson in about 1958

Photo used with permission from Lori English

Appendix Thirteen

1970s Singing Trio of White Oak Springs Baptist Church[46]

The Harvest Trio

This trio was composed of three ladies that were members of White Oak Springs Baptist Church. Pictured from left to right are Virginia Boynton, Bertha Bankstone, and Sue Wix. This is the cover of their first LP (long play) record album. This 33-1/3 rpm record provided about an hour of good southern gospel music.

More information from the back of the LP record cover:

---

[46] Photo used with permission of White Oak Springs Baptist Church, who helped produced the album.

The Harvest Trio is very happy to introduce their first album, the result of many hours of work and planning. The trio consists of Mrs. Sue Wix, lead; Mrs. Bertha Bankstone, alto; and Mrs. Virginia Boynton, tenor and pianist for the group. They are all members of White Oak Springs Baptist Church in Dallas, Georgia. The Harvest Trio feels God has brought them together for the purpose of praising Him in song. "The fields are truly white unto harvest and the labourers are few…"

A big part of the Harvest Trio's work is home missions. God has blessed them to be part of a gospel tent (ministry) which travels throughout the North Georgia area. They also enjoy singing in Nursing Homes, at street services, cottage prayer meetings, and revival services. They have a weekly radio program that has proven a blessing to many people.

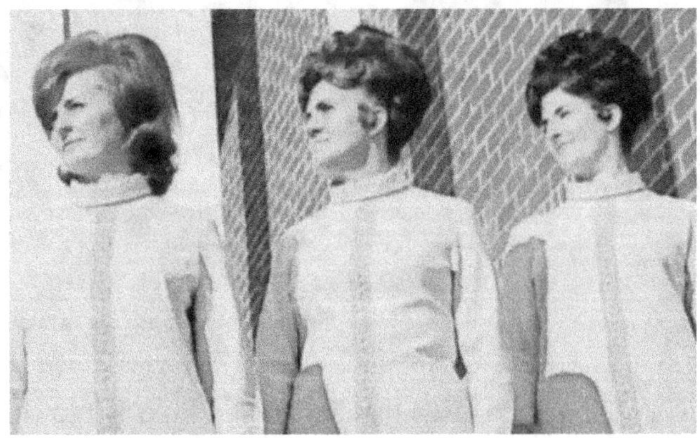

Virginia Boynton, Bertha Bankstone, and Sue Wix[47]

---

[47] Photo taken from cover of their album. Photo used with permission of White Oak Springs Baptist Church, who helped produced the album.

Appendix Fourteen
Why the Primitive Baptist Controversy occurred in Paulding County, Georgia, in 1867

One of the reasons why the Primitive Baptist Controversy came to a head in Paulding County, Georgia, in 1867 and 1868 could be the byproduct of the Chattahoochee Singing Convention that met at Pleasant Hill Baptist Church in Paulding County, Georgia, in 1866. Eight thousand people attended the singing convention at Pleasant Hill Baptist Church, which is in the same county as White Oak Springs Baptist Church. This convention was a fasola singing convention or a noninstrument singing convention.

One of the main doctrines, or positions, of the Primitive Baptists was that no musical instruments were to be used in their services. All music had to be vocal; therefore, Primitive Baptists would have had a strong presence at that meeting. And, as they spoke to other Baptists at the event, they would present their views that singing should be accompanied only by other harmonizing voices. Seeing eight thousand other fasola singing enthusiasts in one place would add support to the Primitive Baptist argument on the use (actually the non use) of instruments in church services.

The following quote comes from page 136 of Buell E. Cobb Jr.'s book the *Sacred Harp: A Tradition and Its Music*. This book was published by Brown Thrasher Books of the University of Georgia in 1978.

In its day the Southern Musical Convention was, in James's words, "the greatest organization of vocal musicians that ever met in Georgia." Similarly, the Chattahoochee remained for decades the largest gathering of singing enthusiasts in its area. Both conventions had suffered during the Civil War years; but while fasola singing in the southern region had generally diminished after the war, the Sacred Harp people in Georgia returned to the great conventions in droves. The 1866 convention of the Chattahoochee Convention was, by James' account, "the largest singing convention held in all the country." The assembly convened at Pleasant Hill Baptist Church in Paulding County, Georgia, on Thursday and dispersed the following Monday. Singers came from several states. The Sunday crowd, James reports, was an immense one—estimated at eight thousand people. As if to substantiate that estimate, James adds, "there were three wells close by, from which water to furnish the crowd was drawn. Before one o'clock they were drawn dry, and it was almost impossible to get water."

Bibliography

Primary Sources

Interview with Clara Mae Baggett on November 13, 2016
Interview with Gloria Caldwell Byrd on January 16, 2017
Interview with Jeff Byrd on January 16, 2017
Interview with Caroline Cohran on January 16, 2017
Interview with Kenneth Cohran on January 16, 2017
Interview with Ernest Gober January 30, 2017
Interview with Sandra Wyatt on April 6, 2017
Interview with Don Wix on April 20, 2017

Cornell, Nancy Jones. *1864 Census for Re-Organizing the Georgia Militia.* Genealogical Publishing Company, 2000.

Georgia. Paulding County. 1850–1920 U.S. Censuses, population schedule. NARA microfilm publication. Washington, D.C.: National Archives and Records Administration, n.d.

Tallapoosa [Georgia] Baptist Association. Yearly Tallapoosa (Georgia) Baptist Association Minutes: 1855–1982. Georgia Baptist Archives located at Mercer University, Macon, Georgia.

Secondary Sources

Austin, Jeannette Holland. *The Georgia Frontier, Vol. 3: Descendants of Virginia, North Carolina, and South Carolina Families.* Clearfield Publishers, 2009.

Cobb Jr., Buell E. *The Sacred Harp: A Tradition and Its Music.* Brown Thrasher Books of the University of Georgia: Athens, Georgia, 1978.

Redmond, LaGroon. *Cemeteries of Paulding County, Georgia.* Dallas, Georgia: Paulding County Historical Society, 1995.

Roberts, Lucien E. *A History of Paulding County.* Dallas, Georgia: self-published, 1933.

Sanders, Sherry Cooper. *My Brother ... My Son Kindle Edition.* Summerday Publishers, 2012.

Townsend, Leah. *South Carolina Baptists, 1670–1805.* Genealogical Publishing Company: South Carolina, 1935.

Voyles, Marie Butler. The First Hundred and Fifty Years of Pumpkinvine Baptist Church, Paulding County, Georgia. Self-published: Dallas, Georgia, 1995.

Warren, Mary Bondurant. Paulding County *Georgia Cemeteries.* Dallas, Georgia, 2009.

Paulding County Heritage Book Committee. *The Heritage of Paulding County, Georgia, 1832-1999.* Paulding County Historical Society. Dallas, Georgia, 1999.

Index of Pastors

Rev. Ed Ballew, 144

Rev. George Barnett, 32, 114, 142, 148, 245, 251

Dr. Walley Bee Bee, 144

Dr. Billy Bell, 164

Rev. E. J. Cain, 32, 116, 126, 245, 251

Elder Burrell M. Camp, 68, 71, 72

Rev. C. R. Campbell, 114

Rev. Paul E. Carter, 32, 124, 137, 245, 251

Rev. Charles Cheek, 31, 57

Rev. A. J. Coalson, 74,

Rev. William Coalson, 31, 73, 74, 75

Rev. Grover Cook, 32, 150

Rev. James A. Crabb, 32, 123, 124, 245, 251

Dr. James W. Crumpton, 144

Rev. J. H. Davis, 32, 83, 92, 101, 107, 108, 109, 147, 245, 251, 280

Rev. Larry G. Davis, ix, 32, 141, 178, 179, 180

Rev. H. M. Eubanks, 44

Rev. Newton Eubanks, 64, 65, 69, 70, 71

Rev. N. W. Eubanks, 31, 44, 64, 65, 68, 70, 71, 72

Rev. S. T. Gilland, 32, 95, 245, 251, 280

Rev. Roy Goodson, 32, 133, 135, 136, 245, 251, 258, 282,

Rev. Clarence Harris, 32, 190

Rev. J. I. Harris, 35, 36

Rev. James I. Harris, 3, 4, 31, (35), 36, 37, 38, 52, 82

Rev. J. J. Harris, 36,

Rev. Jesse Hitchcock, vii, 97, 245, 251

Dr. Curtis Hudson, 144

Rev. Maze Jackson, 143

Rev. G. B. Jenkins, 32, 94, 245, 251

Rev. Robert Jenkins, 144, 236, 237

Dr. Bill Kelly, 144

Rev. J. M. Key, 31, 77

Rev. Keith A. Lee, xi, 32, 107, 164, 165, 238, 239, 243

Rev. Herman H. Long, 32, 127, 131, 133, 245, 251, 280

Rev. George A. Maner, 113

Rev. H. T. R. Marks, 32, 99, 100, 108, 245, 251, 280

Dr. Ken Martin, 31, 193

Rev. T. B. McClung, 32, 96

Rev. Marion B. Moon, 32, (116), 118, 119, 123, 280

Rev. Henry B. Moore, 114

Rev. W. New, 53

Rev. J. H. Ogle, 31, 32, 36, 81, 82, 83, 84, 92, 93, 99, 108, 245, 251, 280

Rev. Earl Partain, 32, 193, 194, 195, 206, 241, 243

Rev. J. S. Reynolds, 31, 58

Rev. John R. Rice, 144

Rev. Luther Rice, 68

Rev. James Roberts, 3, 4, 37, 40, 46, 48, 49, 50, 51, 52, 53, 56, 78, 100, 133, 253

Rev. John Robinson, 32, 191, 192, 193

Rev. Lester Roloff, 144

Rev. Mel Rutter, 144

Rev. Chris Simpson, 32, 218, 234, 243, 272

Rev. Johnny Simpson, 14, 32, 218, 219, 243

Rev. F. M. Smith (also see Francis M. Smith), 31, 60, 61, 62, 63, 274, 275

Rev. Francis Monroe Smith, 60

Rev. J. A. Smith, x, xiv, 277, 278

Rev. Jasper Smith, vii, x, xiv, 97, 245, 251, 273, 274, 275, 276

Rev. John Augustine Smith, 278

Rev. W. B. Smith, 31, 63, 75, 76

Rev. Walter B. Smith, 76

Rev. Roy Stanford, 32

Rev. Ronnie Tibbitts, 164

Rev. Druey Tierce, 32, 190, 191

Dr. Ed F. Vallowe, 144
Rev. Jerry Vines, 143, 144
Rev. M. F. Waddell, 31, 87, 93, 245, 251, 281
Rev. Fred Watts, 32, 192
Rev. G. Fred Wigley, 32, 113, 115, 117, 245, 251, 281,
Rev. Charles Williams, viii, 14, 138, 139, 140, 143, 151, 162, 171, 173, 174, 175, 176, 178, 245, 251
Rev. Toney Willard, 32, 218
Rev. J. Edwin Wix, x, 12, 23, (114), (116), 119, 121, 122, 145
Rev. D. (Duncan) Wortham, 31, 85, 86, 87, 245, 251, 281
Rev. J. W. Womack, 32, 111, 112, 281

Index of Churches

Antioch Baptist Church in Whitesburg, Georgia, 171
Bethlehem Baptist Church in Haralson County, Georgia, 82
Beulahland, Baptist Church in Paulding County, Georgia, 114
Callie Harbin Baptist Church in Villa Rica, Georgia, 171, 175, 176
Corinth Baptist Church, Sumter County, GA, 74
Corner Baptist Church, Powder Springs, Georgia, 149
Double Springs Baptist Church in Paulding County, Georgia, 38
Dugdown Church in Haralson County, Georgia, 178
East Rome Church in Rome, Georgia, 179
Enon Baptist Church, in the Fairburn Baptist Association, 277
Fairview Baptist Church, Rockmart, Georgia, 128, 179
Faith Baptist Temple in Powder Springs, Georgia, 164
Fellowship Baptist Church in Cumming, Georgia, 238
First Baptist Church, Fairmount, Georgia, 83
First Baptist Church, Jacksonville, Florida, 143
Floyd Creek Baptist Church, Polk County, Georgia, 57
Friendship Baptist Church, Paulding County, Georgia, 57
Gateway Baptist Church, Dallas, Georgia, 176
Grace Baptist Church, Powder Springs, Georgia, 193
Happy Valley Baptist Church, Villa Rica, Georgia, 176

Harmony Grove Baptist Church, Dallas, Georgia, 176
High Shoals Baptist Church, Paulding County, Georgia, 114
Holly Springs Baptist Church, Paulding County, GA, 75, 81, 83
Hyde's Chapel Baptist Church, Conyers, Georgia, 193
McPherson Baptist Church, Paulding County, Georgia, 114
Merritt's Avenue Baptist Church, 146
Mt. Carmel Baptist Church, Fort Payne, Alabama, 179
Mt. Creek Baptist Church, Near Paulding County, Georgia, 135
Mt. Moriah Church, Paulding County, GA, 57
Mt. Olivet Baptist Church, Paulding County, Georgia, 57, 80, 82,
Mt. Zion Baptist Church, Cobb County, Georgia, 64, 82
New Georgia Baptist Church, Villa Rica, Georgia, 82, 176, 274
Peoples Baptist Church, Morrow, Georgia, 238
Pineywood Baptist Church, Rico, Fulton County, Georgia, 278
Pleasant Grove of Carroll County, Georgia, 83
Pleasant Hill Baptist Church, Polk County, Georgia, 83
Pleasant Hill Baptist Church, Paulding County, Georgia, 285
Pleasant Plains Baptist Church, Carroll County, Georgia, 38
Providence Baptist Church, Palmetto, Georgia, 277
Pumpkinvine Baptist Church, xii, 5, 6, 37, 40, 51, 52, 54, 65, 66, 72, 114, 115, 122,
Second Baptist Church, Boaz, Alabama, 171
Second Baptist Church, Dallas, Georgia, 149
Second Baptist Church, Douglasville, Georgia, 165
Second Baptist Church, Riverdale, Georgia, 176
Springville Baptist Church, Cobb County, Georgia, 35
Sweetwater Baptist Church, Douglas County, Georgia, 75, 96
Union Primitive Baptist Church, Paulding County, Georgia, 68
University Baptist Church, Brookhaven, Georgia, 238
Van Wert Baptist Church, Polk County, Georgia, 65, 80
Victory Baptist Church, Dallas, Georgia, 171
Victory Baptist Church, North Augusta, South Carolina, 176
Walter's Grove Baptist Church, Lexington, North Carolina, 234

Wayside Baptist Church, Dallas, Georgia, 164

Wimberly Hill Church, Cedartown, GA, 178

Yorkville Baptist Church, Rockmart, Georgia, 98

Index of Newspapers

Atlanta Constitution Newspaper, 98, 121, 149, 230

Atlanta Journal-Constitution, 232

Carroll Free Press, 63, 75

Dallas New Era, 98, 112, 230, 231, 232

Paulding New Era, 7, 14, 17, 19, 20, 43, 84, 85, 86, 88, 90, 91, 254

Christian Index, 73

Cullman (Alabama) Tribune-Gazette and Tribune, 87

Rockmart Journal, 118

Southern Baptist Journey, 171

Sword of the Lord Newspaper, 144

Schools

White Oak Springs School, 17,18, 19, 39

Draketown School, 109

Index

Abercrombie, Cindy, 181, 195, 207

Abercrombie, Crystal, 207,220

Abercrombie, Elaine, 181, 207, 220

Abercrombie, Vickey, 181, 195, 207, 220

Ackerman, Denise, 196, 207, 220

Acklin, Gail, 152, 181

Acklin, Melvin, 181

Acklin, Paul, 152, (220)

Acklin, Randy, 181, 207

Adair, Adaline Gann, 94

Adair, Amanda Sinyard, 94

Adair, Bozeman, 66

Adair, Caroline Evans, 66

Adair, James Lee, 66

Adair, Judith "Judy," 66, 94, 255, 263

Adair, H. R., 112

Adair, M. R., 93, 94, 95, 96, 99, 100, 107, 109, 110, (112), 279

Adair, Milton R., 94, 95

Adair, William Levi, 94

Akins, Glenda, 207, 220

Akins, Paula, 220

Agan, A. V., 152

Agan, Lindal, 152

Alford, Jean, 152

Alford, Johnny, 152

Alford, Sammy, 181, 220

Allen, Amanda, 240

Allen, Andrew, 196, 207, 240, 241

Allen, Ansley, 241

Allen, Cathy, 220

Allen, Dusty, 196

Allen, Eli, 241

Allen, Gene, 196

Allen, John, 207, 220

Allen, Jo Ann, ix

Allen, Joanna, 196, 207, 220, 240

Allen, Ralph, 196, 220, 240, 241

Ammonds, Mary Ann, 196, 207, 220

Ammonds, Mary Jane, 152, 181

Anthony, Donna E., 207

Arnold, C. H., 127

Arnold, Dick, 152, 181, 196, 207, 220

Arnold, Jana, 220

Atchenson, J. T., 135

Atchenson, Jewell, 114

Austin, Betty, 181, 196

Austin, Brenda, 152, 181, 196

Austin, Darcile, 220

Austin, Irma N, 152

Austin, James, 152, 181, 196, 207, 220

Austin, Linda, 152, 181, 196, 207, 220

Austin, Michelle, 196
Austin, Sherry, 196
Avant, Rhonda (Spruill), 207

Baggett, Ashley, 196
Baggett, Aubrey, 119, 125, 141
Baggett, Bell, 181, 196
Baggett, Betty, 181, 208, 220
Baggett, Billy, 181, 196, 208, 220
Baggett, Clara Mae, iii, ix, xi, 22, 118, 120, 141, 168, 180, 181, 196, 208, 221
Baggett, Claudie, 141
Baggett, Donna, 181, 221
Baggett, Edna Fae, 181, 196, 207
Baggett, Ester, 124
Baggett, Fae (Faye), 126, 133, 142
Baggett, Frankie, 196
Baggett, Glen, 117, 181, 196, 207
Baggett, Jessie, 196, 207, 221
Baggett, Kerrie, 196
Baggett, Lowell, 119, 126, 132, 133, 181, 196, 207, 221, 270
Baggett, Nora Lee, 124
Baggett, Rudy, 181, 196, 207
Baggett, Tom, 124, 126, 127, 279
Ballew, Ed, 144
Ballinger, Robbie, 168

Ballanger, Sherri, 168
Bandy, Matt, 102
Bankstone, Bertha, 283, 284
Bankstone, Danny, 181, 196, 207, 221
Bankstone, Kent, 152
Bankstone, Rock, 152
Bankstone, Rocky, 196
Baptist Pioneer Mission, 237
Barber, Dennis, 165, 196, 207, 221, 269
Barber, Jeanette, 208, 221
Barber, Jenny, 196
Barber, Kathy, 196, 208
Barber, Norma, 152
Barber, Travis, 196
Barnes, Roy (Governor), 121
Barnett, Connie, 181, 196, 208, 221
Barnett, George, 32, 114, 142, 148, 245, 251
Bates, Charlene, 196, 208, 221
Bates, Dana, 196
Baxter, Alan, 221
Baxter, Berdie, 279
Baxter, Betty, 196, 208, 221
Baxter, Brenda, 152, 181
Baxter, Buddie, 117
Baxter, C. G., 117
Baxter, Charles Gordon, 115, 117, 149, 260, 267, 279
Baxter, Clindon, 279
Baxter, D., 117

Baxter, Danny, 152, 208, 221, 231

Baxter, David, 152, 181, 196

Baxter, Dewey, 279

Baxter, Douglas, 152, 181, 191

Baxter, E. E., 50, 55

Baxter, Earlon F., 196

Baxter, Emily E., 50

Baxter, Emily "Kelly." 231

Baxter, Evelyn, 152, 181

Baxter, Jewel, 152, 181, 196, 208

Baxter, Jimmy, 231

Baxter, Jimmie Lynn, 152, 181

Baxter, Josie, 128

Baxter, Junior, 181, 208, 221

Baxter, Kimbal, 152, 181, 196

Baxter, Leona, 152, 260

Baxter, Levena, 196

Baxter, Linda, 135

Baxter, Lois, 182

Baxter, Lola, 152, 182, 196, 208, 232

Baxter, Loretta Croker, 231

Baxter, Lottie, 149, 152, 180, 181

Baxter, Lucious, 27, 28, 152, 169

Baxter, Lucious Baxter Lake, 132

Baxter, Marie, 152

Baxter, Marion, 140, 260

Baxter, Maybell, 152, 182, 196, 208, 221

Baxter, Mertha Lea, 149

Baxter, Minnie, 169, 260

Baxter, O. G., 117

Baxter, Randy, 152, 182, 196

Baxter, Sherry, 152, 182

Baxter, Stefanie, 182

Baxter, Tasker, 125

Baxter, Teresa, 221

Baxter, Tim, 152, 182, 196

Baxter, Vealer, 152, 182, 196

Baxter, W. H., 50, 55

Baxter, W. S., 117, 119

Baxter, Whitie, 152, 182

Bearden, Becky, 152, 168, 177, 180, 182, 191, 192, 195, 196, 207, 208, 220, 221

Bearden, Chris, 196, 208

Bearden, Jamie, 196

Bearden, Jason, 208

Bearden, Jean, 152, 182

Bearden, Junior (See Neal Bearden, Jr.)

Bearden, Neal (Junior), 152, 177, 182, 195, 196, 207, 208, 220, 221, 269

Bearden, Tammy Lee, 196, 208, 221

Bearden, Keith, 196

Bearden, Lavenna, 152, 182, 221

Bee Bee, Walley, 144

Bell, Billy, 164

Bennett Bullock's baptismal pool, xi, 27, 28

Beyers, Tonya, 208, 221

Bice, Jay, 152, 168, 172, 173, 174, 175, 272

Bice, Marvene, 152, 172, 175

Biggers, Karen, 208, 221

Blackmon, Rebecca Lynn, 182, 221

Blair, Mildred, 196, 208

Blair, Wanda, 196, 208

Bone, Eddie, 152, 182, 196

Bone, Virginia, 152

Boone, Matthew, 51

Boone, Sarah Roberts, 51

Bowen, Eddie, 208, 221

Bowen, Essie Powell, 196, 208, 221

Bowen, Heather, 208

Bowen, Regina, 208, 221

Bowen, Robby, 208

Bowen, Robert, 221

Boynton, Kenneth. 152, 182

Boynton, Kim, 152

Boynton, Virginia, 153, 182, 283, 284

Brackett, Marcy, 221

Bradley, C. B., 107, 260

Bradley, Edith, 260

Bradley, Ida, 111

Bragg, Lynn, 208, 221

Breedlove, Teresa, 196

Bricken, Connie, 153, 182, 196, 208

Brinson, Barbara Cason, 153

Brock, Lucinda, 256

Brock, Nancy, 256

Brown, Amanda Partain, 118

Brooks, Bobby, 135

Brooks, J. M., 135, 136, 141, 150, 170, 272

Brooks, Jim, 136

Brookshire, Candance, (197), 208

Brookshire, Candice, 197, (208)

Brown, Bessie, 118, 153, 180, 182

Brown, Bobbie, 167

Brown, C., 50

Brown, G. Louvenia Head

Brown, Grace, 119

Brown, H. M., 115, 116, 117, 118, 119, 124, 126, 127, 133, 267

Brown, Henry, 112, 117, 118, 279

Brown, Mrs. Henry, 117, (119)

Brown, Henry M., 260

Brown, J. Homer, 260

Brown, Marlene, 153

Brown, Michael, 197, 208, 221

Brown, Mildred, 208, 221

Brown, Robin, 177

Brown, Sharon, 153

Brown, Thomas J., 118

Brown, Tim, 177
Brown, Tom, 279,
Bryant, Bear (Coach), 193
Buckner, Lynda, 208
Bud Community, p. 90, 98
Bullock, Bennett, xi, 27, 28, 279
Bullock, Bennett Bullock's baptismal pool, xi, 27, 28
Bullock, Brenda K. Haggard, 153
Bullock, Mary Cooper, 55
Bullock, N. T., 55
Bullock, John Pickney, 67
Bullock, Judith "Judy" Adair Carter, 67, 97
Bullock, Linda, 182, 197, 201, 208
Bullock, Nettie, 125
Bullock, Nickalus Hawkin, 67
Bullock, Tom R.,136, 280,
Bullock, William, 67
Bulter, Cinda (Also see Butler), 109
Burmely, Cathy Cohran, 153, 182, 208
Burney, April, 208, 221
Burns, (Mrs.) Frances, 5, 40, 42, 54
Burns, Henry Hayes, 42, 43, 54
Burt, Claud, 170
Bush, Benjamin, 208, 221
Bush, Bonnia, 208

Bush, Norman, 208, 221
Bush, Randy, 208, 221
Bush, Roger, 208, 221
Butler Cinda (Bulter), 109
Butler, Emma, 266
Butler, Lela, 153, 182
Butler, Lonnie, 153, 182, 197, 197
Butler, Richard, 153, 182, 197, 208
Buzzard's Roost, 145
Byrd, Althea, 240
Byrd, Angela, 240
Byrd, Angie, 197
Byrd, Annie, 169
Byrd, Brenda, 153, 182
Byrd, Cainan, 240, 241
Byrd, Cathy, 192, 208, 240
Byrd, Claude T., 153, 182, 208, 221
Byrd, Francine, 153, 168
Byrd, Frank, 145, 146, 147, 148, 153, 168, 182, 192, 195, 197, 207, 208, 220, 239, 240, 241, 245
Byrd, Glenda, 153, 182, 268
Byrd, Gloria, vii, xi, 6, 14, 118, 123, 125, 126, 127, 134, 137, 145, 146, 148, 150, 151, 153, 168, 178, 182, 192, 193, 194, 197, 207, 208, 220, 221, 234, 239, 240, 241
Byrd, Hadassah, 241

Byrd, Hadley, 241
Byrd, Hannah, 241
Byrd, Heather, 240
Byrd, Jeff, vi, viii, x, xi, 16, 24, 107, 121, 122, 124, 127, 134, 137, 145, 146, 153, 179, 182, 191, 192, 195, 206, 208, 221, 240, 245, 268
Byrd, Jonathan, 240
Byrd, Kenneth (Kenny), 153, 171, 180, 182, 191, 192, 197
Byrd, Jane, 153, 182, 197, 221
Byrd, Joann, 153, 182
Byrd, Jr., 182
Byrd, Marcus, 240, 241
Byrd, Silas, 241

Cain, E. J., 32, 116, 126, 245, 251
Cain, Jewel, 126
Caldwell, Claude, 127, 153, 182
Caldwell, Emma, 153, 169
Caldwell, Gloria, 145, 146
Caldwell, Homer, 125, 153, 180, 182, 240, 241
Caldwell, Melissa, 182
Caldwell, Ola, 110, 119, 120, 125, 133, 153, 182, 240, 241
Caldwell, Owen, 241
Caldwell, Pete, 153, 182, 197, 208, 221, 241
Callahan, D. C. 197, 221
Campbell, C. R., 114

Camp, Al, 153, 182, 221
Camp, Burrell M., 68, 71, 72
Camp, Chester, 197
Camp, Diane, 207, 208
Camp, Elaine, 153
Camp, Ella Veal, 230
Camp, Evelyn, 221
Camp, Fannie, 221
Camp, Fannie Mae, 153, 182, 197
Camp, Harold, 208
Camp, Joe, 153, 168, 191, 192, 208, 221
Camp, Joy, 153
Camp, Lynn, 153, 182, 197, 221
Camp, Martha, 153, 182, 197, 208, 221
Camp, Nancy, 255
Camp, William T., 230
Carroll, Brandy, 197
Carroll, Brian, 197
Carroll, Denise, 197
Carroll, Joey, 197
Carroll, Tonya, 197, 208, 221
Carson, Charlie, 182
Carson, Nora, 182
Carson, Kathy, 182, 197, 221
Carson, Charlie, 182
Carter, Addie, 87, 94
Carter, Amanda 197, 209, 221
Carter, B. A., 127, 148, 169
Carter, Ben, 33, 123, 124, (126), 132, 133, 135, 137, 139, 148,

153, 168, 169, 182, 245, 268, 280

Carter, Bennett, 124, 126, 137

Carter, Brittany, 197, 221

Carter, Caleb, 197, 221

Carter, Calvin, 124

Carter, Chris, 153, 182

Carter, Darrel, 135, 137, 139, 141, 272

Carter, Delia, 15

Carter, Denise, 197, 209, 221

Carter, Effie, 116, 117, 124, 126, 135, 137, 153, 164, 168, 180, 182

Carter, Gail, 153, 182

Carter, Hettie, 124, 149, 169

Carter, J., 66, 67, 75, 77, 96

Carter, J. R., 87

Carter, James, 15, 66

Carter, James Rufus, 67

Carter, Janet, 182

Carter, Jennifer, 153, 182

Carter, Jill, 182

Carter, Joann, 197, 209

Carter, Joseph, 66, 95

Carter, John T., 124, 260

Carter, Josephine, 67, 266

Carter, Judith Adair, 255

Carter, Judy, 66

Carter, Mary Emma Wix, 260

Carter, Paul, 32, 124, 135, 137, 139, 141, 153, 169, 170, 182, 245, 251

Carter, R. T., 169

Carter, Richard J., 66, 67, 255

Carter, Richard T., 260, 280

Carter, Roben, 153, 195, 197, 207, 209, 220, 221, 269

Carter, Robert, 135, 139, 148, 153, 168, 180, 182, 191, 192, 197

Carter, Tom, 169

Carter, Thomas B., 67

Carter, Thomas M., 124, 169

Cason, Bertha Mae, 153, 182,197, 209, 222

Cason, Charlie, 127, 128, 268

Cason, Ernest, 153, 182, 197

Cason, Minnie S., 260

Cason, Norma Head, 128

Cason, Pearl, 262

Chambless, Mary Ann, 133

Champman, Bill, 153

Chatman, Hobart, 127, 133, 153

Champman, Retincy Hill, 48

Champman, Ruby, 153

Chappel, Debbie, 182

Chappel, Kay, 182

Cheek, Charles, 31, 57

Chepwood, Valarie 197, 209, 222

Childers, Diane, 209, 222

Clark, Annie Lou, 164, 191, 192

Clark, Annie Cole, 260

Clark, Clara, 117, 136

Clark, Celicie Moody, 20, 105, 153, 183, 197, 209, 222, 260, 264

Clark, Daley, 149

Clark, Fred, 169

Clark, George, 168

Clark, Georgia, 105, 153

Clark, Gertrude, 153

Clark, Irene, 153

Clark, Kimberly, 209

Clark, Lucy Leathers, 20

Clark, Marvin, 153, 169

Clark, Randy, 197, 272

Clark, Rhonda, 197

Clark, Samuel (Sammy), 19, 20, 105, 153, 183, 261

Clark, Sue, 183, 197, 222

Clark, T. W., 132, 135, 137, 139, 148, 191, 245, 271

Clark, Thomas L., 197, 209

Clark, Tommy, 153, 183

Clark, Toni, 197

Clark, W. L., 260

Clark, Wanda, 191, 192

Clark, William M., 20, 260, 261, 280

Clark, Woodrow, 127, 128, 129, 133, 153, 168, 183, 191, 192, 197, 209, 268

Clay, Shelby, 222, 239

Clifton, Connie, 197, 209

Coates, Robert, 148

Coalson, A. J., 74, 101, 109

Coalson, Harriet Eady, 73

Coalson, Oma Lois, 127

Coalson, William, 31, 73, 74, 75

Cobb, Buell E., 285

Cochran, Elise, 153

Cochran, Ethel, 126

Cochran, Fain, 153

Cochran, Mrs. Henry, 117

Cohran, Aaron, 197

Cohran, Amber, 197, 209

Cohran, Anthony, 209, 222

Cohran, Cardine, 148

Cohran, Caroline, 140, 141, 144, 148, 153, 161, 164, 168, 178, 180, 183, 197, 209, 222

Cohran, Denise, 141, 153

Cohran, Fred, 154

Cohran, Gladys, 154, 183, 197, 209

Cohran, Glenda, 154, 155, 183, 209

Cohran, Heather, 197

Cohran, Kathy, 197, 209, 222

Cohran, Kenneth, xi, 11, 25, 33, 111, 119, 134, 137, 138, 139, 140, 141, 144, 148, 154, 160, 161, 162, 164, 165, 168, 174, 175, 179, 180, 183, 191, 192, 195, 197, 206, 209, 220, 245, 268, 287

Cohran, Louise, 154

Cohran, Parks, 154, 183, 197, 209, 222
Cohran, Ruth, 154,183, 222
Cohran, Tony, 154, 183, 197
Cogburn, Fanny Roberts, 51
Cogburn, Zachariah, 51
Cole, Alma, 119, 120, 154, 183, 191, 232
Cole, Ana, 15
Cole, Annie, 260
Cole, Annie Mae, 154, 183, 197
Cole, Babe, 280
Cole, Barbara, 154, 183, 197, 209, 222
Cole, Bill, 154, 168, 183, 209
Cole, Becky, 154, 183
Cole, Betty, 149, 154
Cole, Boyd, 154, 168, 183, 197, 209, 222
Cole, C. A., 117
Cole, Cathy Allen, 209
Cole, Charlie, 129, 130, 261
Cole, Charles, 154, 180, 191, 192
Cole, Christy, 209
Cole, Claudia, 170
Cole, Clifford, 154, 170
Cole, Claude, 197
Cole, Cleveland, 168
Cole, Connie, 280
Cole, Curtis, 137, 139, 141, 150, 154, 170, 171, 180, 183, 191, 192, 197, 209, 222, 272

Cole, Daily, 15
Cole, Dana, 197, 222
Cole, Deanie, 183
Cole, Deloris, 154, 183, 195, 197, 209, 222
Cole, Dennie, 154
Cole, Dicy (Dicey) Sinyard, 89, 90
Cole, Elizabeth (Also see Lizzie Cole), 13, 51, 77, 78, 84, 85, 86, 88, 89, 90, 122, 261
Cole, Elizabeth "Betsy," 13, 51, 77, 78, 84, 85, 86, 88, 89
Cole, Ella, 125, 126
Cole, Elmer, 110
Cole, Floy T., 115, 154, 183, (197), 209, 222
Cole, Floyd, 197
Cole, Fonda, 154, 183, 198, 209, 222
Cole, Francine, 154, 183
Cole, Frances, 183, 198, 209, 222, 231
Cole, Fred Norman, 232
Cole, G. C., 280
Cole, Sr., G. W. Cole, (Also see George W. Cole), (died 1908), 33, 86, 88, 90, 94, 95, 96, 99, 100, 101, 261, 265, 280
Cole, Jr., G. W. Cole, (Also see George W. Cole), 97, 106, 112, 236, 261, 270

Cole, Sr., George W. (died 1908), vii, (33), 86, (88), 90, 91, 101

Cole, Jr., George W., 91, 97

Cole, Mrs. George, 122

Cole, Georgia, 261

Cole, Gertrude, 15,

Cole, Gloria Jane, 232

Cole, H. L., 169, (262), 280

Cole, Hattie, 154, 183, 198

Cole, Henry L., 262

Cole, Henry R., 261

Cole, Herman, 119, 154, 170, 232

Cole, Homer, 109, 280

Cole, J. C., 100

Cole, J. M., 280

Cole, J. T., 133

Cole, J. R., 108

Cole, J. Ray, 232

Cole, J. Robert, 91, 92, 93, 99, 100, 107, 108, 109, 112, 280

Cole, J. W., 280

Cole, Jacob, 13, 84, 85, 89

Cole, Jake, 135, 280

Cole, James M., 89

Cole, James N., 261

Cole, Jane, 15, 154, 183, 222, 262

Cole, Jesse, 103

Cole, Jimmy, 154, 183, 209, 222

Cole, JoAnn, 209, 222

Cole, Jodie, 209, 222

Cole, Joel, 222

Cole, John, 103, 117, 127, 128, 129, 130, 280

Cole, John Marion, 261

Cole, John R., 89, 90

Cole, John T., 268

Cole, John W., 261

Cole, Joy, 198, 209, 222

Cole, Josie, 117, 154

Cole, Kansas, 154, 169, 262

Cole, Kelli (Moore), 209

Cole, Kim, 154

Cole, Kristi (Payne), 209

Cole, Landry, 154, 198

Cole, Larry, 154, 183, 222

Cole, Larry, Jr., 154, 183

Cole, Lafayette, 15, 112

Cole, Leona, 170

Cole, Lessie, 147, 154, 183, 198, 222

Cole, Lincoln, 136, 139, 148, 168, 169, 175, 268, 280

Cole, Lizzie, 154, 183, 191

Cole, Lola, 154

Cole, Louisa Sinyard, 87, 88, 91

Cole, Mahala, 89

Cole, Mary, 89, 103, 124, 198, 209, 222, 261, 262

Cole, Mary Frances Roberts, 103, 124

Cole, Mary Fuller, 89

Cole, Mary Louisa, 261

Cole, Martha, 261

Cole, Mattie, 198

Cole, Maudie, 15

Cole, Melisa, 154

Cole, Mildred, 136, 154, 175

Cole, Milton, 137, 140, 262

Cole, Minnie, 236, 261, 262

Cole, Mollie Wilson, 106, 154

Cole, Monnie, 116

Cole, Nathan, 133, 280

Cole, Oscar, 154, 183

Cole, Pearlie (Pearl), 154, 170, 262

Cole, Peggy, 209, 222

Cole, Quiller, 15, 112, 129, 130, 280

Cole, Radar, 15, 100, 261

Cole, Ralph, 169, 232

Cole, Ramy (Ranney?), 15

Cole, Ranney, 280

Cole, Ray, 133, 145, 147, 148, 154, 168, 179, 183, 198, 209, 222, 245, 268

Cole, Renford, 154, 191, 192, 198, 209, 222

Cole, Roger, 154, 183, 195, 198, 209, 222

Cole, Robert (also see J. Robert Cole), 139, 148, 191

Cole, Rosie, 169

Cole, Roy, 209

Cole, Rusty, 209, 222

Cole, Sabra, 89

Cole, Samuel Melvin, 262

Cole, Sammy, 154, 166, 180, 183, 191

Cole, Sallie, 262, 265

Cole, Sarah, 54, 100, 103, 113, 119, 262

Cole, Sarah M. Waites, 89

Cole, Shane, 154, 183, 191

Cole, Susanah, 89, 90

Cole, Texaner, 264

Cole, Thersey, 149, 262

Cole, Tim, 15, 119, 120, 133, 135, 145, 149

Cole, Tracy, 154, 183

Cole, Vanda, 154

Cole, Venie, 15

Cole, Vonda, 183, 209

Cole, Vernon, 28, 132, 133, 148, 168, 169, 268, 280

Cole, W. B., 47

Cole, W. L., 169

Cole, W. T., 119, 130, 232, (262), 280

Cole, Walter, 102, 106, 107, 112, 262, 267

Cole, Wafford, 280

Cole, Wendy, 183, 209, 222

Cole, Whittic, 261

Cole, William, 89, 90, 232, 262

Cole, Wofford, 100

Cole, Z. C., 107, 108, 109, 280

Connally, W. C. (doctor), 254

Collins, Annette, 154, 209, 222

Collins, Ben, 154
Collins, Kathy, 154
Collins, Kaylie, 222
Community of Bud, p. 90, 98
Cook, Grover, 32, 150
Cook, Larry, 183, 198
Cooper, Amonda, 154, 183, 198
Cooper, C. B., 280
Cooper, Jane, 45, 46, 47, 55, 81
Cooper, James, 45, 46, 47, 55
Cooper, James N., 46, 67
Cooper, John, 45, 46, 47, 55
Cooper, Lavinia, 278
Cooper, Lucy Hitchcock, 46, 55
Cooper, Martha, 47
Cooper, Mary, 45, 55
Cooper, Mary Catherine Wheat, 55
Cooper, Moses, 40, 45, 46, 47, 55
Cooper, N., 40, 45, 58, 66, 75, 77, 78, 80, 81
Cooper, Nathan, 45, 47, 48, 55, 81
Cooper, Sarah, 45, 47, 55
Cooper, Susan Ann, 278
Cooper, Tracy, 222
Copeland, Albert Dewey, 235
Copeland, Shirley, 209, 222
Copeland, Wanda, 222
Copeland, Wayne, 209, 222
Copeland, Willie Mae Lancaster, 235

Crabb, James A., 32, 123, 124, 245, 251
Creel, Elizabeth, 97, 253
Criswell, Billy, 209, 222
Criswell, Diane, 198, 209, 222
Criswell, Linda Fay, 209, 222
Criswell, Sherry, 209, 222
Croker, Candy, 198, 209, 222
Crowe, Joey, 198
Crumpton, James W., 144
Culver, Lynn, 198, 209, 222
Cummings, Denise, 210

Daniel, Annette, 183, 198, 210, 222
Daniel, Emma, 112
Daniel, Ida, 154, 183, 198
Daniel, J. M., 111, 112, 136, 267, (280)
Daniel, John, 280
Daniel, Mrs. J. D., 119
Daniel, Josie, 112
Daniel, Ida, 112
Daniel, Nellie, 154, 183, 198
Daniel, Oda, 112
Daniel, Opal, 112
Daniel, Sam, 112
Darbry, Angie, 183, 198, 210, 222
Davis, April, 198
Davis, Barry, 178, 183
Davis, Clara, 183, 198
Davis, Daphne, 210

Davis, Darlene, 183, 198, 210, 222

Davis, David, 198, 210

Davis, Donnie, 183, 198, 210, 222

Day, Ezell, 154

Dayal, George, 280

Davis, J. H., 32, 83, 92, 101, 107, 108, 109, 147, 245, 251, 280

Davis, Jerry, 198, 210, 222

Davis, Jimmy, 183, 195, 198, 222

Davis, Juanita, 178, 183

Davis, Kaye, 178, 183

Davis, Larry G., ix, 32, 141, 178, 179, 180

Davis, Lisa 198

Davis, Loy 198, 207, 210, 222

Davis, Lynn, 198

Davis, Mary, 210, 222

Davis, Teresa, 198

Davis, Traci, 178, 183

Daughtery, Bob, 135, 272

Day, Larry, 154, 175, 180, 183

Day, Lennie, 154, 183, 210, 222

Davis, Lisa, 210

Day, Margaret, 154, 175, 183, 198

Davis, Martha 198, 210, 222

Day, Pete, 155, 184

Day, Ronnie, 155, 184, 210, 222

Day, Tammy, 184

Day, Vanessa, 155, 184

Day, Veronica, 155, 184

Dean Nathan (Senator), 14

Dean, Mrs. Nathan, 14

Deems, Ann, 210

Deems, Gordon, 198, 210, 222

Deems, Tonya, 198

Denton, Kay, 155, 184, 198, 210, 222

Denton, Patricia, 155, 184, 198, 210, 222

Dockery, Annette, 198, 210, 222

Dockery, Mark, 175, 198, 235

Dockery, Marie, 175, 198, 235

Dockery, Randy, 198, 210, 222

Dodd, Ernie, 192

Dodd, Mary, 223

Dodd, Shar-main, 155, 184, 198, 210

Dodd, W. A., 108, 109, 280

Dodson, Alene, 210, 223

Dotson, J. D., 192

Dudley, David, 198

Drummond, Anthony, 155, 184

Drummond, Pauline, 155, 177, 184

Drummond, Robert, 155, 184

Dudley, Elaine, 198, 210, 223

Dudley, John, 184, 198, 210, 223

Dudley, Lloyd, 198, 210, 223

Dudley, Renee, 198
Duke, Wesley, 155, 184, 198, 210, 223
Dunn, Becky, 198, 210, 223
Dunn, Leeann, 210, 223
Dutton, Ricky, 155
Duvall, Thomas Lee Jr., 210, 223
Dykes, Mildred, 184, 210, 223
Dykes, Anthony, 198, 210, 223
Dykes, Craig, 198
Dykes, Michael, 198, 223
Dykes, Mildred, 198, 210, 223
Dyre, E., 108
Dyer, JoAnn, 184
Dyer, Michael, 198, 210

Eady, Harriet, 73, 77
Earwood, Donna, 210, 223
Earwood, Joel, 210, 223
Edwards, J. H., 35, 40, 43, 54
Edwards, Mrs. J. H., 54
Edwards, John H., 40
Edwards, Tony, 184, 199, 210, 223
Ellis, Becky, 199, 210, 223
Ellis, Debbie, 199, 210, 223
Ellis, Janette, 210, 223
Elrod, Angie, 155, 184
Elrod, Chris, 210
Elrod, Tammie, 155, 184, 210, 223
England, Joan, 199, 210, 223

England, Stephanie, 199
Eskew, Danny, 155, 184, 199, 210, 223
Eskew, Sharon, 155, 184, 199, 210, 223
Estes, Bonnie, 199, 210, 223
Ethenridge, Cynthia, 199, 210, 223
Ethenridge, Marie, 199, 210
Eubanks, Angeline, 44, 54, 68
Eubanks, John Eubanks, 44, 46, 54
Eubanks, H., 40, 45, 58
Eubanks, H. M., 44, 66
Eubanks, Hared, 44, 51, 54, 70
Eubanks, Hosea, 44, 51, 54, 68
Eubanks, Hosea Marion, 44, 68
Eubanks, J. H., 43
Eubanks, James, 44, 70
Eubanks, John, 44, 51, 64, 65, 70
Eubanks, Lenaan (Leann), 44, 54, 64
Eubanks, N. W., 31, 44, 64, 64, 65, 66, 68, 70, 71. 72
Eubanks, Newton, 44, 64, 65, 69, 70, 71
Eubanks, Sarah, 44, 46, 51, 54, 64
Eubanks, Susana B. Leathers, 44
Evans, Caroline, 66
Evans, Debra Thompson, 169

Evans, Irma Ruth (Knight), 232
Evans, Jaynell, 155
Evans, Ruth, 184, 199, 210, 223
Evans, Tammy, 199
Evans, T. C., 155, 170, 171
Evans, Wayne, 210, 223
Everidge, Wayne, 155, 184, 199, 210

Fairchild, Sheila, 184, 199, 210, 223
Fambrough, Jack, 180, 181, 191, 192
Farr, Oree, 155, 184
Farr, Marvene, 171
Farr, Pam, 210, 223
Farr, Randy, 210, 223
Ferguson, Bill, 155, 184, 199, 210
Ferguson, Butch, 155, 184, 199, 210, 223
Ferguson, Edith, 199, 223, 235
Ferguson, Ray, 155, 184, 199, 223
Ferguson, Sandy, 155, 184
Ferguson, Vickie, 155, 184
Fennell (Also see Finnell)
Fennell, Edna, 164, 184, 191
Fennell, Horace, 171, 180, 184, 191, 192
Fennell, Judy, 184
Fennell, Gloria, 184
Ferrell, Adam, 199, 210, 223

Ferrell, Christy, 211, 223
Ferrell, Dixie, 199
Ferrell, Doug, 199
Ferrell, Ginny, 199
Ferrell, Michael, 199
Ferrell, Richard, 199
Fields, Ada, 135
Fields, Cathy, 223
Fields, Edward, 155, 184, 199
Fields, Frances, 155
Fields, Felix, 184
Fields, Jeanette, 199
Fields, Jobia, 199
Fields, Joseph, 181, 191, 192
Fields, Joy, 199
Fields, Kathy, 199
Fields, Lorene, 184
Fincher, Dickie, 155, 174, 272
Fincher, Herbert, 168, 171
Fincher, Melinda, 155
Ford, Macajah M., 89
Ford, Mahala Cole, 89
Fowler, Dan, 199, 211, 223
Fowler, Shirley, 199, 211, 223
Freeman, Chad, 199, 211, 223
Freeman, Chris, 199, 211, 223
Freeman, Florine, 199, 211
Freeman, Lester, 135
Freeman, Rosa, 199, 211, 223
Freeman, Susan, 184, 199, 211, 223
Fristad, Amanda, 211, 223
Fristad, Candi, 211, 223

Fristad, Jim, 211, 223

Fristad, Rhonda, 211, 223

Fuller, Alma, 110

Fuller, Amy, 155, 184, 199, 211, 223

Fuller, Berdie, 155, 184, 199

Fuller, Betty Ann, 155, 184, 199, 211, 223

Fuller, Carrie, 110

Fuller, Dorothy, 168, 211, 223

Fuller, Dossie, 280

Fuller, G. W., 112

Fuller, Hettie, 192

Fuller, J. O., 155, 184, 199, 211, 223

Fuller, Jimmy, 155, 184, 199, 211, 223

Fuller, John, 111

Fuller, Joyce, 155, 184, 199, 211, 223

Fuller, Katie, 110, 112, 264, 264

Fuller, Lizzy, 126

Fuller, Mary, 89

Fuller, Oliver, 280

Fuller, S. Elizabeth (Lizzie), 142, 262

Fuller, Minnie Lee, 199

Fuller, T. J., (also see Tom Fuller), 111, 112, 113, 117, 119, 120, 124, 126, 127, 133, 141, (262), 267, 270, 280

Fuller, Tom, 22, 107, 111, 129, 141, 262, 280

Fuller, Ware, 280

Furr, Angie Lee, 155, 184

Furr, Larry, 155, 184

Gamel, Annie Lou, 129

Gamel, Charles, 133, 135, 148

Gamel, Clifton, 280

Gamel, Clyde, 155, 180

Gamel, Estelle, 168

Gamel, Florence, 122

Gamel, Gene, 133

Gamel, Glenda, 155

Gamel, J. C., 280

Gamel, L. K., 155, 199, 211

Gamel, Mildred, 155, 184, 199, 211

Gamel, Nettie, 112

Gamel, Rufus, 155, 170

Gamel, Snote, 155, 185, 199

Gamel, Snowden, 280

Gamel, Sylvia, 199

Gann, Adaline, 94

Ganues, Jackson, 244

Ganues, Yelenne, 244

Garner, Gerrill, 230

Garner, Foster, 155, 185

Garner, J. S., 77

Garner, Randy, 185, 199, 211, 224, 230, 231

Garner, Randall, 233

Garner, Mary Jo Yearty, 230

Garner, S. L., 77
Garner, Treva, 185, 199, 211, 224, 233
Garnett, Ann, 199, 211, 224
Gault, John, 211, 224
Gaylord, Glenda, 155, 185, 199, 211
Gazaway, Clark, 110
Gazaway, Guy, 132, 133, 135, 137, 139, 140, 149, 270, 271
Gazaway, Mrs. Guy, 117, 137
Gazaway, J. J., 280
Gazaway, Mertha, 139, 148, 149
Gazaway, R. G., 245
Gazaway, R. S., 132, 148, 271
George, Delilah, 155, 185, 199, 211, 224
George, Dorothy, 155
Gilland, S. T. (also see Stephen T. Gilland), 32, 95, 245, 251, 280
Gilland, Stephen T., 95, 280
Gilland, Sarah Ida Wyatt, 95
Glass, Felicia, 199, 211, 224
Gober, Carolyn, 138, 155, 185, 199, 211, 211
Gober, Ernest, 191, 192, 199, 211, 224, 268
Gober, George Edward, 169
Gober, George Ernest, viii, xi, 124, 132, 133, 135, 137, 138, 139, 148, 155, 168, 179, 180,
185, 191, (192), 193, 195, 199, 206, 211, 220, 224, 268
Gober, Steve, 185, 199, 211, 224
Godfrey, Bobbi, 167, 211, 224
Godfrey, Christy, 199
Godfrey, Colin, 167, 200, 211, 224
Godfrey, Connie, 200
Godfrey, Greg, 167, 200, 211
Godfrey, Jeff, 165, 167, 211
Godfrey, Jerry, 168, 180, 200, 269
Godfrey, Lynn, 168
Goodson, Roy, 32, 133, 135, 136, 245, 251, 258, 282
Goosby, Lucile, 155
Gravette, Jeff, 200, 224
Gravette, Kelly, 200, 211, 224
Gravette, Pauline, 185, 211, 224
Gravette, Randall, 200
Gravette, Wendy, 200, 211, 224
Gregory, Tony, 211, 224
Green, Becky, 200
Green, Jimmy, 272
Green, Laynette, 200, 211, 224
Green, Minnie Husley, 149
Green, Missy, 200
Griffith, Christi, 200
Griffith, Dianne, 200
Gray, Joann, 224
Grimsley, Frank, 185, 200, 224
Gulledge, Dusty, 211, 224

Gurley, Annie Mae, 117, 155, 185, 200, 211, 224
Gurley, Martha, 155, 185

Hackney, Teresa, 200, 211, 224
Hagan, Andy, 200, 211, 224
Haggard, Debra Cole, 155, 185, 220, 211
Hale, Hattie, 155
Haley, Nancy Caroline, 81
Hall, Jean, 155, 185, 200, 211
Haney, Belle, 15
Haney, Tabitha, 211
Hannah, Cindy, 156, 185, 200, 211
hard-shell Baptists, 69
Hardy, Alta, 211
Hardy, David, 185
Hardy, Elaine 211, 224
Hardy, Gerald, 185
Hardy, J. C., 137, 156, 185, 211
Hardy, Randy, 156, 185, 200, 211
Hardy, Scott, 224
Harness, Cassie, 185, 200, 211, 224
Harness, Shirley, 185, 200
Harness, Steve, 185
Harness, Stoney, 185
Harper, Hiram, 280
Harper, Mary Alice, 262
Harris, Agnes, 115

Harris, Amy, 5, 36, 40, 42, 43, 54
Harris, Arnold, 263
Harris, Bell, 115, 156
Harris, C., 77, 78, 86, 88
Harris, Celia, 5, 40, 42, 43, 54
Harris, Clarence, 32, 190
Harris, Clinton, 156
Harris, Craven, 5, 40, 41, 42, 43, 45, 51, 52, 54, (77), (78), 274
Harris, D. E., 115, 117, 126, 129, 130, 267, 280
Harris, Daniel Erving, 115, 280
Harris, Daniel T., 42
Harris, David, 42, 99, 263
Harris, D. G., 126, 280
Harris, David G., 126
Harris, Dura, 170
Harris, Elicia, 90
Harris, Elijah, 42, 43, 51, 54
Harris, Elizabeth, 5, 40, 41, 42, 43, 54
Harris, Erving, 263
Harris, Irwin, 119
Harris, Isabel, 180
Harris, Floy T. Cole, 115
Harris, Francis Elizabeth, 42
Harris, Hannah, 42
Harris, James I., 3, 4, 31, 35, 36, 37, 38, 52, 82
Harris, J. D. 117
Harris, J. J., 36, 117

Harris, James, 37, 123

Harris, James J. (born 1847), 36

Harris, Jesse (Jessie), 15, 112, 113

Harris, John D., 117, 263

Harris, Kenny, 156, 185, 200, 211, 224

Harris, Linda, 156, 185, 211, 224

Harris, Lois, 127

Harris, Lon, 119

Harris, Marion, 123

Harris, Myra, 124, 156, 185, 200, 212, 224

Harris, Mary Ann, 42, 99, 263

Harris, Mary Louise Leatherwood, 106, 263

Harris, Metie Lindsey (Meedie Lindsey), 115, 263

Harris, Ola, 125, 240, 241

Harris, Ollie, 129, 130

Harris, Nancy, 41

Harris, Penelope, 5, 40, 42, 54

Harris, Pleasant, 42

Harris, Ralph, 119, 120, 123, 124, 126, 127, 156, 185, 200, 268, 270

Harris, Ruby, 115, 123, 156, 185, 200

Harris, Samuel, 42

Harris, Sarah, 5, 40, 42, 43, 54

Harris, Shirley, 200, 212, 224

Harris, Tempie Rainey, 263

Harris, Thomas, 42

Harris, Thomas A., 42

Harris, Thomas J., 36

Harris, William Alonzo, 42, 106, 263, 280

Harris, W. A., 102, 106, 107, 108, 109, 110, 112, 119, 123, 136, 267, 280

Harris, W. J., 99

Harris, William J., 42

Harris, William Jackson, 99, 263

Hart, Faye, 185, 195, 200, 212, 224

Hart, Jim (James), 185, 200

Hatcher, Ann, 156, 224

Hatcher, Carl, 156

Hatcher, George, 156

Hayes, Dura, 156

Hayes, Joe I., 156, 185, 200, 212, 224

Head, C. O., 15

Head, Dan, 15

Head, Paul, 15

Heath, Debra Payne, 212, 224

Heaton, John R., 64, 65

Hembree, Margaret, 156, 185, 212

Henderson, Arnold, 135, 137

Henderson, Aubry, 156, 280

Henderson, Bessie, 185, 212, 224

Henderson, Emmett, 180

Henderson, Freddie, 156, 185, 212, 224
Henderson, Jean, 156, 168, 185, 212
Henderson, Lois, 185, 212, 224
Henderson, Louella, 130
Henderson, O. J., 109, 110
Henderson, Ola Mae, 156, 185
Henderson, Robert, 185, 212, 224
Henderson, Tony, 156, 185, 191
Henderson, Traci, 224
Herington, Sandra Jo, 224
Herrin, Tabitha, 78
Hicks, Ada Beth Roberts, 100
Hicks, Aileen, 156, 185
Hicks, Barbara, 156, 185, 212, 224
Hicks, Barbara, 224
Hicks, Charlene, 156, 185
Hicks, Debra, 170, 212
Hicks, Dennie, 156, 185
Hicks, Frankie, 185
Hicks, J. B., 156, 185
Hicks, J. C., 156, 185, 233
Hicks, John Columbus "J. C.," 233
Hicks, Josie, 156, 185, 212
Hicks, Kathy, 185, 212, 224
Hicks, Kim, 224
Hicks, Mack, 156, 185, 212, 224

Hicks, Marie, 156, 185, 212, 224
Hicks, Marvine, 156, 185, 212, 224, 232
Hicks, Maudie, 156, 185, 212, 224
Hicks, Nancy, 156, 185
Hicks, O. K., 156, 180
Hicks, Ola, 156, 185, 212
Hicks, Sally, 156, 186, 212, 224, 233
Hicks, S. O., 109
Hicks, Sue, 156
Hicks, Treva Nell, 156, 231
Hill, Luanne, 212
Hill, Stephen, 212
Hitchcock, A. J., 79
Hitchcock, A. Jack, 79
Hitchcock, Alice, 126, 127
Hitchcock, Bell, 79
Hitchcock, Bennett, 156, 186, 191
Hitchcock, C. B., 107, 280
Hitchcock, Carl, 125
Hitchcock, Carolyn, 156, 186, 200, 212, 224
Hitchcock, Carey, 15, 126, 263
Hitchcock, Charles Toler, 79
Hitchcock, Cumi, 11, 79, 253, 254, 255
Hitchcock, Emma Cornelia, 133
Hitchcock, Estella Louisa, 79
Hitchcock, F. E., 79

Hitchcock, Flossie Bell, 263

Hitchcock, Frances Pace, 80

Hitchcock, Hallie, 156

Hitchcock, Henry Grisson, 79

Hitchcock, J., 78, 80, 84, 86, 88

Hitchcock, Jebez Caswell, 79

Hitchcock, Jesse D. Glen, 79

Hitchcock, Jesse, vii, 64, 65, 66, 67, 78, 79, 80, 84, 92, 93, 94, 95, 97, 98, 99, 100, 107, 109, 110, 133, 251, 253, 254, 263, 273, 280

Hitchcock, Jesse William, 78, 97, 98, 254

Hitchcock, John, 46, 51, 64, 67, 77, 78, 79, 110, 112, 133, 263, 280

Hitchcock, John H., 78, 263

Hitchcock, John Matthew, 67, 78, 79, 80, 133

Hitchcock, John Oliver, 79

Hitchcock, Joseph, 79

Hitchcock, Josephine Carter Wix, 67

Hitchcock, Judith "Judy" Adair, 67 79, 94, 97, 263

Hitchcock, Keith, 156, 186, 200, 212, 224

Hitchcock, Leona Madora, 79

Hitchcock, Lessie, 147

Hitchcock, Louise, 78, 79

Hitchcock, Lucy, 46, 78, 79

Hitchcock, Mary, 11, 46, 51, 64, 78, 79, 133, 263

Hitchcock, Mary A., 79, 263

Hitchcock, Mary Jane Toler, 78, 79, 80, 86, 88, 94, 97, 98, 253, 254, 263

Hitchcock, Martha, 79

Hitchcock, "Merucey," 79

Hitchcock, M. S., 79

Hitchcock, Paula, 212

Hitchcock, "Polly" Roberts, 51, 78

Hitchcock, Ove, 265

Hitchcock, Overton Alberton, 78, 79, 80

Hitchcock, Ruby, 156, 186, 200, 212, 224

Hitchcock, Tabitha Herrin, 78, 79

Hitchcock, Talithia Cumi, 79, 254, 255

Hitchcock, Thersey, 262

Hitchcock, William Oscar, 79, (98)

Hitchcock, W. O., 98

Hoffman, Curt, 200, 212, 224

Holcomb, Geraldine, 212

Holcombe, J. A., 83

Holcomb, Jerry, 186, 201, 212, 224

Holcomb, Martha, 186, 201, 212, 224

Holder, Geraldine, 156, 186, 201, 212, 225

Holder, Hollie, 156

Holder, Keith, 156

Holder, Phylis, 186, 201, 212, 225

Holder, Sandra, 156, 186, 201, 212, 225

Holland, Laura, 156, 186, 201, 212, 225

Hollis, Amy (born 1838), 37

Hollis, Burma, 156, 180

Hollis, Evaline, 37

Hollis, Darrell, 225

Hollis, Jane, 36

Hollis, Lillie, 186, 201, 212

Hollis, Lynn, 201

Hollis, Mahala, 36

Hollis, Mary (born 1836), 36

Hollis, Mary Amy Miller (born 1810), 36

Hollis, Sarah, 36

Hollis, W. T., 108, 280

Holmes, Cheyeene, 186

Holmes, Denise, 186

Holmes, Edna, 186, 201, 212, 225

Holt, Alene, 212

Holt, Ronald, 212

Holt, Rayburn, 186, 212, 225

Horner, Betty, 232

Hopkins, E. A., 230

Hopkins, Sharon, 201, 212, 225

Howard, Lucious F., 264

Horton, Sue, 201, 212, 225

Hudgins, Pat, 201, 212, 225

Hudson, Curtis, 144

Hudson, Mary Louisa Cole, 261

Hulsey, Alton, 156, 186, 201, 212

Hulsey, Bernice, 156, 186

Hulsey, Cliff, 156, 186, 201, 225

Hulsey, Debra, 156

Husley, Lillie, 186, 212, 225

Hulsey, Mary, 156, 186, 201, 211, 225

Hunt, Mary Jane, 65

Hurst, LuAnne, 186, 201, 212

Huston, Angie, 201

Hutchenson, Dovie, 156, 186, 191

Hutcherson, Offord, 124

Indians, 46, 63, 247, 249

Israel, Sue, 212, 225

Ivery, Cecil, 186, 201, 212, 225

Ivey, Bufford, 170

Ivey, Cindy, 201, 212, 225

Ivery, David, 186, 201, 212, 225

Ivery, Edna, 186, 212

Ivey, Edith, 201, 225

Ivey, Jackie, 186, 225

Ivery, Randy, 186, 201, 212, 225

Jackson, Hattie, 201, 212, 225

Jackson, Maze, 144
Jackson, Reuben, 135, 136
Jacobs, Jo, 156
Jacobs, Walter, 156
Jennings, Becky, 186
Jennings, Margaret, 237
Jennings, Parnick, 237
Jenkins, Ann, 156, 186, 201
Jenkins, Boyd Lee, 237
Jenkins, G. B., 32, 94, 245, 251
Jenkins, J. A., 280
Jenkins, Luanne, 157
Jenkins, Nancy, 157, 186, 237
Jenkins, Ovie Lee Tidwell, 237
Jenkins, Ricky, 186
Jenkins, Robbie, 157, 186
Jenkins, Robert, 144, 151, 157,
168, 170, 171, 180, 186, 237,
272, (280)
Jenkins, Robert (Mrs.), 168
Jenkins, Roger, 157
Johns, Lillie Mae, 186, 201,
212, 225
Johnson, Lisa, 186, 201, 212,
225
Johnston, Ann, 202
Johnston, Roy, 202
Johnston, Rita, 202
Johnston, Tim, 202
Jordan, Ines, 186
Jones, John, 201, 212, 225
Jones, Juanita, 178

Jones, Larry, 157, 186, 201,
212, 225
Jones, Myrtle, 201
Jordan, Inez Sue, 201, 212, 225
Jordan, J. A., 108, 109
Jordan, Landrum, 157
Jordan, Marie, 157
Jordan, Mildred, 232
Jordan, Martha, 157, 186
Kaplan, Loretta, 201, 212, 225
Kelley, Lena, 167
Kelly, Bill, 144
Kelly, Linda, 157
Kemp, Andrew, 109, 280
Kemp, H. H., 100, 102, 107,
108, 267
Kemp, H. Hendred, 101, 280
Kemp, Nara, 108
Key, J. M., 31, 77
Key, Sherry, 201, 212, 225
Kilpatrick, Charmane, 157
Kilpatrick, Denman, 157
Kinney, Ada, 135, 157, 186
Kinney, H. L. (Red), 132, 133,
(134), 135, 136, 137, 139,
(148), 157, 180, 268, 271, 280
Kinney, Herbert "Red", 134,
139, 148
Kinney, Ross, 157, 186, 212,
225
Kirby, Annie, 157, 186, 201
Kirkland, Jeff, 201, 212, 225
Knight, John C., 232

Knight, Ruth, 157
Koss, Kinney, 201
Kaplin, Loretta, 186
Koplin, Loretta, 157, 186
Kramer, Becky, 157
Kramer, Dan, 168, 171
Kramer, Frances, 157
Kramer, Sonya, 157
Kramer, William, 157

Lacy, Sharron, 201, 213, 225
Lane, William, 157, 186, 201, 213, 225
Lang, Karen, 186, 201, 213, 225
Lanzo, Angie, 213, 225
Lanzo, Sammy, 157, 186, 201, 213, 225
Leathers, Lucy, 20
Leathers, Susana B., 44
Leatherwood, Jesse, 11, 253, 256
Leatherwood, Mary Louise, 106, 125, 256
Leatherwood, W. A., 280
Ledford, Robin, 201, 186, 26
Lee, Amanda J., 238, 239
Lee, Elaine, 213, 226
Lee, Jean, 213, 226
Lee, Jessica, 213
Lee, Kara, 238
Lee, Keith A., xi, 32, 107, 164, 165, 238, 239, 243
Lee, Lisa, 207, 213

Lee, Matthew, 238
Lee, McKenzie, ii, 24, 238
Lee, Megan, 238
Lee, Robert, 195, 207, 213
Lester, J. H., 15, 280
Lenzy, Jas. (also see Lindsey), 107
Lewis, Cindy, 201, 213, 226
Lewis, Glen, 201, 213, 226
Lewis, Wayne, 186, 201, 213, 226
Lindsey family, 145
Lindsey, Catherine, 274
Lindsey, Davis, 186
Lindsey, Ethel, 157, 186, 201, 213, 226
Lindsey, George L., 274
Lindsey, J. M., 107
Lindsey, James M., 107, 264, 278
Lindsey, John, 274
Lindsey, Kelly, 157, 186
Lindesy, Kerry, 168, 171, 180, 191, 192
Lindsey, Linda, 157, 186, 201, 213, 226
Lindsey, Luella (Lula), 274
Lindsey, M., 274
Lindsey, Marion, 157, 186, 201, 213, 226
Lindsey Metie, 115
Lindsey Meedie, 115, 263
Lindsey, Omie, 125, 264

Lindsey, Patsy, 274

Lindsey, Paul, 157, 186, 201, 213

Lindsey, Phyllis, 157, 186

Lindsey, Raymond, 201, 213, 226

Lindsey, Sarah, 274

Lindsey, Speegle, 181

Lindsey, Spurgeon, 157

Lindsey, Susan, 186, 201, 213, 226

Lindsey, Traci, 187

Lindsey, William, 274

Linsey, Lula, p 274

Lipscomb, Frances, 157, 186, 213, 226

Lipscomb, Gene, (133), 137, 140, 141, 150, 272

Lipton Gene, 133

Little, Zebulon, 68

Locklear, Ann, 157

Locklear, Barbara, 201

Locklear, Beverly, 201, 226

Locklear, Cathy, 213, (201), 226

Locklear, Kathy, 201

Locklear, Dana, 201, 226

Locklear, Gene, 201, 213, 226

Locklear, Jeff, 202, 213, 226

Locklear, Michael, 202, 213, 226

Locklear, Randy, 202, 213, 226

Locklear, Stacy, 201,213, 226

Locklear, Wayne, 202, 213, 226

Long, Herman H., 32, 127, 131, 133, 245, 251, 280

Loudermilk, Jenny, 202, 213, 226

Lucious Baxter Lake, 132

Lummer, Kim, 187

Mammenga, J. T., 202

Mammenga, JoAnn Wix, 187, 202, 213, 226

Mammenga, Marsha, 202

Mammenga, Michael, 202

Mammenga, Terry, 202

Mammenga, Tina, 202

Maner, Clameria, 113

Maner George A., 113, 264

Maner, Mary, 157, 186

Maner, Roland, 264

Maner Sally Ida Cole, 113

Maner, Winnie, 262

Maner, William, 264

Marks, H. T. R., 32, 99, 100, 108, 245, 251, 280

Marsh, Mary, 157, 180

Martin, Barbara, 193

Martin, Ken, 31, 193

Massey, Carolyn, 187, 213, 226

Massey, Glenda, 187, 202

Massey, Randy, 202

Matthews, Bonnie, 166

Matthews, Bryan (Brian), 166, 202, 213, 226

Matthews, Keith, 166, 202, 213, 226,

Matthews, Kelly, 213, 226

Matthews, Ollie, 157, 165, 166, 167, 180, 187, 202, 269

Matthews, Willie Mae, 157, 187, 202

Maranatha Baptist Missions, 144, 237

Marks, Henry Thomas Reed, 99

Marks, Mary, 99

McBrayer, Angeline, 44, 68

McBrayer, John H., 44, 66

McBrayer, J. L., 66,68, 70

McBrayer, James L., 68

McBrayer, Mary, 262

McBrayer, Mary C. Moody, 68

Mauldin, Brian, 202, 213, 226

Mauldin, Wendy, 202

Maxwell, Julie, 157

Mayberry, Debra, 157

McCarley, Moses, 64

McCarley, Raymond, 25, 148

McClendon, Betty, 187, 202

McCullough, Minnie Lee, 187

McClung, Debra Brown, 96

McClung, Ruben, 96

McClung, Samuel, 96

McClung, Susan E. Whitehead, 96

McClung, T. B., 32, 96

McClung, Thomas B., 96

McDowell, Jake, 136

McDaniel, Tabitha, 213, 226

McDaniel, Tracy, 213, 226

McDuemon, Christy, 202

McDuemon, Luanne, 202

McDurmon, Robert, 157

McElroy, Cindy, 202, 213, 226, 187, 202

McGurt, Ann, 213, 226

McKenzy, David, 213, 226

McKenzy, Melissa, 213, 226

McKenzy, Paula, 213

McLarty, Cynthia, 187, 202

McLarty, Margie, 157, 187, 192, 202, 213, 226

McKenzy, Melissa, 226

McLaty, Paula, 187, 202, 226

McLarty, Raymond (Ray), 157, 187, 168, 180, 191, 192, 195, 202, 207, 213, 226, 245, 271

McLarty, Rhonda, 157, 187

McMichen, Cleo, 157, 187

McMichen, John, 157, 187

McMichen, Lonnie, 157, 171, 187

McMichen, Virginia, 157, 187, 202, 213, 226

McWhorter family, 76

Meadows, Arthur, 139

Meadows, Jeb, 136, 137, 272

Meadows, Job, 136

Meeks, Terry, 169

Meeks, Ricky (Randy), 157, 187, 202, 213, 226

Miles, Jimmy, 187
Miller, Martha Ann, 60
Mitchel, Chris, 213, 226
Mitchel, Josie, 202
Mobley, Allen, 49, 55
Mobley, Jesse M., 49, 55
Mobley, M., 40, 58
Mobley, Matthew, 49, 55
Mobley, Merida, 49, 55
Mobley, Meridy, 49, 55
Mobley, Newton B., 49, 55
Mobley, Rebecca, 49, 55
Mobley, Susan, 49, 55
Mobley, Willie Mae, 27
Moody, Amy Carolyn, 157
Moody, Billy Rogers, 157, 187, 202, 213, 226
Moody, Calista, 48
Moody, Celicie, 20, 261, 264
Moody, Charlie, 187, 213, 226
Moody, Danny, 168, 171
Moody, Denise, 202
Moody, Elizabeth, 48
Moody, Eller, 48
Moody, Ezekiel, 48
Moody, Franklin, 187, 202, 213, 226
Moody, Greenberry, 48
Moody, Janice, 187, 202, 214, 226
Moody, Joanna, 226
Moody, John, 48, 226
Moody, Leander, 48

Moody, Loretta, 187, 202
Moody, Mary, 48, 68
Moody, Mary Frances, 157, 187, 202
Moody, Marth Jane, 48
Moody, Retincy, 48, 49
Moody, Retincy, 48, 49, 56, 84, 117, 256, 264
Moody, Ricky, 202, 214, 226
Moody, Samuel, 48
Moody, Sarah, 48
Moody, Shirley, 168
Moody, Sophronia, 48, 84, 117, 257, 264, 265
Moody, Thomas, 48, 49, 56, 84, 117, 256, 264
Moody, William, 48
Moon, Marion B., 32, (116), 118, 119, 123, 280
Moore, Henry B., 114
Moore, Linda Whitley, 157, 187, 202, 226
Morgan, Debra, 226
Morgan, J. C., 280
Morgan, Joe, 157, 187, 202, 214
Morris, Brenda, 157
Morris, Irma Ruth Baggett, 157
Moon, Nettie B., 118
Moon, Rosie Fae, 118
Moore, Linda Whitley, 214
Moore, Ruby, 120
Morgan, A. J., 75
Morrow, Doris, 158

Morgan, Joe, 124, 214

Morris, Mildred, 136

Morris, Pam, 202, 114, 226

Morris, Vera Mae, 214

Morris, Vera Mae Cole, 158, 187, 202, 214, 226

Morrow, Doris, 158

Morrow, Ona Pearl, 239

Morrow, Randal, 157, 158, 187, 202, 202, 214, 226

Mosley, W. C., 84

Moss, Martha, 202, 214, 226

Murdock, Edward, 158

Myers, Brenda, 214, 226

Nash, Mary Ann, 46, 47

Nash, Violet, 233

Neal, Jessie, 15

Neal, Geneva, (15), 158, 180, 187

Neal, Lassy, 15

Neal, Ollie Lee, 158, 187

Neighbors, Mary Ann Nash, 46, 47

Neighbors, Thomas, 46, 47

New, W., 53

Newton, Albert, 187, 203, 214, 226

Newton, Debbie, 158

Newton, Evelyn, 158

Newton, Lynn, 158, 187

Newton, Timmy, 158, 176

Newton, Wayne, 158

Newton, Albert, 203

Nix, J. N., 112

Noble, Angie, 203, 214

Noble, Bethel, 165, 168, 187, 203, 214, 268

Noble, Heather, 203

Noble, Lisa, 165, 187, 203

Noble, Mitch, 203

Noble, Pam, 165

Noble, Shirley, 165, 187, 203, 214

Noble, Tim, 165, 187, 203, 214

O'Brian, Sharon, 203

Ogle, J. H., 31, 32, 36, 81, 82, 83, 84, 92, 93, 99, 108, 245, 251, 280

Ogle, John H., 81, 82

Ogle, John Harrison (Also see J. H. Ogle), 81

Ogle, Nancy Caroline Haley, 81, 82

Ogle, Robert, 281

Ogle, Sarah Jane Sander, 81, 82

Old-school Baptists, 69

Osborne, John, 15

Osborne, J. (Press), 15

Osborn(e), Warner, 108, 280

Owens, Sandy, 214, 226

Owens, Terry, 187, 203

Overton, Pamela Cole, 158, 187, 203

Pace, Dennis, 203, 214, 226
Pace, Frances, 80
Pace, Jesse, 187, 203, 214, 226
Pace, John B., 255
Pace, Lynn, 158
Pace, Nancy Camp, 255
Pace, Rex, 203
Padgett, Diane, 187, 214
Padgett, Robin, 187, 203, 214, 226
Palmer, Bennie, 158
Palmer, Bonnie, 166
Palmer, Denise, 158
Palmer, Eddie, 158, 214, 226
Palmer, Edward, 158, 187
Palmer, Franklin, 158
Palmer, Jackie, 158, 188, 203
Palmer, Jeff, 187, 214, 226
Palmer, Shirley, 158, 187, 214, 226
Paris, Trumie, 121
Parker, Amy C., 113
Parker, Randy, 158
Parks, John, 203
Parks, Oree, 177, 203, 214, 226
Parsons, Bertie, 188
Parsons, Gary, 188
Partain, Amanda, 118
Partain, Angie, 214, 220, 226
Partain, Becky, 194, 203, 214
Partain, Carl, 194, 195, 203, 206, 214, 220, 226

Partain, Earl, 32, 193, 194, 195, 206, 214, 226, 241, 243
Patterson, Steve, 203
Pawley, Jackie, 214
Pawley, Mark, 214
Perry, Michael, 226
Peter, Michelle, 203, 214, 226
Pettway, Steve, 230
Phillips, Cynthia, 158
Phillips, Martha, 158
Phillips, Robert, 158
Phillips, Wendell, 136
Pinson, Berdie, 158
Pinson, Donna, 214
Pilgrim, Pete, 188, 214
Pinson, Berdie, 188
Pitts, Chris, 188, 203, 214, 226
Pitts, Etta Mae Baxter, 158, 188
Ploof, Eddie, 188, 203, 214, 226
Pollard, Sandra, 188, 203, 214, 226
Pool, W. A., 84
Poss, Bill, 158, 170, 188, 203, 214
Poss, Dot, 158, 188, 203, 214
Poss, Michael, 158, 188, 203, 214
Postell, Bill, 11
Postell, Mary "Polly" Stuart, 256
Postell, Lucinda Brock, 256
Postell, Nancy Brock, 256
Postell, Thomas, 253, 256

Powell, Bill, 172
Powers, Laura, 214, 226
Prater, Roger, 158, 188, 203, 214, 227
Primitive Baptist Controversy and Doctrines, xiv, 8, 68, 69, 70, 71, 72, 285, 286
Pruett, Claudia, 158, 203, 214, 227
Pruett, Dee Dee, 214
Pruett, Deidra, 214, 227
Pruett, Donald, 158, 203, 214, 227
Pruett, Jane, 158
Pruett, Jennifer, 203, 214, 227
Pruett, Max, 214, 220, 227
Pruett, Penny, 214, 227
Pruett, Teresa, 188, 203, 214, 227
Pugh, Brenda, 203, 214, 227
Puckett, Earl, 158, 188, 203, 214
Rakestraw, G. L., 117
Radcliff, Brenda Holder, 158, 188, 215, 227
Radcliff, Holder, 188
Radcliff, Inez, 158, 188
Radcliff, Jerry, 158, 188
Radcliff, Larry, 158, 188
Radcliff, Marvin, 158, 188
Ragan, Louis, (158), 280
Ragan, Lewis, 158, (280)
Ragan, W. L., 280

Ragan, Will, 126
Ragsdale, Dale, 203, 215, 269
Ragsdale, Elaine, 203
Ragsdale, Jana, 203, 215
Ragsdale, Robin, 188, 203
Ragsdale, Sara, 203, 215
Ragsdale, Sue, 14
Rainey, Bell, 115
Rainey, Ella, 122
Rainey, Jasper, 107, 264, 281
Rainey, Katie Fuller, 264
Rainey, Lois Ann, 180
Rainey, Odesa, 15
Rainey, Ove Hitchcock, 265
Rainey, Peek, 281
Rainey, Miluner, 264
Rainey, R. A., 281
Rainey, Tempie, 15, 263
Rainey, Texaner Cole, 264
Raney (Also see Rainey)
Raney, Lou Ann, 158
Rakestraw, Angelia, 215, 227
Rakestraw, Jeremy, 203, 215
Rakestraw, Jimmie Lynn, 215, 227
Rakestraw, Ricky, 203, 215, 227
Raney, Bell (Also see Rainey), 115
Ray, Bobbie Jean, 158, 188
Ray, Carolyn, 188
Ray, Charlotte, 158, 175
Ray, Dianne, 203

Ray, Henry, 175
Ray, Jessie, 158, 188
Ray, Kelly, 203
Ray, Pattie, 158
Ray, Rhonda, 158
Ray, Ronnie, 158
Ray, Thomas, 158
Reese, Louise, 158
Renfroe, Eunice, 158, 188, 203
Rentz, Peter, 203
Reynolds, J. S., 31, 58
Reynolds, Margaret, 203, 215, 227
Rice, John R., 144
Rice, Luther, 68
Rice, R. L., 170
Riggs, Joan, 203, 227
Roberson, Larry, 207
Roberts, A., 50
Roberts, Alva, 233
Roberts, Arnold, 103
Roberts, Ada Beth, 100, 103
Roberts, B. J., 139, 158, 188, 203
Roberts, Bessie, 115, 124, 126, 136, 139, 148, 158, 168, 180, 188, 203, 215, 227
Roberts, Birma, 265
Roberts, C. A., 107
Roberts, Carolyn, 138
Roberts, Cleveland, 233
Roberts, Cumi, 265
Roberts, Dean, 124, 168
Roberts, Delilia, 53
Roberts, Dewey [Dean] L., 100, 102
Roberts, Edna Fae Cole, 158, 188, 203, 215, 227
Roberts, Elmer, 100, 103, 124, 159
Roberts, G. R., 127
Roberts, George R., 100, 103, 265, 281
Roberts, H. J., 281
Roberts, Hammie, 103
Roberts, Hamon, 11, 50, 51, 52, 53, 56, 100, 125, 126, 253, 265
Roberts, Hamon Jessie, 100, 265, (281)
Roberts, Hugh, 236
Roberts, Ida, 159, 170, 232
Roberts, J., 35, 40, 43, 50
Roberts, James, 3, 4, 37, 40, 46, 48, 49, 50, 51, 52, 53, 56, 78, 100, 133, 253
Roberts, Jean, 233
Roberts, Fanny, 51, 103
Roberts, Frances (Franky), 53
Roberts, June, 53
Roberts, L. T., 233
Roberts, Linda, 159
Roberts, Lois, 188, 203, 215, 215, 227
Roberts, Louise, 233
Roberts, Lucien E., vii

Roberts, Martha, 43, 46, 49, 50, 51, 52, 56, 78, 133

Roberts, Mary, 51

Roberts, Mary Frances, 103

Roberts, M. B. (Also see Moses Barto Roberts), 100, 102, 103, 107,108, 112, 126, 265

Roberts, Moses Barto, 33, 53, 54, 100, 102, 103, (107), (108), (112), (126), 265, 267, 281

Roberts, Myrtle, 159

Roberts, Nancy, 11, 53, 56, 265

Roberts, Nath. C., 100, 102

Roberts, Omie, 100, 263

Roberts, Pauline, 126, 159, 168, 188, 203

Roberts, Pearlie, 100

Roberts, "Polly" (also see Mary Roberts), 51

Roberts, Rebecca, 159, 188

Roberts, Ruben Arnold, 100

Roberts, Ruth, 102

Roberts, Ryland, 50

Roberts, Sarah, 51

Roberts, Sarah "Sallie", 54

Roberts, Sallie Cole, 100, 102, 262, 263

Roberts, Sally, 215

Roberts, Sim, 100, 103, 127, 133, 136, 137, 159, 281

Roberts, Susan, 53

Roberts, Susanne (Susannah), 51

Roberts, Thelma, 159, 188, 203, 215, 227, 233, 235

Roberts, Tyra, 100

Roberts, Tyre, 232, 281

Roberts, Vinnie, 100, 103

Roberts, W. B., 159, 188, 233, 235

Roberts, Wesley Hogan, 51

Roberts, William, "Owen", 235

Roberts, Zellie, 53, 265

Rock of Ages Mission, 144, 176

Robertson, Dianne, 215, 227

Robertson, Carroll, 188, 203, 215, 227

Robertson, Larry, 215, 220, 227

Robertson, Mary, 203

Robertson, Pam Wyatt, 215

Robinson, Annabelle, 215

Robinson, Cindy, 215, 227

Robinson, Colinca, 215, 227

Robinson, Doug, 215, 227

Robinson, Henry, 215, 227

Robinson, John, 32, 191, 192, 193

Rogers, Anita, 215, 227

Rogers, Harriet, 65

Roloff, Lester, 144

Rollins, David, 159, 188, 215, 227

Rollins, Diane, 159, 188, 203, 215, 233

Rollins, Glenda, 203, 215, 227

Rollins, James, 233

Rollins, Jim, 159, 188, 203, 215

Rollins, Steve, 233

Roney, Mrs. Lex, 136

Rose, Dorothy, 159

Ross, Michael, 207, 215

Ross, Rhonda, 215

Rollins, Russell, 203, 215

Rollins, Steve, 188, 203

Rollins, Teresa, 215

Ruff, Gary, 159, 188

Ruff, Linda Ann, 203, 215, 227

Rucker, Helen, 232

Ruff, Lovona, 159, 188

Rutledge, Emma, 159

Rutledge, Sandra, 159

Rutter, Mel, 44, 144

Rutter, Dottie, 144

Sabinas, John Lee, 215, 227

Saladrigas, Joyce, 203, 215, 227

Sander, Sarah Jane, 81, 82

Sanders, Betty, 159

Sanders, Carmen Lee, 203, 215, 227

Sanders, Harold, 159, 171

Sanders, Sherry Cooper, 46, 47

Sanford, Amanda J., 238

Scoggins, Myrtis, 159

Scott, Dean, 215, 227

Scott, George E., 265

Scott, Margaret, 204, 215, 227

Scott, Vinnie R., 265

Sewell, Virginia Louise, 114

Shanks, Joe, 215, 227

Shead, Keith, 188, 204, 215

Shead, Mollie, 159, 188, 204, 215, 236

Sheets, Charles, 227

Sheets, Lisa, 227

Shelton, Virginia Caroline (Jenny), 60, 61, 62

Shelton, Virginia, 60, 61

Shelton, Martin, 61

Shirley, Irene, 159

Shoemaker, Jewell Taylor, 159, 188, 204, 215, 227

Shores, Rodney, 188, 204, 215, 227

Shores, Shelia, 188, 204, 215, 227

Silvey, Francene, 159

Singleton, Doris, 188, 204

Simpson, Brenda, 218

Simpson, Chris, 32, 218, 234, 243, 272

Simpson, Heather, 234

Simpson, Hayleigh, 234

Simpson, Rick, 215, 227

Simpson, Sheryl, 215, 218, 227

Simpson, Rhonda, 218

Simpson, Rick, 218

Simpson, Sondra, 218

Simpson, Weston, 234

Singleton, Elizabeth, 84

Singleton, J., 84

Singleton, James, 84

Singleton S. L., 84
Sinyard, Addie, 125, 149
Sinyard, Amanda S. 94
Sinyard, Annie, 159
Sinyard, Dicy, 90
Sinyard, Jacob, 54, 125, 265, 281
Sinyard, John, 89
Sinyard, Louisa, 86, 91
Sinyard, Susanah Cole, 89, 90
Sinyard, Will, 281
Sinyard, Zellie Roberts, 54, (125), 265
Sinyard, Zilla, 125
Skinner, Amelia, 188
Skinner, Danny, 188
Skinner, Geanene, 204, 215, 227
Skinner, Sandra, 168, 180, 188, 191
Smith, Ann, 275
Smith, Armanda L., 278
Smith, Angie, 204, 215, 227
Smith, B. H., 275
Smith, Bennie, 274
Smith, Benj. J., 278
Smith, Beth, 204, 240
Smith, Carroll, 159, 188, 204, 215, 227
Smith, Catherine, 62
Smith, Charles, 62
Smith, Columbus, 76
Smith, David, 275

Smith, Dennie, 241,
Smith, Diane, 159,188, 204, 215, 227
Smith, Elizabeth, 278
Smith, Emily, 275
Smith, Elijah, 61, 62
Smith, F. M. (also see Francis M. Smith), 31, 60, 61, 62, 63, 274, 275
Smith, Fielding M., 60
Smith, Francis, 62, 275
Smith, Francine, 195, 204
Smith, Francis Monroe, 60
Smith, Hannah Guyton, 61
Smith, Harry, 62, 63, 76
Smith, Henry H., 278
Smith, James, 62
Smith, J. A., x, xiv, 277, 278
Smith, J. C., 281
Smith, Jasper, 97, 245, 251, 273, 274, 275, 276
Smith, Jasper C., 62, 63, 275, 277
Smith, Jasper L., 275
Smith, Jerry, 62, 63
Smith, Jane, 62
Smith, Jimmie, 136
Smith, J. N., 77, 78
Smith, J. S., 78
Smith, John A., 277
Smith, John Augustine, 278
Smith, John M., 275
Smith, John T., 76

Smith, Jon K., 278
Smith, Laura, 204, 215
Smith, Leo, 159, 188, 204
Smith, Lottie, 274
Smith, Lavinia Cooper, 278
Smith, Lucy, 278
Smith, Lula, 274
Smith, Lynn, 204, 215, 227
Smith, Mary, 76, 275
Smith, Mancel, 62
Smith, Martha Ann Miller, 60
Smith, Menbrey, 274
Smith, Nancy A., 275
Smith, Narcissa, 275
Smith, Newton, 275
Smith, Nicy, 62
Smith, Pat, 159
Smith, Posey N., 275
Smith, Simpson, 62
Smith, Sarah, 76, 89, 278
Smith, Sarah M., 278
Smith, Sabra Cole, 89
Smith, Susan, 60
Smith, Susan Ann Cooper, 278
Smith, Thomas, 62, 63
Smith, Virgina, 274
Smith, W. B., 31, 63, 75, 76
Smith, Walter B., 76
Smith, William B., 76
Smith, Willie, 274
Smith, Wyatt, 61, 63
Snelgrove, Heath, 238
Snelgrove, Megan, 238

Sorrel, Emma, 204, 215, 227
Sorrells, Will, 168
Speck, Byron, 204
Speck, Gilbert, 204
Speck, Kathy, 204
Speck, Melody (Melony?), 204
Speck, Stephanie, 204
Speegle, Stanley, 191, 192, 204
Sprayberry, Jamie, 204, 215, 22
Sprayberry, Michelle, 204, 215, 227
Spruill, Rhonda, 227
Stanford, Estelle, 178, 188, 204, 215, 227, 230
Stanford, Roy, 32, 178, 180, 188, 191, 192, 204, 204, 215
Stearns, Shubal, 51
Stearns, Susanne Roberts, 51
Stearns, Thomas, 51
Stone, Grady, 159
Still, Cathy, 189
Still, Robin, 159, 189, 204
Still, Sue, 159, 189, 204
Swafford, Danny Eugene, 189, 204, 215, 227
Swafford, Steve Darrel, 188, 204, 215, 227

Tant, Brenda, 204
Tant, Dale, 204, 216, 228
Tant, Glenda, 204, 216
Tant, Joan, 216, 228
Tant, Travis, 204, 216, 228

Tant, Wayne, 204, 216
Tallent, Gary, 159
Tallent, Jeff, 216
Tallent, Linda, 159
Tallent, Louise, 159, 192, 195, 204, 207, 216, 220, 228
Tallent, Shae, 216, 220, 228, 272
Tallent, Tabitha, 216, 228
Tallent, Tommie, 159, 189, 192, 204, 216, 228, 269
Tapley, Corry, 204, 216, 228
Tapley, Judy, 204, 216, 228
Tapley, Sanford, 204, 216, 228
Tapley, Tonya, 204, 228
Taylor, Hollis, 216, 228
Taylor, June, 216, 228
Taylor, L. T., 118
Taylor, Minnie Lee, 159
Taylor, Sally Field, 118
Teal, Angie, 216
Teal, Debbi, 216
Teal, Tony, 216
Thomas, Charlotte, 204, 216, 228
Thomas, Dewayne, 204, 216, 228
Thomas, Lisa, 177
Thomas, Terry, 177
Thompson, Connie, 159, 204
Thompson, Charlie, 15
Thompson, Jane, 159, 204, 216, 228

Thompson, John, 15
Thompson, Larrin, 228
Thompson, Lizzie, 15
Thompson, Rita, 204, 216, 228
Thompson, Richard, 191
Thompson, Rosy, 15
Thompson, Tabitha, 204
Thompson, Timmy, 204, 206, 216, 228
Thompson, Toby, 204, 220, 228
Thompson, Todd, 204
Tibbits, Anna, 216, 228
Tibbits, Cody, 216, 228
Tibbits, Emily, 228
Tibbits, Mary, 216, 228
Tibbits, Randy, 216
Tibbits, Ronnie, 164, 272
Tierce, Druey, 32, 190, 191
Tierce, Toni C., 191
Todd, John Thomas, 255
Todd, Martha Lucinda Wilson, 255
Toler, Mary Jane, 79, 86, 87, 97, 98
Toler, William, 97
Tomlin, Diane, 189, 204
Touchton, Linda, 216, 228
Touchton, Raymond, 216, 228
Townsend, Wayne, 189, 204, 216, 228
Trapp, Nancy Alice, 105
Treglown, Elizabeth Cole, 89
Treglown, Robert M., 89

Tucker, L. J., 50
Tumlin, Dianne, 216, 228
Turner, Charlotte, 204, 216, 228
Turner, Jackie, 189, 204, 216, 228
Turner, Jamie, 204, 216, 228
Turner, Linda, 216, 228
Turner, Lisa, 216, 228
Turner, Mary, 189, 204
Turner, Marty, 216, 228
Turner, Rainey, 216, 228
Turner, Richard, 216, 228
Turner, Todd, 216
Turner, W., 84
Tyre, Ben, 241
Tyre, Sue, 216

Upton, Bobbie, 189, 205
Upton, David, 189, 205, 216, 228
Upton, J. R., 205, 216, 228
Upton, June, 189, 205, 216, 228
Upton, Lora Lee, 189, 205, 216, 228
Upton, Patti, 189, 205
Upton, Robert, 189
Upton, Samantha, 216, 228
Upton, Sandra, 216
Upton, Stephanie, 228
Upton, Tony, 189, 205
Upton, Wendell, 159, 189, 205, 216, 228

Vaughn, Cheryl, 189
Vaughn, Jamie, 205, 216, 228
Vaughn, Janice, 189, 205, 216, 228
Vaughn, Lamar, 205, 216, 228
Vaughn, Melissa, 205, 216, 228
Vaughn, Tammy, 216, 228
Verner, Betty, 189, 205, 216, 228
Verner, Jack, 189
Verner, Melody, 189, 205, 216, 228
Vines, Jerry, 143, 144
Voyles, Scott, 216
Voyles, Stacy, 216

Waites, Sarah M., 89
Waddell, M. F., 31, 87, 93, 245, 251, 281
Walker, Angie, 205
Walker, Cathy, 205, 217, 228
Walker, Loretta Baxter, 159, 189, 217, 228
Walker, Richard, 159, 205, 217, 228
Walker, Sharon, 205, 217, 229
Wall, Sharon, 217, 229
Wallace, David, 217
Wallace, Jessica, 217
Wallace, Shirley, 217
Warrenton Baptist Mission, 237
Wash, Carey, 205, 229
Wash, Gary, 217

Watts, Dennis, 159, 205
Watts, Fred, 32, 192
Waters, Betty, 192, 217, 229
Waters, Carolyn, 189, 205
Waters, Denise, 205, 217
Waters, Susan, 229
Weather, Lynn, 159
Weatherington, Herman, 159, 171, 189, 205, 217, 229
Weatherington, Joe, 159, 189, 205, 217, 229
Weatherington, Junior, 148, 159, 168, 180, 189, 205, 217, 229
Weatherington, Kenneth, 168
Weatherington, Lela, 159
Weatherington, Margie, 159, 189, 205, 217, 229
Weatherington, Nancy, 159, 168, 180, 189, 205
Weaver, Patricia, 189
Weaver, Rachel, 205, 217, 229
Weaver, Tommy, 205, 217, 229
Webb, Sharon, 205, 217, 229
Weeks, Isaac (also see Wix), 257
Weeks, Missouri E., (also see Wix), 257
Wehunt, Gregg, 159, 189
Wehunt, Jackie, 169
Welborn, Johnny, 237
Weldon, Mark, 217

Wells, Addie, 86, 87, 94, 95, 96, 99
Wells, Erastus, 86, 87, 95, 96
Wells, J. H., 87
Wells, L. E., 87, 94, 95, 96, 99
Wells, Mary A., 64
Wells, W. W., 64
Wells, William Wilder, 64
Wentz, Jamie, 205, 217, 229
Wentz, Janice, 205, 217, 229
Wentz, Marion, 205
Westbrook, James, 168
White, Andrew, 230
White, Bill, 159, 189
White, June, 159, 189, 205, 217, 229
White, Katherine, 159, 189, 205, 217, 229
White, Larry, 159, 189, 217, 229
White, Louise, 169
White, Lula, 230
White, Osara, 160, 189, 205, 217, 229, 230
White, Penny, 217, 229
White, Steve, 160, 189, 205, 217, 229
White, William, 191
Whitely, Sherrie, 205, 217, 229
Whitely, Vicky, 205, 217, 229
Whitton, Levoy, 171
Wigley, Clarence F., 114
Wigley, Fred Lee, 114

Wigley, G. (George) Fred, 32, 113, 115, 117, 245, 251, 281
Wigley, Gay Lewis "G. L.", 114
Wigley, James Robert, 113
Wigley, John Jefferson, 113
Wigley, Lillian, 160, 189, 217, 229
Wigley, Lona, 113, 115
Wigley, Maud, 114
Wigley, Ruthie Ann Miller, 113
Wigley, Paul Albert, 114
Wigley, Rilla Mae, 114
Wigley, Vennie, 114
Wigley, Virginia Louise Sewell, 114
Willard, Toney, 32, 218
Williams, Aline, 160
Williams, Amber, 217
Williams, Ancy J., 239
Williams, Anita Neal, 217
Williams, Becky, 151
Williams, Charles, viii, 14, 84, 138, 139, 140, 143, 151, 162, 171, 173, 174, 175, 176, 178, 245, 251
Williams, Jean, 151, 164, 168, 176, 177
Williams, Joshua, 217, 229
Williams, Homer Lee, 176
Williams, Mark, 160
Williams, Martha Jean Smith, 176, 177
Williams, Micah, 217
Williams, Sara Frances Browning, 176
Williams, Sherry, 189
Williams, Steve, 177, 190, 217, 220, 229
Williams, Terry, 177, 207, 217, 229
Williams, Tracy, 190
Willoughby, Brandi, 217, 229
Willoughby, Carla, 229
Willoughby, Cory, 229
Willoughby, Hollie, 217, 229
Willoughby, Rhonda, 217
Willoughby, Wesley, 217, 229
Wills, Shirley, 165
Wilson, Annie, 160, 190
Wilson, Allen, 190, 217, 229
Wilson, Becky, 190
Wilson, Billy, 190, 217, 229
Wilson, Bob, 15
Wilson, Dora Harper, 266
Wilson, G. O., 133
Wilson, George W., 117, 265
Wilson, H. R., 107, 108, 112, 117, 281
Wilson, Harvey Rose, 117, 266
Wilson, J. A., 110
Wilson, J. O., 115, 117, 119, 126, 127, 129, 130, 267, 281
Wilson, John Oliver "Dutch", 116, 265
Wilson, J. R., 112
Wilson, Joyce, 160, 190, 217

Wilson, Joshua, 217

Wilson, Karen, 217

Wilson, Lillie, 15, 160, 190, 217, 229

Wilson, Mark, 217, 229

Wilson, Mary, 112

Wilson, Martha Dora Harper, 117

Wilson, Martha Lucinda, 255

Wilson, Mellie, 15

Wilson, Mollie, 106

Wilson, Monnie Cole, 106, 116

Wilson, Oscar, 15, 112, 281

Wilson, Randall, 160, 217, 229

Wilson, Randy, 160, 190

Wilson, Rebecca, 160

Wilson, Rodney, 190, 217, 229

Wilson, Ruth, 126, 160

Wilson, R. H., 112, 117

Wilson, Sherrie, 217

Wilson, Sophronia Moody, 84, 257, 264, 265

Wilson, Vonnie, 110, 160, 190, 192

Wilson, Willie, 180

Windward Island Mission, 176

Wingers, Linda, 217

Wines, Kathleen Denise, 217, 229

Winters, Gregory, 217, 229

Winters, JoAnne, 160, 190, 217, 229

Winters, Linda, 160, 190

Winters, Tommy, 160, 190

Wintz, Marion, 217, 229

Wisner, Debroah, 160, 190

Wisnener, Debroah, 190

Wisner, Joyce, 229

Wisener, Shirley Pace, 190

Witcher, Theresa, 160, 170

Wix, Alan, 160

Wix, Alma Annie, 105

Wix, Anne, 15, 217, 229

Wix, Adarine, 104, 105

Wix, Bennett, 160, (280)

Wix, Betty, 132

Wix, Benjamin, 104

Wix, Bud, 272

Wix, Cecilia Moody Clark, 105

Wix, Charlie, 105, 266

Wix, Diane, 190

Wix, Donnie, 160, 190, 217, 229

Wix, Don Edwin, v, x, 12, 122, 257

Wix, Eddie, 217, 229

Wix, Emm Butler, 266

Wix, Gerald, 160, 190

Wix, Georgia, 15, 105, 160, 190, 191

Wix, Mrs. George, 119

Wix, Gina, 217, 229

Wix, Grace, 160

Wix, Herbert Loring, 105

Wix, I. L. V., 266

Wix, Isaac, 15, 104, 257, 266

Wix, J. Edwin, x, 12, 23, (116), 119, 121, 122, 145, 257, 272

Wix, J. M., (John Newton), 105

Wix, James, 131, 148, 160, 163, 164, 167, 168, 190, 217, 229, 231

Wix, Jean, 167

Wix, Jennifer, 229

Wix, J. H., 105, 107, 122

Wix, Joseph Hiram, 105, 122

Wix, John, 106, 149

Wix, John Edwin, 105

Wix, J. N., 32, 102, 105, 112, 115, 116, 117, 119, 124, 126, 127, 133, (266), 267, 281

Wix, John Newton, 105, 266, 281

Wix, Joseph, 266

Wix, Joseph H., 104

Wix, Joseph Hiram, 104, 105, 122

Wix, Josephine Carter, 67, 266, 271

Wix, Julia Ann, 104

Wix, Lena, 160, 167, 190, 229

Wix, Leonard (Bud), 129, 130, 160, 170, 171, 190

Wix, Lilla, 125

Wix, Lizzie, 142

Wix, Lois, 106

Wix, Lorsing (Also see Loring Wix), 106

Wix, Loring, (106), 117, 119, 127, 160

Wix Luther, 160, 190, 281

Wix, Martha, 122

Wix, Mary E., 104, 260

Wix, Marion, 104

Wix, Mildred, 160, 190, 229, 231

Wix, Missouri E., 104, 266

Wix, Nancy, 266

Wix, Nancy Trapp, 105, 122

Wix, Newton, 104

Wix, Oliver, 105

Wix, Oma Lois, 105

Wix, Pauline, 106

Wix, Pearl, 15

Wix, Ralph, 160, 165, 167, 168, 180, 269

Wix, Rebecca Larena, 104

Wix, Roger, 220, 229

Wix, Ruthie, 105

Wix, Salley Jane, 104

Wix, S. C. (Sarah), 105

Wix, Sandra, 160

Wix, Silas, 280

Wix, Sue, 160, 190, 283, 284

Wix, Trumie Paris, 121

Wix, Velma, 160, 190, 231

Wix, Vera I., 105

Wix, Mrs. Virgie, 119

Wix, Wayne, 160, 180, 181, 191

Wix, William, 104, 105, 266

Wix, Zachariah, 67, 104, 122, 213
Wix, Zannie, 15
Womack, Elizabeth, 190, 229
Womack, J. W., 32, 111, 112, 281
Womack, Georgia Morgan, 111
Womack, Sue, 190
Womack, Vassie J., 114
Wood, Lois, 160, 190
Wood, Spurgeon, 160, 190
Wooden, Cordie Guffey, 231, 232
Wooden, James Blanco, 231, 232
Woods, Roy E., 190
Woods, Tommy, 190, 229
Woods, Wanda, 190
Woody, Earnest, 160, 190
Woody, Lee, 190
Woody, Orlee (Ora Lee), 160, 229
Workman, Judy, 190, 229
Wortham, D. (also see Duncan Wortham), 31, 85, 86, 87, 245, 251, 281
Wortham, Malinda, 85
Wortham, John, 85
Wright, Kristina, 233
Wright, Gail, 190
Wright, James, 190
Wright, Letitia, 190
Wyatt, Angie, 229

Wyatt, Eddie, 160, 176, 190, 229, 272
Wyatt, Sandra, 136, 160, 175, 176, 190
Youngblood, Sonja, 230